## McGraw-Hill Bulletproofing Series

0-07-067620-8  WEADOCK • *Bulletproof Your PC Network: Solving the 210 Most Common Problems before They Happen*

0-07-067631-3  WEADOCK • *Bulletproofing Windows 95: Solve the Top 160 Problems before They Happen*

0-07-067621-6  WILKINS/WEADOCK • *Bulletproofing NetWare: Solving the 175 Most Common Problems before They Happen*

## McGraw-Hill Related Titles

0-07-005996-9  ALLEN/BAMBARA/BAMBARA • *Informix: Client / Server Application Development*

0-07-001697-6  ANDERSON • *Client / Server Database Design with Sybase*

0-07-005664-1  BERSON • *Client / Server Architecture, 2e*

0-07-006080-0  BERSON/ANDERSON • *Sybase and Client / Server Computing*

0-07-913267-7  BLOCK/BROWN/GREEN/GASIN/TAUBER • *Powersoft Foundation Class Library Sourcebook*

0-07-024469-3  BROWN/GREEN • *PowerBuilder 5: Object-Oriented Design and Development*

0-07-011662-8  CLIFFORD • *Mastering Sybase SQL Server 11*

0-07-016736-2  DEWIRE • *Second Generation Client / Server Computing*

0-07-913255-3  HORWOOD • *Optima++ Developer's Toolkit*

0-07-912982-X  JONES • *Developing Client / Server Applications with Microsoft Access*

0-07-038118-6  LIGON • *Client / Server Communication Services*

0-07-053999-5  ROSEEN • *InfoMaker 5: A Guide to Developing Client / Server Applications*

0-07-071173-9  WISE • *Client / Server Performance Tuning*

# Bulletproofing
# Client/Server Systems

Richard J. Martin

Glenn E. Weadock

Illustrated by Emily Sherrill Weadock

**McGraw-Hill**

New York   San Francisco   Washington, D.C.   Auckland   Bogotá
Caracas   Lisbon   London   Madrid   Mexico City   Milan   Montreal
New Delhi   San Juan   Singapore   Sydney   Tokyo   Toronto

**Library of Congress Cataloging-in-Publication Data**

Martin, Richard J.
    Bulletproofing client/server systems / Richard J. Martin, Glenn E.
Weadock.
        p.    cm.
    Includes index.
    ISBN 0-07-067622-4
    1. Client/server computing.    2. Debugging in computer science.
I. Weadock, Glenn E.    II. Title.
QA76.9.C55M39        1997
004'.36—dc21                                                                97-4056
                                                                            CIP

*McGraw-Hill*

*A Division of The McGraw·Hill Companies*

1 2 3 4 5 6 7 8 9 0    DOC/DOC    9 0 2 1 0 9 8 7

ISBN 0-07-067622-4

*The sponsoring editor for this book was John Wyzalek and the production supervisor was Pamela A. Pelton. It was edited and set in New Century Schoolbook by TopDesk Publishers' Group.*

*Printed and bound by R. R. Donnelley & Sons Company*

McGraw-Hill books are available at special quantity discounts to use as premiums and sales promotions, or for use in corporate training programs. For more information, please write to the Director of Special Sales, McGraw-Hill, 11 West 19 Street, New York, NY 10011. Or contact your local bookstore.

 This book is printed on recycled, acid-free paper containing a minimum of 50% recycled de-inked fiber.

# Contents

# Chapter 3.   Why Client/Server? 33

# Chapter 4.   Bulletproofing Client/Server Design 53

## Chapter 5.  Bulletproofing Client/Server Performance

## Chapter 6.  Bulletproofing Client/Server Security                                              **145**

## Chapter 7.   Bulletproofing Client/Server Fault Tolerance                                                 185

# Chapter 8.  Bulletproofing Client/Server Support                               217

# Chapter 9.  Intranets and Extranets                                   249

# Bulletproofing
# Client/Server Systems

# 1

# Beyond Troubleshooting: The Bulletproofing Philosophy

This book is a new entry in McGraw-Hill/Computing's new "bulletproofing" series. Bulletproofing books share a common philosophy, namely that troubleshooting computer systems doesn't really work and the only practical way to manage today's computing environment is to design and configure it for reliable, successful operation before most problems even have a chance to appear.

Although it shares this overall "world view" of business computing, *Bulletproofing Client/Server Systems* is a little different from the other books in the series. The biggest difference you'll see is that this book is not product specific: You'll be able to apply its ideas and suggestions to nearly any client/server environment. Another major difference is that this book is designed to be read from front to back, whereas other books in the series are more in the nature of reference works. Finally, the subject matter for this volume is much broader than for the other books. Client/server computing is a huge topic, but we have found enough commonalities between client/server systems to identify five key bulletproofing areas: design, performance, security, fault tolerance, and support.

## Welcome to Bulletproofing

In this section, we'd like to present the backdrop for the bulletproofing approach.

### New Challenges in Information Technology

Several trends have made the job of building fast, secure, reliable, and supportable client/server systems a nearly overwhelming challenge for technical professionals:

- Network software and hardware adds several layers of complexity to the computer environment, and distributed processing increases complexity even further by requiring clients and servers to share computing tasks across platforms and by distributing data from a central repository to multiple locations, which must now be tracked and coordinated.

- Another trend is "downsizing" or "rightsizing," in which companies move older, sometimes mission-critical, mainframe-based applications down to client/server systems for cost savings, performance benefits, and (most of all) greater accessibility. There is therefore increasing pressure on client/server systems to handle more and more of a company's computer workload—and to provide the levels of security and reliability that mainframe systems have had 40 years to refine.

- The third trend changing the business computer landscape is the plunge in price/performance ratios, particularly in the microcomputer world. The result has been twofold: a population explosion of machines more capable than early mainframes and able to shoulder many processing-intensive tasks at the client, and a new class of processor- and memory-intensive applications (multimedia, CBT, etc.) unheard of in mainframe days.

- The fourth trend is the development of faster, more sophisticated data communications systems that permit more data to move to more users at speeds permitting distributed processing.

These four trends combine to create a computing environment that is much more complex, running many more applications on much more capable client systems that can communicate faster than ever before. As a result, many organizations are moving to client/server systems in droves and at high speed, during a period when user populations and application workloads are skyrocketing.

Complexity can be managed with experience. However, whereas IS departments have had 40 years to learn to manage mainframes, the widespread deployment of client/server computing is only two to three years old. The experience base isn't there yet, nor are the modeling tools. As a result, many organizations are making mistakes when migrating to distributed processing. Those mistakes create underperforming systems of such complexity—a complexity often hidden from users and managers alike by aesthetically pleasing graphical user interfaces—that they require a tremendous investment in troubleshooting and support to keep them afloat. The Gartner Group has estimated that the hardware and software costs of moving to client/server comprise 3% of the total, most of the balance being labor—the labor of those setting up and supporting the system, and of those learning and using it.

The *supply* of full-time troubleshooting and support assistance, however, has been shrinking. The software industry is beating a hasty retreat from free technical support, and even paid support doesn't mean prompt support anymore. IS department personnel budgets were cut during the last nationwide recession, and they haven't bounced back. Computer technicians are so busy installing new systems that they haven't time to troubleshoot existing ones.

Even in companies where computer support staff has grown, it hasn't typically grown fast enough to keep pace with the four trends. There are over 200,000 people now providing technical support as a full-time job. Many of these individuals are fighting a losing battle: to transform improperly designed and deployed systems of enormous complexity into efficient data-processing organisms.

The consequences of losing that battle are becoming more serious with every new business function being automated. As companies computerize more and more of their core business operations, they become more dependent on their client/server systems to take orders, ship goods, design products, pay bills, and so on. The organization may leave itself open to lawsuits if it cannot meet contractual obligations because of network failure, or, more simply, it may just lose all its customers.

### Better than Troubleshooting

Because traditional troubleshooting isn't enough, bulletproofing emphasizes ways in which businesses can design and configure their computing systems to guard against the more common problems a priori. This approach is not just advisable in the multivendor world of distributed processing, it's essential.

Even though client/server technology is in its infancy, we already know about many of its problems by now. How can an organization create a successful client/server architecture? How can latency be minimized so that the system performs fast enough for user needs? How can organizations ensure security in what is inherently a less secure environment than the centralized mainframe? And how can companies build in fault tolerance so that the system generates fewer errors and does not suffer from the errors that do occur?

We also know, in reasonably good detail, how the typical client/server system "looks." For example, they nearly all run some version of Microsoft's Windows operating system on the client platform and some form of relational database management system on the server platform.

In short, we now know enough about client/server systems to be able to point out how to avoid many of the common pitfalls.

Bulletproofing may be thought of as adding an immune system to the computer system organism, preventing problems without intervention by users or specialists, and making a graceful recovery more likely in those cases when intervention is required. It's more like forest management than firefighting. Making client/server systems less vulnerable to common problems can be a much more cost-effective strategy than hiring more troubleshooters, pumping ever more technical details into the aching brains of overworked support staff, or throwing money (in the form of hardware, software, infrastructure, etc.) at endemic problems, and cost-effectiveness is paramount in a business climate driven by the bottom line.

We can no more expect to design a 100% effective bulletproofing plan for a client/server computer system than we can expect to find a living being with a 100% effective immune system. To use another analogy, if a mainframe is like a railroad, with clearly defined tracks guiding the flow of data at every step, a client/server network is like the interstate highway system, where cars and trucks crash all the time. We use the interstate highway because it provides a level of flexibility that the railroad does not, and we recognize that it is an inherently riskier way to get around. By applying some of the bulletproofing suggestions in this book to the client/server systems we build, we might be able to avoid 90% of the common problems as opposed to 50% of them, and that could be the difference between a highly successful computer system and a disastrous one.

We'll go further and assert that bulletproofing is the only long-term hope of creating manageable information systems out of today's exploding, mutating client/server networks. Using the bulletproofing philosophy will make client/server networks more reliable, more productive for users, and less of a hassle for technicians, troubleshooters, and managers. Like most worthwhile things, it requires a little more up-front effort, but pays off handsomely over the long term.

## Welcome to This Book

Client/server computing is largely a reaction against the continued high costs of mainframe systems and their slowness in adapting to a user-dominated computing model—explaining why mainframe revenues have dropped by half over the past four years. Client/server is a more user-centered set of technologies that focuses on fast access to lots of information and often to new *kinds* of information (e-mail, fax, graphics, videoconferencing).

Client/server computing is not one technology, but rather a set of technologies: data communications, distributed databases, transaction processing, groupware, middleware, servers, PCs, client workstations, networks, network management, intranets, fault tolerance, backups, security, and so on. It is inherently complex for several reasons: It splits computing chores across multiple platforms; it attempts to deliver data (whatever and wherever it may be) quickly to users (wherever they may be); and its world is one of multiple vendors and many competing standards.

*Bulletproofing Client/Server Systems* is about deploying and managing distributed processing systems so that they work well from the start and so that problems get fixed permanently rather than temporarily. This book will help organizations avoid common problems and build systems that make sense as a whole rather than just at the component level. It will help companies improve speed, security, and reliability, and it will reduce client/server support costs.

This book covers the what, why, and how of client/server systems in a logical progression. Each chapter stands alone, and it's not necessary to read the book from front to back; however, readers who do will find a smooth flow of topics answering these questions:

- What are client/server systems?
- Why implement them?
- How does one build them?
- How can one make them fast enough?
- How can one ensure their security?
- How does one build in reliability?
- How should one support them once they're in place?

The last chapter deals specifically with bulletproofing intranets and extranets, which (as we'll see) comprise a new, popular, and powerful form of client/server system.

The references and resources section at the end provides additional help for client/server implementers, including print, CD-ROM, and online resources as well as a listing of prominent client/server software and hardware companies with addresses, phone numbers, and World Wide Web addresses.

We've tried to write this book in clear, precise, yet conversational English. Though there's no jargon for jargon's sake, the book assumes a basic familiarity with computer terminology. New concepts are explained carefully in the early chapters, and a complete glossary of technical terms and acronyms at the end makes this book useful even for those new to client/server computing.

Many of the suggestions offered here are based on the experiences of technical managers who have attended our seminars. Many have come from our own consulting activities. We invite readers to share their bulletproofing techniques to make the next edition of this book even better.

The first task we will tackle is defining in greater detail just what we mean by "client/server systems"—the subject of Chapter 2. Let's get to it.

# 2

# Defining Client/Server Computing

Now that we've explored the concept of computer system bullet-proofing, we must define this book's central subject—*client/server computing*. For a subject so widely written about and frequently discussed, client/server computing is surprisingly difficult to define except in a technical sense. Perhaps the best way to begin is to consider six vignettes from modern life.

1. It's lunchtime at the neighborhood Boston Market restaurant. The normal mix of customers has come in, ordering sandwiches, meatloaf platters, quarters of chicken. It's only 11:45 a.m., but the line is already pretty long. In the kitchen, a CRT screen tells the cook to put another rack of chicken into the oven, so that it will be ready when the current stock is exhausted, about 12:35 p.m.

2. You call a toll-free telephone number that you found in a catalog of casual clothing. The customer service operator answers, asks you for your customer ID number (for reasons of marketing referred to as "priority code"), verifies that you haven't changed your name or mailing address since last month, and asks how she can help you. You ask about the wool content in a sweater on page 26; she answers with a complete breakdown of fabrics in that item. You want to know whether the kids' overalls on page 55 are available in size 6X, maroon; she says that there are none in stock right now, but that another shipment should be in on Tuesday. You order the sweater and two pairs of overalls, give shipping instructions, and remember that you have an item to return from a previous order. The operator gives you the address for returning merchandise, collects information about the reason for the

return, gets your credit card information for the new order, tells you about some unadvertised specials (you're not interested, but it's nice to know), double-checks your shipping address for UPS (your mailing address is a P.O. box), and thanks you for your business....

3. A mortgage originator ("loan officer") walks into his office at the end of a long day. He plugs his notebook computer into its port replicator, turns it on, and logs into the network. All the information about the six loan applications he took earlier is copied from his hard disk onto the network, where it will automatically become part of the mortgage processing staff's workload. Various people in the company will take steps to verify the applicants' employment, income, assets, and other characteristics listed on each loan application. Based on the outcome, the branch manager (in her role as the "loan committee") will determine whether or not to grant each loan, and at what interest rate. In the long term, the originator's commission depends on the outcomes, and he'll talk to the various processors to make sure the information looks favorable, but right now it's Miller time....

4. A U.S. Army technical specialist, on station somewhere in the Balkan peninsula, needs to repair a component of an advanced weapons system. He has been trained on this class of system but never actually needed to repair one in the field before. He has tools, he has access to a parts depot, but he needs the technical manual and engineering drawings for the system before he can figure out just what needs adjustment or replacement. He goes to his computer, enters a string of numbers that he finds on the component itself, and retrieves the necessary technical information online from the databases maintained by the weapon's original manufacturer....

5. A concerned taxpayer and parent recently walked into the office of his county Superintendent of Schools to ask a question. Because of a recent redistricting proposal, he wanted to know how many classes the county was running in kindergarten through grade 5, by grade level, in each of its 28 elementary schools. By the look on the administrative assistant's face, he knew this was a question no one had ever asked before. Based on the nature of that particular bureaucracy, he was willing to bet that it was not the job of anyone in the entire building to know the answer to his very simple

question. However, the administrative assistant calmly typed a query into his PC, generated a matrix of numbers, and printed the result on a nearby laser printer. With the information in hand, the parent left the office a satisfied (and, truth be told, placated) citizen....

6. In some country of the world, on some date and time, a person will decide to transmit a television signal from one continent to another. That person will inquire about the availability of high-frequency transponders (receivers linked to transmitters) on various geostationary satellites orbiting 22,000 miles above the equator. The inquiry will specify the date and time in question, and the specific satellites of interest; it will be entered in a standard format into a standard PC. The PC will respond with a bar chart indicating transponder availability over the time period in question. If the desired transponder or satellite is available and there is no other traffic using the satellite at that time that would interfere with the television transmission, then a transaction reserving transponder capacity will be submitted online, and the database that records transponder utilization will be updated. If not, then maybe there's another satellite available, or maybe another time slot would be acceptable....

These half-dozen little stories may seem to have nothing in common, but they all demonstrate uses of client/server computing, the increasingly dominant computing architecture of the 1990s. Each centers on the ability of a worker to get a job done using information retrieved or maintained via a personal computer, but stored or processed on some other computer or computers on a network, and in each case the worker is doing a job that could not easily have been done before the advent of client/server.

## Clients, Servers, and Networks

In its most basic form, client/server technology centers on a network of computers, some of which are clients and at least one of which is a server.

*Clients.* The client computers are the ones most visible—typically desktop computers (most often PCs, sometimes Macintoshes) dedicated to the needs of a single human being.

If the human users' jobs don't require full-time access to a computer, then clients can be shared on a walk-up basis (just as you share the ATM across the street from your office with a lot of other bank customers), but more often each human user has a dedicated client machine.

*Servers.*   Server computers, on the other hand, are virtually always shared. The server provides services to some or all of the clients hooked up to the network. In the simplest client/server network, the server provides the following services:

- Shared *disk space* for applications and data files
- Shared *printers* via managed queues

Today's more evolved client/server networks add one or more of the following to the list of services:

- *Security* services for access control, backup, and virus prevention
- Shared *communications* services for outbound access to mainframes and online information providers, and inbound access for remote users, customers, and suppliers
- *Messaging* services such as e-mail and e-mail gateways
- *Directory* services to facilitate access and administration in multiserver networks
- *Management* services to help technicians detect problems earlier and fix them faster

*Networks.*   The set of programs that runs on the network server and provides the services just described, is known as a Network Operating System (NOS); commonly used NOSs include Novell NetWare and Microsoft Windows NT Server as well as Microsoft LAN Manager, IBM LAN Server, and various Unix-based operating systems. The aggregate of clients, servers, and the interconnecting infrastructure is what we'll call a *network*.

## HOW DO PROGRAMS COMMUNICATE ACROSS A NETWORK?

The element of client/server computing that many people familiar with the mainframe, the mini- or midrange computer, or the standalone PC environment often have most difficulty understanding is the communication between computers (or, more correctly, between programs running on different computers).

Of course, there's nothing magic about programs communicating across a network. Most people are aware that it's possible (even common), but that doesn't mean that they're comfortable with *how* the communication takes place.

The industry-standard way of explaining how programs communicate from one computer to another is best represented by a seven-level partitioning known as the "Open Systems Interconnection Reference Model," or just the "OSI Model." The seven levels of partitioning simply imply that there are seven major tasks such that, if we can solve each of the seven in a coordinated way, communication can be achieved.

The OSI Model is generally depicted as a seven-layer stack or wedding cake (see Figure 2.1), implying not only partitioning among component tasks but also an order in which the tasks should be addressed.

In a pair of production programs, each level would be occupied on each computer by two modules, one for sending messages and the other for receiving messages. All modules on the same level would be designed according to a common protocol, or set of agreements about how the specific task(s) in question would be addressed.

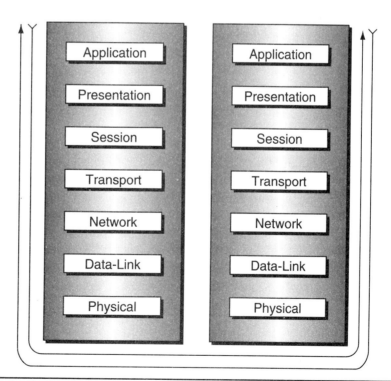

**Figure 2.1:**  The OSI Model

The OSI model is comprehensive and detailed, but we can give a nutshell description of the main responsibility of the module running at each level:

- The *Application* level controls the form and nature of the interaction (or "conversation") as it appears from the perspective of the application program.
- The *Presentation* level takes care of data representation (ASCII vs. EBCDIC, 16-bit vs. 32-bit, etc.).
- The *Session* level keeps track of all the various conversations that are going on and allocates appropriate resources to each.
- The *Transport* layer deals with the limitations of any particular network—things like maximum packet size (the greatest number of bytes that can be sent at once). Messages longer than a particular network allows are divided up into multiple packets that are sent across the wire individually and reassembled into the original message on the other side.
- The *Network* layer deals with addressing and routing—putting "to" and "from" addresses on each packet so that it can be delivered accurately and efficiently.
- The *Data-Link* layer is the "quality assurance" layer, making certain that any transmission errors that occur are promptly detected and corrected.
- The *Physical* layer transforms each packet from its RAM format to whatever is appropriate for a particular network: high and low voltages to go over copper cable, light impulses for fiber optics, radio waves for wireless networks.

To get from an application program running on one computer to a corresponding application on another computer (e.g., from the client half to the server half of a client/server application), any message goes from the application program on the first computer through the protocols in order (application, presentation, session, transport, network, data-link, physical) on that same computer, across the network to the second computer, through the protocols in reverse order (physical, data-link, network, transport, session, presentation, application), and finally to the application program on the second computer.

Communication from the server back to the client will be handled in precisely the same manner.

## Client/Server Computing vs. Client/Server Networking

A network with a NOS that runs on a dedicated server is known as a *client/server network*, and many people think that any computing that takes place on a client/server network is inherently client/server computing.

However, client/server computing is more complex than just using a network server as an electronic file cabinet or to avoid having to buy multiple printers (or multiple connections to the mainframe). It often makes use of server computers entirely separate from the common network server. Client/server computing typically requires such network services as messaging and security authorization, but it also makes use of services that go far beyond.

Client/server computing is a form of *cooperative processing*, that is, the closely coordinated use of more than one computer to solve any given business problem. By way of contrast, then, solving a business problem using the services of only a single computer (such as a mainframe or minicomputer) might be termed "uncooperative processing." (If you identify yourself as a mainframe or minicomputer specialist, you may find this term somewhat objectionable, but if you've used a lot of mainframe or minicomputer systems over the years, you know exactly what we mean!)

## Cooperative Processing, Pro and Con

The good news about cooperative processing (in any of its forms) is that to solve your business problem, you *get* to use the services of multiple computers. If the computers are of different types, sizes, models, and hardware architectures, they probably have different strengths. By using more than one type of computer, you can apply each computer to that part of the task for which it is best suited. You can come up with a more complete, easier to use, more informative solution than would be possible using only a single type of computer hardware.

The bad news about cooperative processing (in any of its forms) is that to solve your business problem, you *have* to use the services of multiple computers. That means that your system must take on the overhead tasks of coordinating and communicating between multiple programs, possibly written in multiple programming languages, running on multiple hardware platforms, under multiple operating systems. Modern client/server technologies can achieve this communication and coordination, but the overhead processing unavoidably adds to the complexity of the application system and the computing environment. Depending on a number of considerations (which we'll go into), the overhead of client/server coordination and communication can increase a system's technical complexity by two to three times or even more.

## Cooperative vs. Distributed Processing

Cooperative processing is often confused with *distributed processing*, with which it often overlaps. Distributed and cooperative processing have much in common, and both terms imply the use of multiple computers, but beyond this the emphases of the two terms are quite different.

Distributed processing, as the name implies, emphasizes that the two (or more) computers are located in multiple physical sites. Distributed computer systems are often designed to allow for the fact that human work goes on in multiple locations and to locate computer processing near the work to which it relates.

In fact, we've been designing and developing distributed computer systems since the 1960s, at least. A manufacturing company with multiple factories in several regions collects production statistics within each factory, verifies the data at the factory to assure its accuracy, and then sends it to the appropriate regional office. The regional staff summarizes the data, produces regional production reports for regional management, and sends a summary file to headquarters. The headquarters staff then summarizes the data from all regions to produce a national or corporate production report.

Such a system could truly be termed "distributed," for each type of location (factory, region, headquarters) has its own computer and each location performs its own appropriate processes within an overall framework. However, the data might get communicated between locations via the U.S. Postal Service, and the whole system might take 30 days to crank out a monthly production report. (By the end of April, corporate management would know what March's production had been!)

*Cooperative* processing implies a much closer, or at least more interdependent, link between the various computers. True cooperation requires more communication than just sending data files through the mail, and cooperative processing systems often perform complete tasks in seconds, not months!

Modern cooperative processing systems typically involve multiple brands and models of computers, and often unpredictable combinations of computer types. They address business problems and tasks that are not as fixed, predictable, and well understood as monthly production reporting. Sometimes they even address multiple business problems simultaneously.

So, in cooperative processing, the emphasis is not on having multiple computers in various locations, but on having multiple computers that work closely together. The computers may be geographically distributed, but in cooperative processing, that's not the point.

## Forms of Cooperative Processing

There are several forms of cooperative processing, but the two most common are client/server and peer-to-peer (see Figure 2.2). Much of the popularity of the client/server form is because it gives more guidance and assistance in the coordination of multiple computer programs than the alternatives.

Client/server computing is the subset of cooperative processing that is based on a simple, stable, hierarchical control relationship between any two cooperating programs, which may be running on two separate computers. Simply stated, the control hierarchy is based on the following rules:

- Coordination is always achieved between exactly two computers.
- Of the two computers, one is the client and the other is the server.

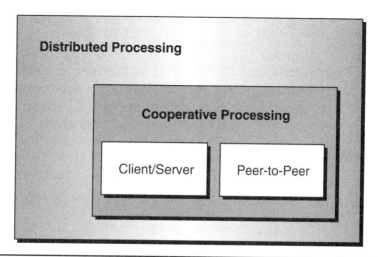

**Figure 2.2:**  Distributed and Cooperative Processing

- The client is always in charge.

These are simple rules, defining a simple building block (the pairing of client and server), but the building block is as versatile as the one pioneered by Lego Systems and the rules turn out to be as restrictive, yet as useful, as the one that says we all drive on the right-hand side of the road.

- Observation: Driving only on the right-hand side of the road is terribly inefficient. No matter where or in which direction you wish to proceed, fully 50% of the pavement is unavailable to you. On the other hand.... (Readers in Japan or the UK please adjust, as appropriate!)
- Observation: There is nothing in the world that cannot be built from Lego blocks. If you doubt it, visit Legoland in the Mall of America near Minneapolis.

The client/server relationship is far more structured than the *peer-to-peer* relationship, in which two programs (which may be running on two computers) coordinate and determine, from moment to moment, which one of them is in charge. Peer-to-peer computing can be very powerful and has been successfully implemented in such fields as communications and scientific calculation, but having a defined client in charge of any particular interaction simplifies control processing and has become the most widely practiced method for business-, administrative-, and database-related cooperative processing.

## Components of a Client/Server Business System

The facts that the client/server building block is simple and involves only two programs (or two computers) do not mean that client/server computing systems are necessarily simple. Each program—the one running on the client and the one running on the server—may be incredibly complex. There may be a large number of client computers, each simultaneously communicating with any number of servers. Taken as a whole, the amount of computer power necessary simply to coordinate all the clients and servers in a large system may exceed what's necessary to run a typical mainframe application.

To make matters worse, there's no single way of dividing an application system to determine what logic runs on the client and what runs on the server. To see some of the more common ways that client/server applications get divided up, let's look at the basic components of the common, garden-variety business application system.

In a sense, virtually any business application system can be divided up into three basic components: *user interface, process logic*, and *data storage*.

## User Interface

*User interface*, sometimes called *presentation logic*, is concerned with getting information from the human user into the computer, or from the computer out to the human user. The user interface includes

- Data entry (such as keying of data at a keypunch, an online terminal or a PC)
- Automated data capture (such as is performed by a bar-code reader or a document scanner)
- Character display (such as a matrix of numbers that appears on the screen of an online terminal or a report printed on green-bar paper)
- Graphical display (such as a pie chart printed on a laser printer, a still or moving picture displayed on a CRT screen or a construction "blueprint" created on a digital plotter).

User interface involves all forms of input and output between humans and computers. The user interface may make certain that data is in the right format (assure input is numeric, transform output from a table of numerics to a bar chart), but it does not edit the data to make sure it makes sense (job title and job grade match up for a new hire, or we're buying our supplies from a company that in fact sells those particular items).

## Process Logic

*Process logic* implements the business rules that characterize or constitute the business application. For an accounting application, the process logic implements accounting principles. For a purchasing system, the process logic implements purchasing policy. For a personnel system, the process logic assures compliance with the latest laws on hiring and firing (you hope).

Process logic is the hardest of the three components to define and talk about directly, but it's absolutely critical to the success of any business computer application. Process logic tells the computer what combinations of data are allowable, and what steps can automatically be taken (add a new employee to the payroll, issue a purchase order) based on the successful completion of previous steps (hire a new employee, approve a procurement request).

## Data Storage

*Data storage* is the long-term memory of the computer application. It stores the information that the system captures, updates old information as newer data become available, and makes appropriate information available when a question (or "query") is asked.

Data storage may be *passive or active*. Passive data storage consists of files of information into which the process logic or user interface can enter records and from which they can scan records. Active data storage consists of modern databases, which accept new data as it becomes available, store it as appropriate, and scan their own information for the answers to queries.

### WHAT'S A RELATIONAL DBMS?

Client/server systems often capture, collect, manage, and report data. To store this data, they typically use the services of a database management system or *DBMS*. The most popular type of DBMS at the moment, and the form generally used in client/server computing, is the relational DBMS.

A relational DBMS differs from earlier types of database management system in that it supports an almost infinite number of relationships among its data records. For instance, in a personnel system containing information about employees, positions, work locations, departments, and divisions, a relational DBMS could easily report data in any of the following formats:

- Employees by position
- Employees by work location
- Employees by department
- Employees by division
- Positions by work location
- Positions by department
- Positions by division
- Work locations by department

- Work locations by division
- Departments by division
- Division by department
- Divisions by work location
- Departments by work location
- Divisions by position title
- Departments by position title
- Work locations by position title
- Division by employee
- Department by employee
- Work location by employee
- Position by employee

Earlier forms of DBMS might have been able to report data easily for some or most of these combinations, but none could typically support all the combinations. The reason is that earlier forms of database management systems predetermined what links to store between one type of record and another. These links would arrange a database into some sort of logical pattern, such as a hierarchy or network.

*Hierarchical* databases (such as IBM's IMS product) tried to fit everything into a pyramid structure. In our example, the top of the pyramid would probably be the division, with department records subordinate to the record for the division to which the departments belonged. Position records would exist "within" (subordinate to) departments, and employees would be recorded within positions. Finally, work locations might be recorded only within a particular employee record. Such a database would have difficulty reporting employees by work location, positions by work location, or even exactly how many unique work locations existed.

*Network* databases (such as Computer Associates' IDMS) attempt to alleviate some of the restrictions of the hierarchical model by allowing the database links to follow a pattern other than a hierarchy. With a well-designed network consisting of bidirectional links, a network DBMS might be able to generate most of the previous lists of data. (Note that the term "network," as used here, has nothing to do with Local Area Networks or data communications. It merely refers to a diagramming of database links that does not resemble a hierarchy.)

The advantage of hierarchical and network databases, and the reason why they're sometimes still used,  is that they are extremely fast and efficient in executing preprogrammed transactions and inquiries. Unfortunately, they are inefficient in the execution of ad hoc transactions and inquiries, and in many instances simply cannot support them at all.

Hierarchical and network databases were a good fit for information systems that performed only a few types of transactions, knew in advance just what those transactions would look like, and had to process large numbers of transactions per day.

*Relational* databases are not as efficient at processing predefined transactions, but they are much easier to use in an ad hoc situation, or when a new production use for the data comes up. With a relational database, system users are not restricted by the imagination of past system designers—they can use a database for purposes the original designer never envisioned.

How do relational databases work? All relational database management systems arrange the information they record into two-dimensional (2D) tables. Our little personnel database would have a table of employees, one of position descriptions, one of work locations, one of departments, and one of divisions.

No record in any table would be "linked" (as with a hierarchical or network DBMS) to any other record or table. On the other hand, records might carry data fields that would allow a user (or a relational DBMS) to find appropriate information in another table. For instance, an employee record might carry coded fields indicating the employee's position, work location, and department; a department record might carry a field to indicate which division the department belonged to. By following these "foreign keys," any user or program can find an employee and then find (from the position table) all the information about the employee's position, or (from the department table) all about the appropriate department, or....

With a relational database, a user can ask any sort of query ("Which department has the most employees over 6 feet tall and under 25 years old?"), whether or not the need for such a query ever occurred to the designer of the system. The trade-off is that, to achieve such flexibility, relational DBMSs have to interpret the query when it is asked, decide which relationships (implemented as foreign keys) are appropriate to determining the query's answer, and trace down data according to those relationships. All of this begins when the user submits the query and must complete before an answer is presented. As a result, relational databases are far slower than either hierarchical or network databases for any task that each can perform equally well. However, because relational DBMSs can perform tasks other DBMSs cannot, speed is not the only issue, and when speed is important, relational database performance can be improved by the liberal application of hardware—you can always put the relational DBMS on a faster server.

## Why These Components Are Important

These three basic components—user interface, process logic, and data storage—have characterized many business applications since the early days of business computing. Implementation technologies have changed—user interfaces have gone from punched cards to high-resolution color graphics—but the basic tasks have remained the same.

For the past 30 years, dividing a computer application into these three components, in most cases, was not a particularly useful task. It could be done, but you really didn't know any more about the system or the program after you finished separating the components than you did before. In most cases all three components were implemented on a single computer in a single programming language—sometimes they were all part of a single computer program.

With the advent of client/server computing, though, the distinctions between user interface and process logic, and between process logic and data storage, become very significant indeed. The dividing lines, the interfaces, among these basic components become the simplest and most widely used locations for splitting an application between client and server platforms. That is, the communication and coordination that is at the heart of client/server computing typically takes place between user interface and process logic, or between process logic and data storage. This is not to say that all client/server systems look the same.

## Different Ways to Divide the Components

The most common varieties of client/server applications have names that have entered the vernacular: *fat client, thin client* (or, in less polite circles, *skinny client*), and *three tiered*. These terms are widely used (and almost as widely understood); they simply refer to different ways of dividing client/server applications along the two most common interfaces: the presentation interface (between the user interface [or "presentation" component] and the process logic component), and the data interface (between process logic and data storage).

### Fat-Client Systems

*Fat client* systems place the user interface and all the process logic on the client (see Figure 2.3). That is, for each user of a fat-

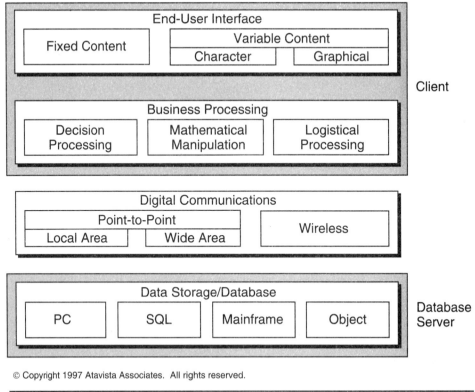

**Figure 2.3:**    Fat-Client Systems

client application, the programs that capture, display, and process all the data that user handles or looks at run on that user's desktop computer. If you have three users, you have three client PCs. If you have three hundred users, you have three hundred client PCs. The data storage, typically residing on a database server, will be commonly accessed and shared among all users, no matter how many, but most of the processing for each user is right where the user is, and affects no one else.

Fat-client applications are the most common business client/server applications, because they're relatively easy to implement, they're relatively easy to scale (that is, to accommodate to a larger or smaller user community), and they're supported by the most popular client/server development tools.

However, fat-client applications have a number of long-term disadvantages, all stemming from their positioning of process logic on the client platform. Because they distribute all the process logic to as many client computers as there are human users, fat-client systems can have significant configuration-management problems. The larger the application (the more components) and the larger the user community (the greater the number of physically separate copies of each component), the more difficult it is to keep track of each component. If the application is volatile, so that versions of at least some components need to be updated continually, configuration management can become a particular problem.

Similarly, fat-client applications not only place their process logic on the user's personal (desktop or portable) computer, they also place it under the user's direct physical control. Sophisticated users can gain access to the program code, for whatever purpose. Unless explicit steps are taken to preclude unauthorized version changes by individual users, distributed process logic is subject to being "hacked." Even if users are prevented from altering the code, they can still examine it, perhaps discerning production algorithms that were better kept secret.

Finally, fat-client applications can place an unacceptable processing demand upon personal computers. With today's high-speed PCs (ever faster hard disks, 32-bit operating systems, 200 MHz processor speeds, symmetrical multiprocessing on the desktop), it may seem unlikely that any application would overwhelm the available hardware, but companies have found that employees who become adept at using client/server applications often use them in combination. The combinations are hard to predict, and they often include programs from three, four, or half a dozen different applications. Under those circumstances, if each application demands that the client computer support all its process logic, it becomes possible to overload even the most capable desktop hardware.

### Thin-Client Systems

*Thin-client* systems put only the user interface component on the client (see Figure 2.4). They keep all the process logic on the server, along with the data storage. To the human user, thin-client and fat-client systems may look identical, but to systems designers and managers the two present quite different challenges. Thin-client systems have more in common with traditional mainframe- or minicomputer-based terminal/host systems than do fat-client systems.

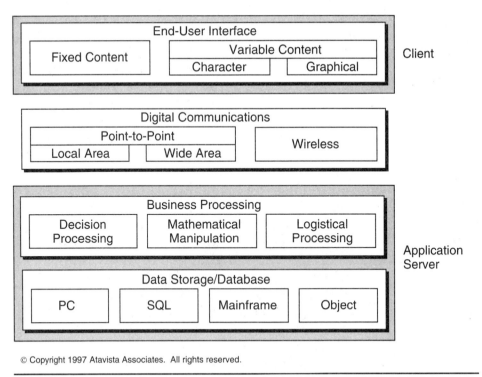

**Figure 2.4:**    Thin-Client Systems

Nonetheless, thin-client systems are popular in the Unix community and where process logic code is security sensitive. The
reasons for thin-client popularity with Unix devotees (Unix is
not merely an operating system, it's a minor nontheistic religion)
are mainly historical. The popularity for applications with security-sensitive process logic, however, is strictly rational and
intentional. By keeping the processing code on a centralized
server, out of the physical control of the human user, systems
designers create a more secure application, even with a sophisticated and untrusted user community.

This points up the rationale behind the most common use of
thin-client applications design today, applications ("pages") on
the World Wide Web. Web browsers are universal (or at least,
standardized) pieces of thin-client software. When a netizen connects to a particular Web page, the Web server downloads a set
of parameters to the Web browser program on the user's PC. The
browser program then interprets the parameters and displays
the appropriate information according to its own capabilities (as
standards evolve, some browsers are more—or differently—
capable than others). The browser is concerned only with input

(mouse motions or keying) and output (graphical or character display); all data storage and any process logic usually remains on the Web server.

When a Web page is more complex than a single server can handle, for instance when it provides access to a huge database or a library of information, then it becomes an example of the last commonly implemented Client/Server design: three-tiered applications.

### Three-Tiered Systems

*Three-tiered* applications are ones in which each basic application component (user interface, process logic, and data storage) has its own computer, or its own logical tier of computers (see Figure 2.5). In a three-tiered design, each component can be imple-

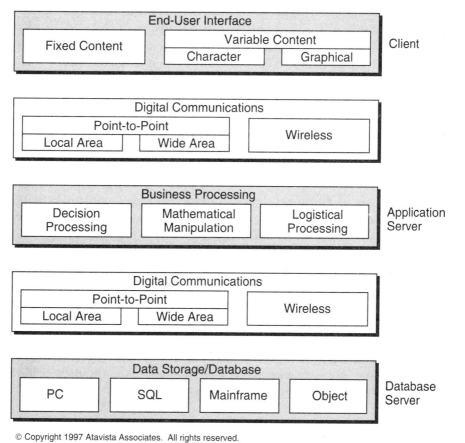

**Figure 2.5:**   Three-Tiered Systems

mented on hardware specifically selected or designed to perform its specific task. Data storage can be on a machine with tremendous magnetic or optical memory capacity and sufficient input/output capability, but minimal calculating power and no graphical capabilities at all; process logic can be installed on a machine with virtually no hard disk or graphics ability, but with lots of random access memory and a particularly fast processor; and the user interface can exist on a machine with great graphics but nothing else.

Three-tiered applications are more complex to design and manage than either fat- or thin-client applications (both of which are known as "two-tiered" designs). They are also at a disadvantage because they generate greater network traffic than two-tiered applications. However, given a knowledgeable system designer, they can achieve higher total throughput and/or faster transaction response time than simpler designs, they are easily integrated with both fat- and thin-client applications (as we will discuss in Chapter 4), and they are often created as the natural outcome of a stepwise application migration from a host-based environment to a client/server environment.

### WHAT IS MIDDLEWARE?

Most of the technologies used in client/server computing can also be used in host-based, or other single-platform, computing systems. The general exception is *middleware*.

The term "middleware" is used by almost everyone in the client/server arena, not always 100% consistently. Some use it to refer only to a very specific type of products; others to reference a much broader range.

In general, middleware, as the name implies, is whatever goes in between two other technologies to allow them to work together (when, otherwise, they wouldn't). In this sense, there can be GUI middleware, file-handling middleware, and probably even number-crunching middleware.

In the client/server world, however, middleware has taken on the more specific meaning of software that helps clients and servers to communicate and cooperate, that is, of application-level protocols for client/server computing. In this sense, there are two common forms of middleware: database middleware and more general module-to-module middleware (such as remote procedure calls, for instance).

Finally, because of the dominance of the fat-client model and the prevalence of database servers, many use the term "middleware" to refer only to database middleware, based on SQL.

In any given context, both parties are likely to understand the term the same way, but some care should be taken to avoid miscommunication.

More technical permutations exist than these three, so there are more varieties of client/server systems than just fat-client, thin-client, and three-tiered, but a more complex design is usually only justifiable on a case-by-case basis. More complex designs mean more complex system administration, maintenance, and management. As we'll soon see, the client/server environment is quite difficult enough to administer, maintain, and manage without unnecessary complexities. A key element of bulletproofing is to avoid complexity where it does not add valuable functionality.

In fact, one of the ways companies run into trouble as they move from simple client/server networking to real client/server computing is by failing to deal with the additional complexities of a cooperative processing environment.

## Client/Server Complexities

Technology salespeople have been proclaiming the simplicity of client/server for so long, and so loudly, that some IT managers simply don't understand what they're getting into. The predictable result is unhappy users (which, in turn, can lead the IT manager into an opportunity to make new friends in the workplace).

The most common symptom of an overly simplistic plan for the transition to client/server computing is an overloaded network, usually a local area network. As network traffic (the demand for and utilization of network capacity) builds up, response times for every user on the network get longer and longer. Tasks such as retrieving a file or loading a program from the network server, which used to take only a couple of seconds, begin to take a minute or longer. Signing on to the network at the busiest time of day may take five or ten minutes. Sending a large report to a network printer may take half an hour, even if the printer itself is sitting idle. To make matters worse, the network crashes or locks up more and more often.

Network capacity is fixed by the particular network technology in place. A client/server network that has given fully adequate service (response time, reliability, etc.) to 40 or 50 users may be quite inadequate for the same number of users doing client/server computing. Each user generates more network traffic in a cooperative processing environment—the direct result of having to coordinate and communicate between two programs that were once running on a single computer, but aren't anymore.

## From Condos to Suburbs

To understand the situation, think of a small town in which everyone lives in a single condominium complex. Additionally, everyone works in a single office complex, located right next door to the condominium. Such a town would need a system of roads, so that people could shop, travel, and receive visitors from other locations, but it would have no rush hour. A network of two-lane roads would be quite adequate to support all the traffic.

Now take those same people and move them to single-family detached homes in the suburbs. They still work in a central office complex, but now each one of them has to commute. Rush hour becomes a concrete reality, and traffic increases at all hours of the day. Stores and services have to support a more distributed population and so become more distributed themselves. Once the suburban model takes hold, every trip requires vehicular traffic. The number of people hasn't gone up, but the formerly adequate network of two-lane roads is now completely overwhelmed.

In many companies with client/server networks, the local area networks are like a system of two-lane roads. They may be totally adequate for their intended purpose of allowing users to share files, share printers, and send messages to one another, but the more efficiently they serve that set of purposes, the more certainly they will be overwhelmed by the shift to client/server computing. The network will need to be redesigned, and in the worst case completely rewired.

In our small town analogy, we presumed that everyone continued to work in a single location. That location, the destination or starting point of most rush-hour trips, corresponds to the server in a typical client/server setup. However, in a mature client/server computing environment, there is often more than one server. Network services may be provided by one server computer and database services by another (or by a number of others). As a result, not only does network traffic volume increase, the *pattern* of network traffic gets more complex. The network becomes harder to design and manage for efficiency.

In a client/server networking environment, most users interact only with a single server that is located logically near them on the network. (All the users on local area network A will be served by the server on A; all the users on local area B will be served the server on B, etc.). With client/server computing, users will be interacting with multiple servers at multiple locations on the network. Sometimes, a user at one end of the network may need to communicate with a server at the other end. Traffic gets more complex, and the traffic on every portion of the network between one end and the other will increase.

So, as the use of client/server computing increases, the likelihood of communications running across the network from server to server goes up. Not only does this increase the number of trips across the network, these server-to-server communications tend to carry a higher volume of data than client-to-server traffic. As a result, they use up a larger share of the available network capacity and slow other traffic down even more.

## WHAT IS A DATA WAREHOUSE?

To hear some people talk about it, client/server computing is all about applications that retrieve, format, and present data, but that perform no data capture or update functionality.

This might seem like a rather narrow view, but the fact is that many companies use client/server computing solely to provide flexible access to data that is still maintained by host-based applications. If their business plans require them to compete on a low-cost (rather than a high-differentiation) basis, their limited use of client/server probably makes sense.

What many of these companies end up establishing are "data warehouses." Data warehouses are (typically) relational databases, physically separate from the databases and files that the operational systems update on a regular basis, and intended solely to support data retrieval, analysis, and presentation.

Data warehouses contain data that is copied, extracted, summarized, and/or "snapshotted" from the company's operational data and, in some cases, from external data sources as well. Warehouse data is often summarized, because over 90% of all inquiries can be answered with summarized data; it may be "snapshotted" (a "snapshot" is an image of the data as it existed at a certain time, but not necessarily as it exists currently) in order to facilitate apples-to-apples comparisons across classes of information (sales versus accounting, for instance); and it is physically extracted to a separate copy in order that large-volume inquiries against the data warehouse not degrade the response time that operational users experience as they enter the data that will be summarized tonight, to appear in the data warehouse tomorrow.

## Responses to Complexity

The nature of communication between two programs, closely cooperating across a network, is more sophisticated than the "read a file, write a file" messages that dominate the client/server networking world. As a result, application-level protocols in client/server computing are more complex. They require more explicit design decisions, more integration work, more testing, and more maintenance and management. If you have multiple client/server applications on your network (and you will), a decision has to be made: Will all applications use the same set of protocols, or will different applications use different protocols? This decision will have a significant long-term impact on the manageability of your network environment. If your organization uses a mix of fat-client, thin-client and three-tiered applications, this is not an easy decision to make.

Speaking of fat-client systems, the more process logic gets distributed to the desktop computer, the more capable that computer has to be. As client/server applications get bigger and more complex, and as individual users start to interact with more and more applications simultaneously, desktop hardware typically has to be upgraded. Companies that previously were able to buy a workstation PC and plan on that PC lasting 5 years or longer, often find themselves replacing or upgrading client PC hardware every year or two. The obvious result is additional expense (although not as much as you might expect). The less obvious result is additional system management complexity.

In a cooperative processing network, every computer has to be able to interact/cooperate with every other computer. The more types of physically different computers you have, the more types of interactions are required, and the more difficult it is to keep everything working smoothly and reliably. A common technique used by system managers and network administrators everywhere is to try to standardize desktop computers—to limit the number of different hardware and software configurations they have to support. Unfortunately, the faster desktop hardware changes (is updated or upgraded), the harder standardization becomes.

Finally, client/server computing changes the way people use information and computers. Because client/server makes more information, and more processing power, directly available to the user, people tend to use automated information more. They do their jobs better, they do different jobs, and both the job and the method of performing it tend to evolve over time. As a result, applications in a client/server environment can be far more subject to change than applications in a host-based or client/server networking environment. Because much application software now resides on the desktop computers of the various users, simply keeping up with rapidly changing versions, keeping all the users in sync so that everyone is using the same version of the software, can be a major challenge.

Any way you look at it, client/server computing is more complex than client/server networking. The technical community has learned a lot about designing, implementing, and managing client/server networks. Now the technical and business communities need to learn how to handle the complexities of extending the client/server model into application software.

In this chapter, we've defined what client/server computing is and hinted at what it implies. In the next chapter, we'll explore the benefits of client/server computing more fully, so that we can bring our goals for these new systems into focus. Once we've articulated those benefits and goals, we'll have a solid framework for discussing ways to achieve them by making good decisions from the start in the areas of design, performance, security, fault tolerance, and user support.

# 3

# Why Client/Server?

The previous chapter closed with a fundamental explanation of client/server complexities. If client/server computing is so complex, why is it so popular? Why are companies running toward it and not away?

## Complexity Is Hidden

The short answer is that the complexity of client/server computing is apparent only to the information technician—the Help Desk analyst, support person, or programmer who has to understand enough about the internals to make them work—to the mechanic, if you will. Consumer technologies don't become popular because they appeal to mechanics, they become popular because they appeal to consumers. In today's world of information technology, the consumer is the end user.

## "Consumers" Benefit

Numerous recent studies of the popularity of client/server computing have turned up some very consistent results. What consumers like most about client/server is its ability to provide them with the following benefits:

- Seamless access to corporate data
- Ease of use
- Consistent look and feel for end user access
- Better applications/tools for users

Consumers find client/server easier to use and vastly more capable than previous forms of computing.

If you haven't personally used an online host-based business application recently, a couple of examples from the retail sector may help explain.

One of the stores Rick frequents is a cooperative. He's not only a customer, he's also a member and (to a very small extent) an owner. At the end of each year, he gets a distribution check, paying him back a small percentage of his total purchases. Hence, every time he buys something at the coop, he makes sure that they associate it with his membership account.

Like most of the coop members, Rick doesn't carry his membership account number around in his head. This situation is so common that the online retail system that the coop uses has an alternate key—the telephone number. Rick simply provides his phone number and the system looks up his membership number.

The problem is, the phone number (or membership number) has to be the first thing entered at the cash register, before any of the items are rung up. Once the first item is scanned, there's simply no way to go back and enter membership information without canceling the entire transaction and starting over.

Glenn lives about an hour from the nearest big city and so frequently uses catalog discounters. One in particular has a very sophisticated direct mail operation; the company collects and maintains a good amount of customer information. The key to the customer record, again, is the telephone number. Here, the clerks have been trained to ask for phone number before ringing up any items (apparently their system has the same limitation on processing sequence).

The problem arises when Glenn pulls out his checkbook. He doesn't have his phone number imprinted on his checks. The store wants a phone number on all checks. Of course, they already have his phone number in the computer...but it's no longer on the screen!

In order to pay by check, Glenn has to give the cashier his phone number twice—once at the beginning of the transaction (to identify him as a customer), and once at the end (to write on his check). This strikes at least some customers as inefficient and inconvenient.

The reason that the two host-based retail systems require a phone number at the beginning of the transaction (and don't allow it to be entered more flexibly, whenever it's convenient) is that both systems are programmed in a very procedural manner.

Host-based (typically mainframe or minicomputer) online systems are designed and implemented to control their human users.

## Computing Philosophies

Host-based applications are the end product of a computing philosophy that has been with us since the 1950s. The unwritten rule of this approach is that *computers are expensive and people are cheap.* As a result, systems are designed to make most efficient use of the computer and to force people to accommodate themselves to the machine.

Client/server computing, on the other hand, became popular after computers had become cheap and people relatively expensive. Client/server applications take advantage of technologies that at least attempt to accommodate themselves to human efficiency (sometimes called "ease of use") and are designed to expend some computer resources in the effort.

Guess which systems people prefer to use? Ease of use goes far beyond "look and feel." It reflects client/server's use of the latest Windowslike graphical user interfaces, allowing users to control the sequence of processing rather than being restricted by procedural programs, and even letting them interact with multiple programs at a time. Ease of use also includes consumers' ability to access all sorts of data, both through fixed (production) programs and through variable (ad hoc) inquiries. In the client/server world, consumers can combine the ability to access production data with the power to massage and manipulate that data on their personal computers. Although the thought of this uncontrolled situation may give IT professionals pause, users feel like they've died and gone to heaven.

## Cost Savings?

Ironically, ease of use (and all it implies) was not the original motivation for many companies that adopted client/server, and it's still not the number one objective in the minds of some non-technical managers. Probably the biggest myth concerning reasons to go client/server is the one that says, "You'll save money on your computers." It ain't so.

In the early days of client/server computing, it was commonly said that C/S would allow an organization to save much of its computing budget. Some companies even managed to cut their Information Technology (IT) expenditures by 40% or more. The savings were supposed to come from decreased hardware prices (PCs, even lots of PCs, cost less than a mainframe), decreased software prices (PC software is a competitive market—no more IBM monopoly pricing), and decreased operating staff costs (PCs don't require dedicated computer operators). The myth survived for a couple of years because companies that believed it trumpeted their reduced IT department budgets.

However, the savings are imaginary. They're an accounting fiction. They don't really exist. The IT budget has gone down because a large portion of the cost has been transferred to other departments, largely user departments. G2 Research Inc. puts the per-user cost of client/server systems at roughly twice that of mainframe systems. The British consulting firm Compass pegged 1995 mainframe user costs at 1750 pounds sterling per year, and client/server user costs at 6400 pounds sterling per year. The best U.S. estimates we have of the total cost to an organization of providing a client/server computing capability is $10,000 per year per user desktop, plus the cost of any custom applications (Gartner Group).

Why are costs so high when PC hardware is so cheap? Well, only about $2000 per user annually is spent on hardware. Twice that much is spent on formal PC and network administration and support costs, and another $4000 annually is the real cost of labor provided by the user department itself—training costs, support and informal "help" costs, learning costs in the form of temporarily decreased productivity, et cetera, et cetera. (See Figure 3.1.)

Some organizations have documented an overall savings from their client/server applications, but the savings come exclusively from increased user productivity, particularly in the form of redesigned and rewritten job descriptions.

## Reengineering for Synergy

More sophisticated companies are taking advantage of client/server specifically so that they can redesign people's jobs—so that they can rethink and reengineer the way they serve their

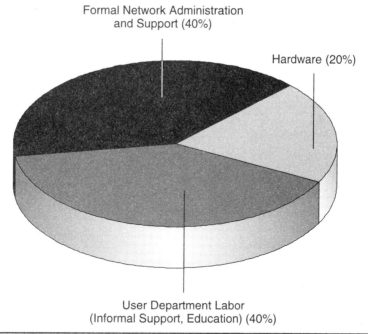

**Figure 3.1:**   Desktop Costs

customers and produce goods. It's been said that "client/server makes reengineering possible, and reengineering makes client/server necessary." (See Figure 3.2.)

The real savings from client/server computing come only to organizations that are willing to change the way jobs are designed. The largest savings from client/server computing come to organizations that actively look for opportunities to make such changes. Of course, the redesigning of jobs has to be for the purpose of making better use of information, and the information has to be used better to serve an identifiable business purpose. For instance, some organizations use client/server applications to help them acquire and retain customers better. They use flexible access to information (both regularly formatted and unformatted information) to facilitate their marketing, sales, and customer-retention efforts.

## Customer Retention

Customer retention is a fairly common use of client/server technology for purposes of marketing. Conventional wisdom says

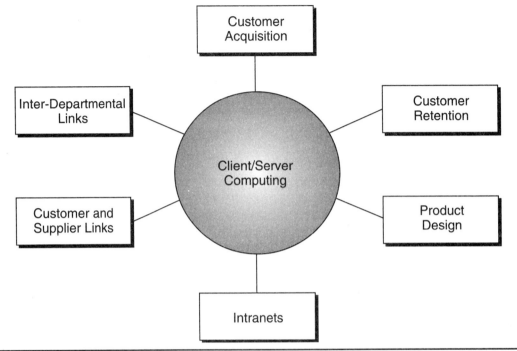

**Figure 3.2:**   Client/Server and Business Redesign

that it's typically 10 times as costly to acquire a new customer as to retain an existing one, and companies can build up large bases of information about their existing customers—information that they can then turn to their advantage.

Have you received personalized grocery coupons in the mail or at the cash register as you check out? Not just checkout coupons for savings on alternatives to products you bought that day, but coupons for alternatives to products you bought last week or last month? Perhaps even coupons with your name printed on them?

Have you thought about how the coupon printer knew your name and what you bought at the grocery store last week? Do you think it might have anything to do with that "loyal customer" card with the bar code imprinted on it?

Because grocery chains have no way of predicting precisely which of their stores you'll shop at next, the data for printing the coupons has to be stored in a central location, but the printing has to take place where you are, as does ringing up the order and decrementing the shelf inventory—Just one innovative use of information, made practical by client/server technology.

## Customer Acquisition

A slightly unusual example of a client/server system for customer acquisition was built by a large Eastern university. The university already had an enviable endowment, one of the largest in the country, but financial projections indicated that it needed more, to offset the costs of an aging infrastructure and allow it to offer more in the way of financial aid (college costs being what they are). The university set up a special marketing/sales task force, with the goal of raising some $200,000,000. The funds were to be raised from alumni over a 2-year period.

The efforts of the special marketing staff were to be made largely on the phone and with the assistance of a special database. The alumni office identified some 2000 former students who were candidate "customers." The database was populated with all the available information about these prominent citizens and then updated daily from news clippings and other sources.

The campaign consisted of calling these wealthy alumni (after all, you can't raise $200 million by calling impoverished alumni) on behalf of the university, on a regular basis over the two-year period. The calls started out with birthday or holiday wishes, continued with greetings on wedding anniversaries and the birthdays of children, and culminated in timely congratulations on business successes or similar newsworthy events.

During the 2-year period, relationships were built. Some relationships were stronger than others, and the weak ones were culled from the database (not the weak individuals, necessarily—the weak relationships). By the end of the 2 years, the plan was to trim the database from 2000 names to 20. Then, each of the 20 survivors would be asked to pony up 10 million dollars! (We presume that, like the O. J. Simpson jury, the plan left a number of alternates in the pool, in case someone said, "Thanks, but no thanks!")

A critical feature of the alumni wheedling system was its flexible access to information. During the phone call, the solicitor would have immediate access to everything in the database regarding the prospect on the other end of the line. As the conversation progressed, virtually any data on store might be required, in no predictable order.

How has the new system worked? In a word, splendidly. The university received over $300 million in gifts in 1995 alone. The retrieval flexibility characteristic of good client/server applications was an overwhelming benefit. In fact, it made the whole marketing approach possible—to build successful relationships, the solicitor had to act as if he or she knew personally everything there was to know about the prospect. After all, the whole operating philosophy was that flattery will get you anything!

Other companies make more mundane, but still quite profitable, use of client/server technology for marketing purposes. For example, every major hotel chain has a toll-free number you can call to get information and make a reservation. The customer service operators who answer the phone are typically paid straight commission—if you don't reserve a room, they don't make any money.

As a result, the operators want to make sure they have access to all sorts of information about every hotel, and because there's no way of predicting what order a caller will ask questions in, there's no way of restricting or structuring information queries.

- How far is the hotel from the airport?
- How many nonsmoking rooms are there? Can you guarantee that I'll get one of them?
- Is there a Baptist church within walking distance?
- Does the restaurant have a breakfast buffet during the week?
- Is there a car rental counter in the lobby?
- When were the sleeping rooms last refurbished?

All of this information is in play even before the conversation turns to rate negotiation. Here, the customer service operator can say "wait a minute, let me check." The customer knows that the operator is sitting in front of a computer monitor and doesn't care, but the operator doesn't get to say, "I don't know that information," much less, "I'm sorry, you should have asked me that question first. I'm past the point on the screen where I can get the answer."

### Product Design

Manufacturing companies use client/server computing to allow them to design products and get them to market more quickly. Chrysler Corporation has all sorts of client/server applications throughout its new product design center. Partially as a result, Chrysler's oldest design (at this writing) is a 10-cylinder sports car that looks like something out of the 21st century!

Client/server computing allows the combination of various information technologies, using each to its best advantage. The product design process offers a good illustration.

Product design can be sped up by accomplishing it online. Development engineers can look at, and modify, technical drawings in no time flat. A number of engineers, in different locations, can be making changes to a design simultaneously. The era of totally redrawing a blueprint because some portion of it changed is gone forever. For that matter, so (increasingly) is the era of 2D engineering drawings. After all, the product under design will be three dimensional, why shouldn't the design model be 3D as well?

Client/server computing can dedicate powerful graphics workstations to presenting and manipulating a graphical model—a 3D design drawing. The drawings can be stored on a central, shared, universally accessible, powerful database server. The workstations and database server all need to communicate, but they need not be colocated, and when the thing's ready to prototype, the specifications can automatically flow into a digitally controlled prototype production process!

Such client/server systems make product design *changes* easier, too. For example, boat manufacturer Chris-Craft created a 24-foot version of a 26-foot boat in only four months by scaling the computerized drawings down by 8%. The same system controlled the machinery that cuts the boat components, dramatically reducing time to market.

### The Expanding "Need to Know"

More and more of U.S. business has nothing to do with manufacturing. According to the U.S. Department of Commerce, since 1992 we've spent more capital dollars every year on computers and communications equipment than on equipment for manufacturing, agriculture, transportation, farming, and natural resources combined. The United States is increasingly an information economy, and the U.S. worker is increasingly an information worker.

Information workers are most productive when they have complete access to all the necessary data. What data is necessary? Well, that depends on what the job is, and the job, increasingly, is to solve the business problem du jour.

Leading edge companies are finding that their workers are incredibly productive, given free access to virtually all the company's internal information. In the past, workers were too often limited in their ability to find out what was going on within their own company. Knowledge was parceled out on a "need to know" basis—not because it was in any real sense classified or sensitive, but because the knowledge was buried within computer applications and computer applications were big, expensive and complex. Most employees had access only to those computer applications that some systems analyst or manager felt were necessary to do a particular job in a particular way.

The opposite philosophy is taking hold in companies that have implemented *intranets*. Intranetting is a form of client/server computing, defined by the use of technology originally developed for the Internet, but deployed for internal use and internal customers.

## WHAT IS AN INTRANET?

The hottest topic in client/server computing is *intranetting*. Intranetting, in a nutshell, is the use of technologies that were developed for the Internet, but on an internal network for internal customers. Such popular Internet applications as the World Wide Web and e-mail can readily be used to make all sorts of information available to a company's employees, customers, suppliers, and stockholders. Intranets and the Internet can be interconnected, or they can be totally separate. Databases can be made accessible across an intranet, both via custom programming and via off-the-shelf utility software.

Intranets are appealing largely because they use the same client-side tools that users have been learning in order to access the Internet, so there's no need for employees to learn a new program in order to use a corporate or departmental intranet. From the administrator's standpoint, one builds an intranet much as one would build an Internet-based Web site or mail server, so here again the organization can leverage its Internet technology experience and tools.

Because intranets, as well as "extranets" (intranets that are also available to outsiders such as suppliers and customers), are so exciting and promising, we've devoted a special chapter to them at the end of the book.

### Intranets

Intranets, using things like electronic mail, Usenet newsgroups, and Web pages, make available just about every type of corporate information to all corporate employees. The Human Resources Vice President's salary and bonus may still be closely guarded, but all sorts of other information is online at the click of a mouse.

Formatted, structured information, such as is normally stored in a database, is available online for regular or ad hoc retrieval, but unformatted, unstructured information—letters, memos, notes, drawings, diagrams, books, manuals, other reference works—is also accessible online. Search engines, designed to look through all the information on the Internet in a matter of seconds, have little difficulty scanning through a company's total 1995 correspondence looking for references to a particular product, customer or event (see Figure 3.3).

The direct value of such applications may seem difficult to measure, but a slightly indirect measurement is relatively easy. These applications provide value to the organization by making information more readily accessible. Their minimum value can be calculated, then, by comparing the percentage (or hours) of time spent searching for and retrieving information before and after intranet implementation. A factor must then be applied to adjust for the fact that employees knew, before implementation, that certain data was simply not available. As a result, they didn't spend time looking for it; research and retrieval time saved will

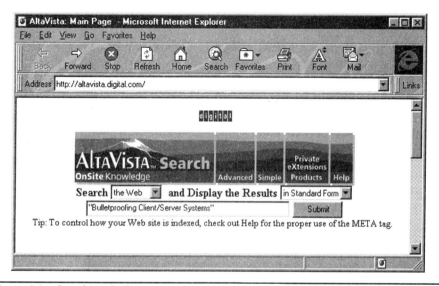

**Figure 3.3:** Searching the Internet

not fully account for the value of doing what was previously impossible!

For some workers, the search for information goes farther afield. Researchers, analysts, and information technologists all benefit from regular use not just of intranets, but of the Internet itself. All sorts of technical journals, white papers, product information, and library contents are available online. Although much of this data is irrelevant to most businesses, the Net (and complementary information services) is still the quickest way to get the most recent information on a wide range of topics, and most Internet technology is inherently client/server.

### Supplier and Customer Links

Companies are using client/server applications to link themselves to their major suppliers and (perhaps more important) to their biggest customers. Online information exchange can allow separate companies to work so closely together that they appear almost as one. The savings in time and paperwork can be huge.

For example, at least two of the Big Three automobile manufacturers have instituted a system whereby suppliers of key components no longer receive purchase orders. Instead, suppliers use a client/server application to look into the manufacturer's production planning database, to determine just how many cars, of what models and options, will be assembled on which assembly lines on what dates. Based on this ability to access information, the suppliers are responsible for getting their respective components to the proper plants and assembly stations, just in time to go into the cars.

The jobs of ordering, receiving, and paying for automotive parts are significantly different than in the past. Ordering, as a separate job function, has been eliminated. Receiving is significantly simplified—there is no longer a need to match goods received against anything, or even do a detailed accounting of what was delivered, and Accounts Payable no longer has to do its dreaded "three-way match": trying to put together one or more each of purchase orders, receiving tickets, and approved invoices to determine which bills can be paid.

Streamlined purchasing procedures made possible by client/server systems can even help companies compete on the basis of convenience. For example, grocery stores in Chicago and San Francisco now sell to homebound individuals who have PCs by allowing them to order electronically for home delivery. Andersen Corporation, a large window manufacturer, puts client PCs in home improvement stores where customers can size, price, and order their windows all at once.

### Interdepartmental Links

Other manufacturers are going even further. They are taking advantage of client/server's ability to combine various technologies to break down the "Chinese Wall" that has separated shop floor operations from administrative and management systems for years.

For the past two decades, both the office environment and the manufacturing shop floor environment have become steadily more automated, but information interchange between the two has often taken the form of reports printed on one system, only to be rekeyed as input data into the other system. The reason, very simply, is that different types of computers, different technologies, have been used in the two environments. Integration, even interfacing, has often been difficult. One food-processing company, for example, has taken advantage of client/server computing to automatically integrate their production planning and digitally controlled processing operations. The plans are prepared and approved on a desktop PC (built up largely by cutting and pasting pieces of previously approved plans). Once approved, they are stored on a Unix/RISC server, in a relational database.

Each digital plan includes in its description the time period and equipment for which it is to be effective. When that time approaches, another PC-based client will retrieve the plan from the database, convert it to a format that the digitally controlled food processing equipment can understand, and automatically control shop floor operations based on data from the "management" side of the house.

This example points up an interesting quality of client/server systems: their tendency to break down traditional boundaries between one application and the next. For another example, consider Attachmate Corporation, which provides mainframe emulation software. Its support organization receives and logs almost 200,000 calls a year, a database that would traditionally have served only the support group, but because Attachmate has client/server capabilities that permit other groups to "mine" the support database for information with their own applications, the company's new product developers can discover what limitations customers are calling the support group about and design new products that overcome those limitations.

## "Stovepipe" Applications

One of the truths of systems reengineering, handed down through the generations as "Ackoff's Law," is that "things are the way they are because they got that way." Applied to typical host-based application systems, Ackoff's Law tells us the pattern of those application systems is as it is because, at some time in the past, it made sense to someone to establish just such a pattern.

Those of us who have been in the systems field long enough can even tell you what the pattern is and how it evolved. It is often referred to as "stovepipe," referring to the vertical integration and almost complete lack of horizontal interface (much less integration), whereby each system addresses exclusively the needs of a single, identified user community.

Stovepipe applications were developed to serve single-user communities because that's the way the user communities were already organized. We have departmental systems (Human Resources, Accounting, Purchasing) that each address a distinct business function because people were already organized into functionally defined departments. If you go back far enough, you find that employees are organized into functionally defined departments because that was the only way to successfully manage a large organization in the days before computers even existed.

Well, it's not the only way, or even the best way, to manage a large organization now.

Increasingly, companies are asking their employees to do more work in less time, to do more than one job, to take on a wider range of duties. As a result, a long-term employee who has spent the past twenty years interacting only with the Payroll application may now find herself expected to use both the Payroll and the Personnel systems. An accountant who has specialized strictly in General Ledger may find himself addressing Accounts Receivable issues as well. A manager who was always able to count on the Facilities people to manage her building may find herself with a sudden additional responsibility. Everyone is expected to help identify better, faster, more efficient ways of doing business.

In today's environment, treating your job description as something never to be altered is a good way to become a statistic. As a result, more and more computer users are interacting with multiple applications, performing more complex business functions using the computer, and even combining bits and pieces of several functionally defined application systems to solve an ad hoc business problem.

## The Need for a Consistent User Interface

Back when each application had a defined user and each user interacted only with a single application, it didn't matter if the Payroll system had a different "look and feel" from the Personnel system or if the Facilities system and the Accounting system operated on entirely different equipment, but now, when single users need to be able to access unforeseeable combinations of application software, consistency at the user interface has become essential.

Users generally will not tolerate having multiple computers (or terminals) on their desks, simply so that they can access multiple applications. Unreasonable individuals that they are, customers now expect to be able to access any and all applications by using a single computer, and once they start to access multiple applications simultaneously (for instance, in different windows open at the same time), it becomes necessary for those applications to share a common set of operating rules—what is often referred to as a common "look and feel."

To understand this latest need, simply think of the alternative: You're the personnel clerk for a small company. For the past three years, you've updated and maintained information on all the employees in a computer database. You have other duties as well, but entering data into the personnel system is a large part of your job. (See Figure 3-4.)

Now the company has decided to outsource its payroll processing. The Payroll department, which was never more than one person anyway, is being eliminated. Paychecks will be produced by a large service bureau, and keeping the payroll information up to date has just become part of your job. You're a little concerned

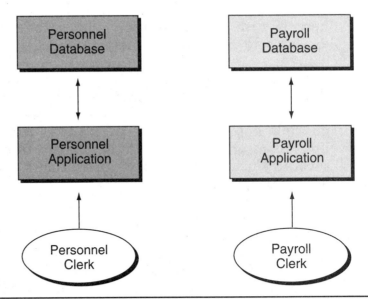

**Figure 3.4:**   Personnel and Payroll before "Reengineering"

about taking on this new responsibility. You're pretty sure you could do the task, but you're busy already. It just seems that "reengineering" means overworking the employees that are left after firing a few randomly selected folks. At least, all the data you've got to put into the payroll system is familiar to you. It's basically the same information that you've always been keeping in your personnel system, just in a different format. You turn on your computer, click on the new dollar sign icon, which is labeled "Payroll," and find yourself looking at the Payroll system.

After you enter your user ID and password, the dialog box that appears is pretty straightforward. Employee name and ID number, mailing address, salary/wage rate—stuff like that. Of course, the Payroll user interface isn't as attractive or as well designed as your Personnel system's user interface. The boxes are the wrong color and shape, and the control buttons (Add, Update, Delete) are on the right-hand side of the data rather than at the bottom where they should be. The control buttons aren't as clearly labeled as your personnel system buttons (Hire Employee, Terminate Employee, Change Employee Information). However, you've been using the personnel system for so long that you don't click on those control buttons much anyway. You prefer using the shortcut keys: F1 to Hire, F2 to Terminate, F3 to Change, F5 to Print, F12 to Exit.

You enter the payroll data for the first new employee and press F1. The cursor changes to an hourglass, you can hear the hard disk bumping and grinding, and a long list of possible help topics is presented to you. You finally figure out that pressing the Escape key will get you back to your data entry, but to get that new employee hired, you have to use the mouse.

In time, you find yourself using the mouse more and more. At first, you simply try to remember to use it when you're entering payroll data, but your fingers keep going to F1, F2, and so on, and every time you use one of your familiar shortcut keys while you're entering payroll data, the system does something wrong, so you start using the mouse all the time—not just in Payroll, but in Personnel as well. You enter the data, tabbing through the fields so that you can keep your fingers on the keyboard. Then you take your right hand off the keyboard, find the mouse, move the cursor to the right control button, and click.

Within a month, not only are you doing more data entry (Payroll as well as Personnel), but your data entry speed with your good old personnel system has slowed by 20%. Each task that used to take you 5 minutes is taking 6. You used to be able to enter the personnel data for 12 employees in an hour, now it takes an hour and 12 minutes, and now you've got the payroll data entry to do, as well! (See Figure 3.5.)

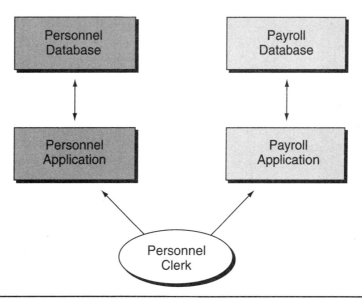

**Figure 3.5:**  Personnel and Payroll after Reengineering

Reengineering, whether of systems, of business processes, or of organizations can make us all more efficient and more productive, but only if the technology we use lets us do more by working differently. For most customers, the minimum requirement is that all the applications they use must look, feel, and act the same way. People can get very good at using computers, and people can even get good at using computers with badly designed user interfaces, but most people cannot get comfortable using computers if they have to be constantly asking themselves, "Now, what rules am I playing by at the moment? What key do I push to make an inquiry, print a report, or exit?"

## The Disappearing Application

Absolute consistency in user interface look, feel, and activity is a key principle when it comes to bulletproofing a suite or set of client/server systems. The effects of interface consistency go further than simply preventing user confusion and inefficiency. Consistent user interfaces encourage users to be adventurous—to explore systems, and parts of systems, and data, and capabilities that they never otherwise would have dared touch.

If you are suddenly granted access to a whole suite of new computer systems, your attitude toward those new applications will probably be determined by your early experiences with them. If your first experiences are positive, then you'll look on the new systems as being a set of tools, or perhaps even toys. If your first experiences are negative, you'll react to the new systems as burdensome, perhaps even dangerous, and nothing causes a new system, or set of systems, to be regarded as positively on first impression as a familiar user interface—the same screens, the same colors, the same layout, the same way of interacting, the same appearance whenever change occurs. If a new application has an interface that appears familiar, you'll explore it. You'll look around and see what this new thing can do. You'll be pretty comfortable, because you feel you can control it. Even if you get into some portion of the functionality that you don't really understand, you're not likely to get into serious trouble.

Looking around is the best way for many people to learn what a piece of software can or will do. A familiar user interface, by encouraging people to explore, speeds the day when the applications are no longer "new"—when they're just another part of the system. That is when change really occurs!

When employees become sufficiently familiar with a number of different applications, and particularly when those applications have a consistent appearance, then the employees often stop thinking about those applications as being separate or distinct. The same set of programs that the Information Technology department categorizes as three or four applications, the users will categorize, and use, as one large application. When that happens, the users are right!

How might separate applications become consolidated or combined by users, without any help from the IT department? Well, let's put you back in the role of being that Personnel clerk who now has Payroll data responsibility. Guess who's going to get the opportunity to respond to any sort of ad hoc question that needs personnel or payroll data as part of the answer?

How are you going to answer these ad hoc questions? As much as possible, you will do so by using tools with which you are already familiar. If the Personnel system can give you part of the answer and the Payroll system can give you part of the answer, sooner or later you're going to figure out how to get part of Personnel running right alongside part of Payroll. You're going to start dragging and dropping (or at least cutting and pasting) data from one window to the other. You're going to start responding to ad hoc problems with ad hoc solutions, cobbled together from bits and pieces of production systems.

Once users start creating their own ad hoc applications, the concept of "application" becomes so fluid and flexible as to be meaningless. Programs, rather than being fixed quantities that can only be executed under a prescribed set of circumstances, become automated tools that allow users to apply familiar techniques to an ever broader universe of data. Employees become more capable, the organization becomes both more productive and more flexible. A paradigm shift has occurred.

So we return to the question that started this chapter, "Why client/server?" No one knows what the ultimate value of client/server computing will be. We're not at that point yet. But penultimately, the value of client/server computing has proven to be in its ability to empower users, to give them ever better access to ever greater ranges of information, and to put them in control of the computer, rather than the computer in control of them. To achieve this value, client/server systems need to be bulletproof. They need to be fast, reliable, easy to use, predictable, always available, secure, honest, loyal, steadfast and true.

The remaining chapters of this book will tell you how to design and construct systems with those qualities. We won't tell you what specific tools to run out and buy—toolsets come and toolsets go—but we will tell you what to do with those tools, what the final product should look like, how to tell if it's right, and how to get it right the first time.

# 4

# Bulletproofing Client/Server Design

Design is the process of determining not *what* an application system is going to accomplish, but *how* the system will accomplish that task. For many client/server development projects, the design phase is where things start to go wrong, so the design phase is where serious bulletproofing needs to begin.

## The Challenge

Designing a client/server application is a larger task than designing a typical host-based system, because client/server design has to address a larger range of issues. The increased technical complexity of client/server computing means that there are more options to consider, more choices to make, more technologies to evaluate and (possibly) select.

Additionally, as we just saw, the real benefits of client/server computing often come not from a single application (as defined by the system development or project management community), but from *combinations* of applications created by the user community from moment to moment. As a result, some of the key client/server design decisions must be made to affect multiple "applications;" that is, they must be made at the architectural level.

Client/server design is further complicated by the fact that each system design must address a wider range of requirements than was necessary in the host-based computing environment.

Host-based applications were typically designed to run in a predefined and well-understood technical setting. The hardware was defined and familiar. The operating system was already chosen and in place. The terminal network already existed, and its capabilities were known. The programming language to be used was probably an old friend (or at worst an old and familiar adversary). Users already had the necessary hardware, knew the basics of its operation, and knew what to expect in terms of "look and feel." Indeed, users had often so internalized the specifics of this technical environment that they were not consciously aware that an alternative might exist.

Host-based applications were often developed by following a well-trod path. Sometimes it was a published path (a formal methodology), and sometimes it was an unpublished path ("the way we do it here"), but in all but the smallest systems development organizations, there was a well-understood set of expectations about how the development process would proceed. This set of expectations was based on some history, some common understanding about the approach that had been successful on previous projects and that could be expected to succeed on future projects.

As a result, many host-based application development projects concentrated only on fulfilling a set of functional requirements. Their system designs addressed only the questions of what data to capture, what formula to apply, and what information to select and display. Nowhere in these designs was any mention made of the need to address a specific number of transactions, a specific volume of data, a particular processing speed or response time, a definite mode of operation, or a defined operating environment.

To build a bulletproof client/server application, all of these issues must be addressed explicitly. Some of them, as mentioned, are best addressed *before* concentrating on any individual set of business processes. The design choices made to affect multiple applications, perhaps all client/server applications within an organization, form a part of the client/server architecture. Making these choices before developing specific applications allows us to build client/server systems that fit well into our chosen environments; waiting too long to make architectural decisions simply requires us to go back and rework systems that are already developed.

## System Requirements

Regardless of when or for how many applications at a time each individual design decision is made, four general categories of

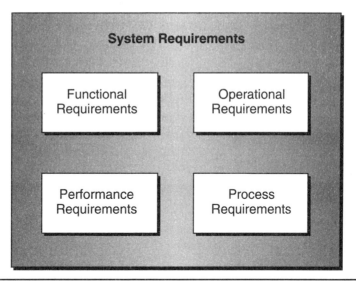

**Figure 4.1:**   System Requirements

system requirements must be addressed for a client/server design to be bulletproof (see Figure 4.1).

- *Functional* requirements are perhaps the most familiar. They specify the nature of events or transactions to which the system must respond and the required outcome of each such response. Functional requirements include the information content of each incoming transaction or request, important formulas or algorithms that must be applied under defined circumstances, and the content (and, perhaps, format) of reports and graphs to be produced in response to user inquiries.

- *Performance* requirements specify not so much what task the system must perform, but how many times, or how fast, or how reliably the system must perform that task. How many incoming transactions per unit of time? Response within what chronological interval? What percentage of the time? Support for how many simultaneous users? What volume of data? Growing at what rate?

- *Operational* requirements address characteristics of the environment in which the system must operate—not just the technical environment (hardware and software) but the surrounding environment as well. What do we know about the anticipated user community? How familiar are they with the job function? With computers? How much training will be provided? Will all users be trained, or only some? What about the physical environment in which the system must operate? Must it be accessible by a remote user? A mobile user? What security is required?

- *Process* requirements speak not of the system that will be delivered, but of the process by which the system will be created and approved. Where will the work be done? Who will participate? When must a system be delivered? What support services will be available? What sort of testing, demonstration, and/or pilot production is required? What budget is available? What documents or other deliverables must be produced?

If it is to lead to a bulletproof system, a client/server system design must address all major requirements in all categories. In this chapter, we will concentrate our attention on addressing functional and some process requirements. The critical issue of system performance, in all of its variations, will be the subject of Chapter 5. Because system and data security are key concerns (and key bulletproofing issues), these are addressed in a chapter of their own. Fulfilling other critical operational requirements will be the subject of Chapters 7 and 8, which concentrate on fault tolerance and system and user support.

## Architectural Decision Making

In their early client/server efforts, many companies fail to lay out any explicit architecture. They often undertake their first client/server development project on the mistaken premise that client/server computing is simple, or purchase their first client/server package presuming that the vendor has expertise and will have decided on an appropriate architecture. In each such case, the company has abdicated much or all of its decision-making responsibility, at least as regards client/server computing.

- Deciding not to decide—developing one or more client/server applications with no thought to consistency or compatibility of technical approach—is a little like marrying someone you've never met before. The technologies you pick for your first application will be part of your computing environment for a long time. So will the technologies you pick for your second application, and your third, and so on. All of these individual technologies will be operating on the same network, at the same time, supporting (at least some of) the same users. You're going to be living with this mix of technologies as long as you use the applications. The success of any future technology choices you make will be affected by the mix already in place. The reliability and performance of both current and future applications will feel the impact.

- Letting someone else decide—choosing a commercially available software package based on cost and how well it fits your functional requirements—is like marrying someone who was selected for you not by your parents, but by some distant marriage broker. Your parents may make a choice based on their concerns for your long-term happiness, but someone not so close to you is choosing based solely on his or her own agenda. Some companies semiconsciously decide to select an off-the-shelf client/server application, and then adopt whatever architecture the application uses as "our corporate architecture." Such a decision entirely misses the point that the software vendor's priorities, constraints, technical abilities, and business objectives are not necessarily the same as your own—"Marry in haste, regret at leisure."

- The first step in bulletproofing your company's client/server systems is to take a step back from your project(s) and make some architectural decisions. This process should not take long—2 to 4 weeks is usually sufficient—but it needs to be *your* process, making your decisions about your architecture based on your priorities, constraints, abilities, and objectives.

## Setting Priorities

Priorities typically come at three different levels: long-term business strategy, middle-term business plans, and short-term technical objectives.

### Long-Term Business Strategy

Designing an architecture to fit your long-term business strategy starts with understanding the business that you're in and what competitive role you've decided to play in the marketplace. Are you competing based on low price, or are you somehow differentiating your products in the minds of the consumer? If you've chosen a differentiation strategy, how are you different?

Are you targeting your products to a particular niche market? Do you bring new products out faster? Do you overwhelm the competition with the range or variety of your new products? Do you specialize in mass customization? Are you committed to maintaining a technology lead?

Different business strategies dictate differing use of computing, and hence differing client/server architectures. For example,

- Producers of undifferentiated commodity goods and services must compete primarily on price. Information and information processing are of relatively little value to them, and must be delivered on a low-cost basis. New or otherwise risky technologies should be avoided, standardization should be emphasized, application systems should be purchased off the shelf, and continuing support costs should be minimized. Information processing should be limited to administrative management plus those applications (manufacturing, logistics, etc.) that are sufficiently standardized to offer a good range of commercial application packages and reliable payback within a short time.

- Companies that follow one of the differentiation strategies, however, have quite different computing needs. Their architectures must support a wider range of information technologies, because information is a critical resource to them. Although standards are still very important, a greater technological variety may be justified. Some amount of technology risk must be accepted. Applications and application components should be bought off-the-shelf when possible, but some software—that which directly supports the company's differentiation strategy—will probably need to be developed on a custom basis. Support costs will be higher for these companies, but the value of the information provided should more than offset the increase.

### Middle-Term Business Plans

Your organization's middle-term business plans can be understood within the context of your longer-term strategy. What competitive tactics will you be emphasizing over the next 2 or 3 years? What uses of information will allow your people to succeed in those tactics?

- Will you be competing primarily on the basis of value (quality and features for a given price) or customer service?

- Are you trying to protect your market share or expand it? If the latter, how fast? How?
- Is your emphasis the retention of existing customers or the acquisition of new customers?
- Are you enhancing the products you already produce, extending established product lines, or introducing entirely new products?
- What technologies, not currently available in-house, would your key information users particularly like to have?

### Short-Term Technical Objectives

As regards this last question, your organization's short-term technical objectives should also be understood. What motivates your shift to client/server from some other form of computer processing?

- Are you reengineering large parts of the company, and if so, to what end?
- Do your users need better access to internal information, external information, or both?
- Are you trying to establish electronic linkages with major customers or suppliers?
- Are there pockets of expertise, located within your organization, that need to be made more generally available?
- Is there a way to add value to a good or service by adding information?
- Is your business changing faster than your application support people can keep up with?

All of these priorities taken together—the long, middle and short term—will not tell you what specific applications must run in your client/server environment, but that's not necessary for architectural design. What you need to know in order to design a good client/server architecture is not the specific applications that will be supported, but rather the *types* and *general mix* of applications that will be supported.

## Defining the Application Mix

Client/server computing has been successful, in part, because of its ability to economically address a wide range of applications.

|  | Database Retrieval Only | Stand-Alone Update & Retrieval | Integrated Update & Retrieval | High-Volume Update & Retrieval |
|---|---|---|---|---|
| Ad hoc Applications | | | | |
| Single-user Applications | | | | |
| Workgroup Applications | | | | |
| Departmental Applications | | | | |
| Enterprise Applications | | | | |
| Mission-Critical Applications | | | | |

**Figure 4.2:** Application Matrix

Many applications within this potential range were not economically addressable on mainframe platforms (they were just too small to be worth the cost and effort), or technically addressable on PC platforms (they needed to serve and coordinate too many users, or too many transactions). As a result, most information technology professionals are not used to thinking about the full range of client/server applications.

A matrix, such as the one shown in Figure 4.2, can be a useful tool for looking at the type and mix of applications that your client/server architecture must support. This particular matrix, intended to characterize and group client/server database applications, looks at the issues of database access pattern and system size as a proxy for robustness requirement.

Horizontally, the matrix divides applications into four categories, based on their interaction with appropriate or central data stores.

### Database Retrieval Only

The first column, "Database Retrieval Only," contains all applications that present information to users regularly or on request, but that (with the possible exception of an audit trail or administrative history) themselves don't capture or retain any information. These applications provide access to stores of information that are created, updated, and maintained by other systems. Sometimes known as Executive Information Systems (EIS), Employee Information Systems, Decision Support Systems (DSS), and OnLine Analytical Processing (OLAP), these applications are becoming increasingly popular. They are often relatively straightforward to develop (OLAP aside) and can provide tremendous value in relation to their implementation cost.

The other three columns all contain applications that both maintain and present information. These applications have primary or partial responsibility for creating and maintaining a record of some sort of material or activity. They provide a portion of the company's records, or "corporate memory."

### Standalone Update and Retrieval

*Standalone Update and Retrieval* systems are ones that, from a business perspective, are only indirectly related to major business processes. From a technical perspective, this means that these applications capture and maintain no data that should be shared, or integrated, with mainstream applications. It also implies that the user interface to these systems need not be able to be integrated with user interfaces to other applications. A practical test to determine whether an application fits in this column is the simple question, "If the organization has fully standardized on PCs, all of which are networked, would it be acceptable to the users for us to implement this application on a nonnetworked Macintosh?"

### Integrated Update and Retrieval

*Integrated Update and Retrieval* systems, on the other hand, are those that directly relate to major business processes. Perhaps they automate the performance of a major business function or administratively track a business function. Perhaps they maintain data that must be available for the performance or tracking of a business function. Whatever the specific situation, the data stores maintained by these applications should (some would say *must*) be integrated with data maintained by, and supporting, a number of other applications. Users can reasonably be expected to access these applications at the same time, and in response to the same business problem, as they access other, related, applications. As a result, the user interface to these applications must exhibit a common look and feel, and it must be accessible on a common platform.

### High-Volume Update and Retrieval

*High-Volume Update and Retrieval* systems are also integrated update and retrieval systems. What distinguishes applications in the fourth and final column is the fact that their processing load, combined with their performance requirements, seems likely to pose an unusual challenge to the client/server infrastructure. There is no numerical cutoff for what is considered "high volume" and what is not, but this column might contain the physically most demanding 10 to 25% of your update and retrieval applications. The presumption is that your network and infrastructure will be engineered to suffice for the majority of client/server update and retrieval systems; although applications in the third column will have explicit performance requirements, those performance requirements will not be the primary drivers of system design. For applications in the final column, however, the ability to achieve adequate system performance is in question; performance requirements must be kept high on the list throughout the system design and development process.

Vertically, the matrix divides all applications into six categories, based on the size and nature of the user community and, by implication, the robustness requirement of the applications themselves.

### Ad Hoc Applications

The top row contains ad hoc applications—those that will be created, used successfully (we hope) once, and then thrown away. Ad hoc applications abound in the client/server world. They are used only once for a range of reasons. Some are created to solve a problem that, it is expected, will never recur. Others address problems that will recur, and therefore have the potential for reuse, but are so simple to create that it's easier to throw them away and re-create them when needed than to save them and have to find them later. Still others fall in between—pretty easy to re-create and fairly unlikely to be needed again.

### Single-User Applications

Single-user applications, on the other hand, are ones that are worth saving in such a manner that we can find them again. They may even be worth enhancing with a few features that make them more reliable, or easier to use. Whereas ad hoc applications are most often of the retrieval-only sort, single-user applications are as often update and retrieval, and fairly often standalone.

### Workgroup Applications

Workgroup applications, by contrast, tend to have integration requirements. Workgroups tend to have anywhere from two or three to a dozen or more members. Workgroup responsibilities, and therefore workgroup system functional requirements, tend to be tightly focused and homogeneous, but organizations typically don't have workgroups dedicated to activities unrelated to primary business functions. If the task is related to other functions, then the automation is best integrated with other automated applications.

Ad hoc applications are typically written by one person, who will run them once and then throw them away, in other words, the end user. Single-user and workgroup applications are also often the products of nonprofessional developers. As a result, their designs will rarely be bulletproof, but usually that's OK. These smaller applications tend not to require a lot of robustness, because their user communities are small, tightly knit, and forgiving (because of a sense of ownership). Bulletproofing becomes critical when workgroup applications begin to be used by a larger community, or if the system developer(s) depart the scene. If either event seems likely, the safe course is to treat workgroup applications as if they were departmental.

### Departmental Applications

Bulletproofing becomes expected once we get to departmental applications. To understand the nature of systems in this row of the matrix, simply think what the major departments are in your organization. You have an accounting department and an accounting system; a purchasing department and a purchasing system. A human resources department, a shipping department, and a system for each. Any application that fully automates or significantly supports the major function of a department is a departmental application.

### Enterprise Applications

Enterprise applications go even further. Their functionality is necessary to all the employees in the company, not just those in a single department. (In practice, we tend to categorize systems that support one or two departments as "departmental," and those that serve three or more as "enterprise.") Enterprise applications often provide functionality that is not the central focus of most jobs, but is used by, and important to, a large number of employees. A classic example is a timecard reporting system— we would hope that no one's first job responsibility is "fill out your timecard," but for some reason people get upset if the system is down and they can't report their hours worked!

### Mission-Critical Applications

Finally, we have mission-critical applications. These may have smaller user communities than enterprise applications, but they are more critical to the business. The defining characteristic of a mission-critical application is this: If it's off the air, you're out of business. Maybe your entire company isn't out of business, and maybe you're not out of business permanently, but for some customer, for some period of time, you cannot provide your basic product. The classic example of a mission-critical application is online order entry—for example, in support of a 1-800 customer service center or accessed electronically via the customer's computers). A common characteristic is that the user community extends beyond your organization's employees; if the system goes down, people outside your organization know about it as soon as you do.

Professionally developed systems—commonly, those in the bottom half of the matrix—are expected and required to be more robust than end user systems. As we move from departmental, through enterprise, to mission-critical applications, the user community gets larger and more diverse, and the robustness requirement goes up significantly.

A bulletproof client/server architecture will support all six sizes of applications. It will make creation of ad hoc and single-user systems easy and inexpensive; it will support workgroup and departmental systems without being stressed in any way; and it will provide the performance and reliability necessary for enterprise and mission-critical applications.

A natural tendency for professional system developers is to evaluate an architecture only on the basis of how well it supports the largest and most demanding applications. A truly bulletproof architecture, on the other hand, will do that while not imposing unnecessary costs on the smaller systems. Because different sizes of applications tend to exhibit different deployment schemes (fat client, thin client, three tiered), a bulletproof client/server architecture must do a good job of supporting, and potentially integrating, a number of simultaneous applications, each with its own deployment pattern.

## Architectural Interfaces

What differentiates a fat-client application from a thin-client one, or a two-tiered application from a three-tiered one, is the number and logical placement of the interfaces from one platform to another. The most common architectural interfaces are those that fall between the user interface (or presentation) logic and the business application processing, and between the business application code and the data storage (or database).

*The biggest single contribution to bulletproofing a client/server design comes from standardizing these architectural interfaces, from setting rules and guidelines about how each application will handle communication, and from coordination between client and server modules.*

Standardization should ideally occur at all levels of communication and connectivity. However, in the context of the Open Systems Interconnect (OSI) model of the International Standards Organization, any functioning network has already done significant standardization at OSI levels 1 (Physical), 2 (Data-Link), 3 (Network), and 4 (Transport). Standardization at these levels is necessary to achieve usable connectivity.

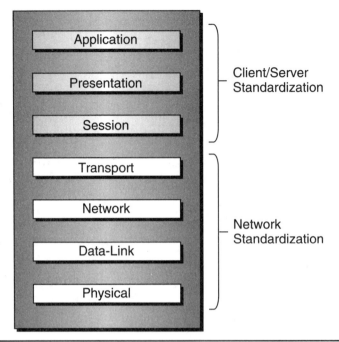

**Figure 4.3:**   Client/Server Design and the OSI Model

Client/server architecture, then, concentrates on standardizing the higher communication levels: 5 (Session), 6 (Presentation), and 7 (Application). Establishing standards at these levels, in practical terms, reduces to choosing *middleware* (see Figure 4.3).

Middleware is a broad term for software that mediates and standardizes the connections, or interfaces, between different parts of a client/server system's communications pathways. The types of middleware a company needs to choose, based on the interfaces that must be standardized, depends on the mix of deployment scenarios (fat client, thin client, three tiered) that must be supported. These three deployment schemes locate and identify two primary networking interfaces: the ones between the data storage and the business logic, and between the business logic and the user interface (or presentation) layer (see Figure 4.4). Standardizing these two primary interfaces is sufficient at the architectural design level.

The relative importance of the two primary networking interfaces is determined by the proportion and criticality of applications that will be fat client, thin client, and/or three tiered. Fat-client applications use only the interface between data storage

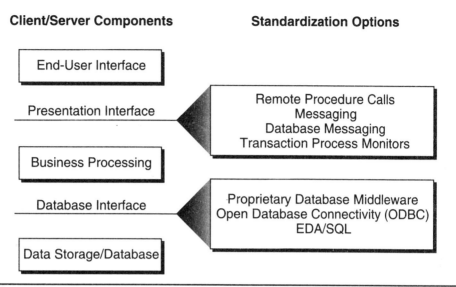

**Figure 4.4:** Client/Server Interface Standardization

and business logic; communications between business logic and user interface are handled within a single computer (the client), and need not cross the network. Thin-client applications use only the interface between business logic and user interface; their data storage and business logic communicate within a single platform (the server). Three-tiered applications, of course, must use both primary network interfaces.

How do you determine the mix of deployments your architecture should be designed to support? Well, in addition to the inherent advantages and disadvantages discussed for each deployment scenario in Chapter 2, there are clear correlations between the location of any application on the matrix in Figure 4.2 and its likely deployment scheme.

To begin with, virtually all user-developed client/server applications are fat client. Each user can control his or her own development environment, because it exists solely on the user's personal computer. The fat-client model simply fits with the objectives and operating realities of end user development, and the tools that end user developers typically use, combined with the degree of expertise they can be expected to achieve and maintain, typically limit applications to fat-client deployment. Similarly, the majority of retrieval-only database systems follow the fat-client model.

At the other end of the spectrum, the biggest and most complex client/server applications—mission-critical integrated, enterprise high volume, and mission-critical high volume—are most often implemented using three tiers. The ability of the three-tiered deployment to throw lots of processing power at a business problem, to use truly optimal hardware, to be managed and tuned continually, and to provide multiple levels of redundancy often outweighs the cost of the increased network traffic that the approach entails.

In between the two extremes, the pattern is less clear. For departmental database update applications, enterprise standalone and integrated applications, and even mission-critical standalone applications, the relative advantages and disadvantages of fat-client, thin-client, and three-tiered deployment must be evaluated.

- If your company emphasizes (or needs to emphasize) individual responsibility and creativity, or has many mobile employees who must be productive even when not connected to the office, then a fat-client approach may be warranted.
- If you're more interested in control and security—for example, a university making course scheduling and registration applications available to students over the network—then a thin-client approach is recommended.
- If you will be migrating most of your departmental systems from a host-based processing environment, then (as we will see) even your smaller professionally developed and supported systems may end up being three tiered.

Look at the matrix. Plot the major applications that you foresee for client/server computing. Plot specific applications that you can identify uniquely and general types of applications that you anticipate will evolve. Talk to the more technically astute users, and find out what use of client/server computing they anticipate. Estimate the relative impact of systems in each cell of the matrix, based on number of applications, number of users, amount of data, volume of transactions, complexity of processing, and so on. No, you won't develop an accurate prediction of what your application mix will be two years in the future but you will achieve a better understanding of the general characteristics, the flavor, of that mix. For architectural purposes, that's what you need to go forward.

Of course, if your company is relatively small or your intended use of client/server computing is relatively simple (for instance, client/server will be used only by end users for ad hoc and single-user applications, primarily data retrieval), then only one primary interface—the one between the data storage and the business logic—need be standardized. This "database interface" must be standardized for every company using client/server systems; addressing it is the most common bulletproofing step. On the bright side, there are a number of standardization options, each with its own set of advantages. Less fortunately, there are a number of choices that must be made.

### WHAT IS SQL?

SQL (or the Structured Query Language) is the industry-standard command language for communicating with relational DBMSs. All the commands that are necessary to establish, maintain, manage, and retire a relational database can be (and generally are) expressed in SQL.

SQL started out in the 1970s as the command language for IBM's DB2 relational DBMS. However, in the 1980s it was selected as the basis for the command languages of all relational DBMSs, as is the case today. SQL is kind of like a cross between English and the language of mathematical logic. A simple SQL command might say: "SELECT NAME, EMPLOYEE_ID FROM EMPLOYEE WHERE DEPARTMENT = 30." More complex SQL commands would create databases, create tables within databases, grant users the authority to read or update the new tables, and automatically calculate the value of a certain column (field) on the database, based on the values of other fields.

Industry standards for the SQL language exist, but most database vendors have implemented the standard SQL and more. These DBMS vendors want to differentiate their products by offering features their competitors can't match. As a result, the SQL supported by differing DBMSs, although largely overlapping, is not identical.

## Standardizing the Database Interface

The technique used to standardize the database interface, almost without exception, is to select a standard language and set of high-level protocols that all client programs will use to communicate with server-based databases. The problem, then, has two parts: What language should be used? and What protocols should communicate database commands written in that language to the database management software?

The language in which your client programs issue database commands might seem to be a moot issue. If your database is a relational database, you're almost certainly talking to it using some version of the Structured Query Language (SQL) (see "What Is SQL?").

The major difficulty arises from the phrase "some version of." There are almost as many versions of SQL as there are relational database management products. Oracle offers Oracle SQL. Ingres has INGRES/SQL as well as Open SQL and a couple of proprietary access languages. Sybase SQL Server supports TRANSACT-SQL and APT-SQL. Microsoft's version of SQL Server accepts only TRANSACT-SQL. Gupta SQLBase understands SQLTalk. INFORMIX offers INFORMIX-SQL. Some of these are ANSI/SAG compliant; others are not. To make matters worse, there are a succession of ANSI standards rather than just one.

A second problem arises because not all databases are relational. Indeed, not all "databases" are supported by full-function database management systems (DBMSs); some are supported, instead, by file processing software that mimics DBMS functionality but is far less powerful.

## One DBMS, Now and Forever?

If your company uses only a single DBMS and cannot foresee the likelihood of ever using any other DBMS, then your choice of database access language is already evident—you're almost certain to use the version of SQL (or proprietary non-SQL database language) that goes along with your database management system. The advantages of such a choice are legion. You'll be using the full suite of software provided by your database vendor, who can be expected to provide knowledgeable support should you run into difficulties. You'll have available all the SQL extensions and other special features that may have caused you to choose your particular DBMS in the first place. Access to your database will be as fast as can be achieved in the client/server environment.

However, be careful about the statement, "We'll never use a different DBMS." Never is a long time, and there are a number of circumstances under which you may be forced to revisit your DBMS selection.

- Your DBMS vendor could go out of business or be acquired.
- Your DBMS might no longer be enhanced and could fall significantly behind the market leaders in functionality.
- Your DBMS vendor could undergo a significant change in business strategy (as when Microsoft and Sybase parted ways and the guarantee of full compatibility between SQL Server products vanished).
- Your organization could acquire a commercial application package that supports only a different DBMS.
- Your company could acquire (or be acquired by) another firm that is heavily invested in a different DBMS.
- Your company, after having standardized on a PC-based nonrelational database, could grow rapidly and suddenly need more robust data management capabilities.
- And many more.

If, in spite of all this, you're comfortable with your choice of and commitment to a single database management system, your life is truly blessed. Depending on your choice of DBMS, you will be able to take advantage of such proprietary features as triggers, stored procedures, SQL extensions, and the ability to support distributed databases. You may even be able (as we'll discuss later) to use your DBMS as a key component in addressing your other middleware requirements. On the other hand, if your company is currently using a number of database management systems, or anticipates the need or wants to retain the ability to use multiple database management systems in the future, you need "open" database middleware.

## Open Database Middleware

Think of what would be required with proprietary middleware. An application system is developed in-house, using Oracle as its database management system. A second, related, application is purchased off-the-shelf; it is only available for Sybase SQL Server. Now a third application needs to access data from each of the first two. It has to issue Oracle SQL calls against one database, TRANSACT-SQL calls against the second, and handle any integration necessary to identify records required from one database based on the contents of data retrieved from the other! Open database middleware is designed to allow an application program to access and/or update data in any one of a large number of commercial DBMSs. The application program doesn't need to, and in fact shouldn't, know in which DBMS the data resides (see Figure 4.5).

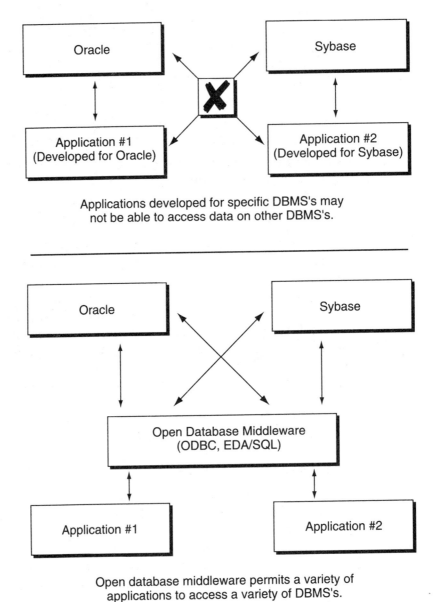

Applications developed for specific DBMS's may
not be able to access data on other DBMS's.

Open database middleware permits a variety of
applications to access a variety of DBMS's.

**Figure 4.5:**   Open Database Middleware

Whereas proprietary database middleware is defined by the database management system it supports and the matching version of SQL it processes, open database middleware is defined by the standard that allows its various pieces to interoperate. With proprietary middleware, all the pieces that run on various client and server platforms need to be purchased from a single vendor. Using open middleware, however, pieces can be bought from any reputable supplier, so long as they conform to the appropriate standard.

Open database middleware achieves standardization in three different areas or dimensions. However, these areas of standardization impose a constraint on application programs that use the middleware:

- First, open database middleware can interact with, and invoke the services of, any of a wide range of DBMSs. The most successful open database middleware standards (see below) are supported by virtually all relational database manufacturers; drivers even exist for a number of significant nonrelational databases.

- Second, open database middleware causes all database servers to look the same to client applications. Data can be moved from one server to another, or from one database to another, without creating a need to modify client applications.

- Finally, open database middleware causes all client applications to look the same to database servers. A piece of logic that was developed for one application can readily be reused by a portion of another application.

To achieve this degree of standardization and interchangeability, open database middleware supports only ANSI-standard SQL with no vendor extensions.

Companies that standardize the database interface by choosing an open database middleware standard gain the ability to use different DBMSs for different databases without forcing applications programs or system users to keep track of which data resides under the control of which DBMS. They use open middleware to present a common face to the client program, regardless of how the data is physically stored. By supplying end users with data inquiry and system development tools that conform to the middleware standard, they greatly simplify the task of end user computing in a multi-DBMS client/server environment.

### ODBC and EDA/SQL

Currently, far and away the most widely supported standard for open database middleware is the Open Database Connectivity standard initially developed by Microsoft. All major relational DBMSs support ODBC; the DBMS vendors supply their own ODBC drivers. ODBC drivers exist for major nonrelational DBMSs such as IMS and CA-IDMS, and many vendors of front-end client application development tools have delivered ODBC support.

ODBC offers a low-risk approach to open database middleware, but it is often a low-speed approach as well. As with many first-generation open software products, the initial emphasis has been on compatibility and functionality—performance considerations will be addressed in a later version of the standard, and of the software.

Organizations that want open database middleware, need better performance than ODBC can currently provide, and are willing to move slightly out of the mainstream have another option, a "de facto" open middleware product known as Enterprise Data Access (EDA)/SQL. Developed and sold by Information Builders Inc., EDA/SQL establishes a gateway server to which client applications issue their database calls. The EDA gateway then interprets and resolves those calls by issuing native SQL commands to any of a wide mix of database servers and DBMSs. The EDA productis widely used for ad hoc and other database retrieval, but it has not been adopted by as many firms for database update applications. Far more client application development tools support ODBC than support EDA/SQL.

For standardizing the database interface, then, there are three possible outcomes:

- Use the proprietary database middleware provided by your client/server database vendor, so long as you have only one client/server database management system and you can reasonably expect that situation to continue.

- Use ODBC middleware if you have, or anticipate, multiple client/server DBMSs, provided that you evaluate the performance of ODBC middleware and can tolerate its low speed at least until the next release.

- Use EDA/SQL middleware if you must support multiple client/server DBMSs and cannot live with ODBC's performance limitation, even for a short time. Less ideally, use EDA/SQL as an adjunct to proprietary database middleware; use proprietary middleware for update and EDA/SQL for retrieval-only applications.

## Standardizing the Presentation Layer Interface

Choosing a database middleware approach may seem somewhat complex, but it is far simpler than the other interface standardization necessity: choosing an organization-standard approach to handling the interaction between a client that automates the Presentation (user interface) layer and a server that automates application business logic.

When you're talking to a DBMS, there are only a limited number of commands that make sense: store some data, retrieve some data, tell me something about some data. On the other hand, if you're giving commands to any and all sorts of automated business logic, your vocabulary needs to be far broader. Business logic has a far wider possible range of actions, and your command language needs to be able to specify them all.

As a result, the Information Technology industry has had far less luck standardizing the Presentation layer interface than it has the database interface. This is not to say that there haven't been valid efforts. In fact, there may have been too many valid efforts! As a result of some of these, you have four legitimate approaches to choose from in your standardization decision:

- Remote Procedure Calls (RPCs)
- Messaging
- Database Messaging
- Transaction Process (TP) Monitoring

### Remote Procedure Calls

One of the earliest successful approaches to client/server middleware, and perhaps still the closest thing we have to an industry standard for the Presentation layer interface, is Remote Procedure Calls (RPCs). A remote procedure call is based on the idea of a procedure call, which is simply C language terminology for a program call, module call, subroutine call, or subprogram call. C programs are called "procedures," and one procedure can call, or invoke by name, another.

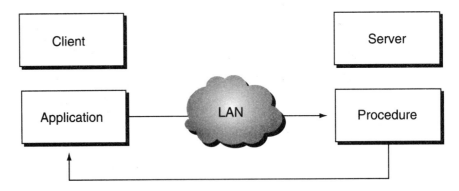

Remote Procedure Call (RPC) is a synchronous client/server
connection that depends on LAN speed for performance.

**Figure 4.6:** Remote Procedure Calls

Remote procedure calls are procedure calls in which the procedure being called is at least potentially on a different computer from the calling procedure. The calling (main or master) procedure is the client program, and the called (or subordinate) procedure is the server program. The fit is pretty clear: The client and the main program are both in control, and the server and the subordinate program are both passive until and unless invoked (see Figure 4.6).

RPCs are available from a number of sources, and the Open Software Foundation (OSF) has created a standard for RPCs as part of its Distributed Computing Environment (DCE) product line. RPCs are thoroughly tested, successful at linking different computing platforms and technologies together, and easy for programmers to understand. DCE and other successful RPC implementations automatically generate all the program code necessary to link a particular client program to a specific server program.

RPCs have disadvantages as well. They are popular in the Unix/C language community because that's where they originated. All the program code generated by a typical RPC facility is in C; if your main programming language is C or C++ that's great, but if you're a COBOL or BASIC or PowerBuilder shop, this is less useful.

The RPC model of client-to-server invocation, like the main program/subprogram model on which it is based, is logically synchronous. That is, when a main program calls a subprogram, it typically waits for the subprogram to execute before regaining control and resuming its own execution. In an RPC, the client typically calls the server, then waits for a return of control. This isn't necessarily bad, and for applications where the client doesn't want to wait, many RPC facilities allow the invocation to be asynchronous (the client calls the server and immediately gets back to work), but the mental model that most programmers have is still the synchronous model; changing the way it works destroys the familiarity that is one of its basic advantages.

## Messaging

Perhaps the simplest form of middleware to understand, messaging is just what it sounds like—to achieve interoperation, one program (the client) sends a formatted message to another program (the server). By previous agreement—that is, in accordance with the application design—the server knows what action to take upon receipt of each format of message. A message in a predefined format, which includes some sort of (trans)action identifier and the associated data fields or strings, is known generically as a "datagram." The implications of this—a telegram, the contents of which are application data—help explain just how simple messaging communication is.

Computers, and application programs running on them, send and receive messages all the time. Perhaps the most familiar example of this is electronic mail—the transmission of character messages, sometimes with files of data attached, across a network. Say "e-mail" to some people, and they think about communicating across the Internet, or CompuServe, or America Online. Others think immediately about the electronic mail capability provided by the local area network (LAN) at their workplace. Many people have experienced, and come to depend on, some simple sort of computerized messaging capability.

The visible face of electronic mail—the text editor that the sender uses to compose the message and the text browser that the recipient uses to read it—is not directly applicable to the scenario wherein a client application program sends a message to a server application (or vice versa). Text editors and browsers are sophisticated software programs that allow computers to interact visually with human beings; application programs have no need to physically display or key-enter words and data. However, all the other components of a functioning electronic mail system have their counterparts in messaging-oriented middleware. Indeed, in some cases, electronic mail software has been used directly as messaging middleware!

To work properly and reliably, an electronic mail system must solve a number of basic problems:

- It must translate a recipient's "name" (e-mail ID) into a network address so that the message can be properly delivered
- It must store the message for later delivery if the intended recipient is not immediately available
- It must translate the message contents from one format to another, based on the mix of computers in use (for instance, a message created on a PC and sent to a mainframe user will be translated from ASCII to EBCDIC)
- It must keep track of numerous messages, sent from many users to many recipients simultaneously
- It must maintain various conversations or "threads" of messages over time
- It may be required to notify the recipient upon receipt of a message

Substitute "program name or identifier" for the name of an e-mail sender or recipient, and the under-the-cover functionality of an e-mail system sounds a lot like middleware. Instead of sending a message from a text editing application to a text browsing/display application, middleware sends a message from a client application to a server application, or back again (see Figure 4.7).

The implementation of messaging middleware varies. Some organizations use the native messaging capabilities that are provided by their Network Operating System (NOS). Others use the extended capabilities of one of the commercial add-on electronic mail packages. Still others use proprietary messaging-oriented middleware packages, such as the MQ product from IBM. There are as yet no standards-based products on the market that are specifically written to be messaging-oriented middleware. There are messaging middleware products, but they are all proprietary. There are standards-based products, but they are really intended for e-mail rather than messaging. Nonetheless, messaging remains a popular approach to communication between clients and servers. Most major e-mail programs provide

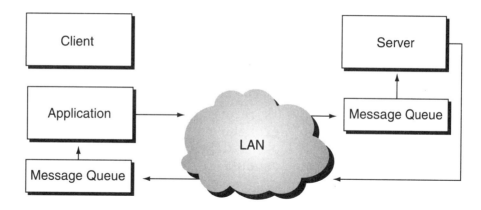

Message-oriented middleware (MOM) is asynchronous, using an e-mail type facility for store-and-forward operation. In database messaging, a separate DBMS constitutes a shared message "post-office".

**Figure 4.7:** Message-Oriented Middleware

Application Program Interfaces (APIs) that make it easy for one program to send a message to another, and messaging coordination of clients and servers has the arguable advantage of being inherently asynchronous.

Asynchronous coordination is the opposite of synchronous coordination such as is typical of RPCs. It is difficult for some people to think about in the context of computers and computer programs—many programmers have been too close to the synchronous model for too long—but asynchronous coordination is easy to think about in many other contexts. When you write a letter to someone, you don't sit and wait, unable to do anything else, until you receive a reply. You go on with the rest of your life. Any action that directly depends on information that you requested in the letter, and that you expect to be contained in the reply, may be postponed, but actions that do not directly depend on such information can go on very nicely, thank you. Designing an application to use asynchronous coordination, as we will see, is a little different, but such applications, properly designed, can achieve high transaction rates and very high efficiency.

### Database Messaging

Another form of asynchronous coordination, popular particularly with larger organizations and larger, more complex or more widely distributed applications, is messaging achieved through database software. Database messaging achieves very much the same result as e-mail messaging. However, it uses one or more client/server databases as message repositories. Instead of sending an e-mail message to another program's in-box, this approach inserts a row (or record) into another program's database. The DBMS then alerts the receiving program, or the receiving program simply looks at the database and notices the message.

Three points should be immediately understood about database messaging:

- First, the database being discussed is not part of the application database. If you're building a personnel system, this is not a personnel database. If you're creating an operations management system, this is not an operations management database. The database being discussed is a messaging database, treated as part of the client/server infrastructure.

- Second, the database into which a message is inserted will typically reside on the same computer as the program to which the message is being sent. Because this is generally not the same computer as is running the sending program, some sort of database middleware will be used to effect communication. In a nutshell, we can use database middleware to serve the purpose of module-to-module middleware; for reasons of performance, we typically use proprietary database middleware.

- Third, because the return message (from server to client) typically gets inserted into a database on the client platform, and because there can be dozens or even hundreds of client platforms in use for a single application, database messaging can turn into a significant configuration management and database administration problem. Some companies have addressed this issue by defining a single large messaging database that is distributed across all client and server platforms on the network. Other companies have defined separate databases for each client and server.

The database messaging approach may seem a bit artificial, and unduly complex, but it can simplify a large client/server architecture while providing a good measure of industrial-strength technology. Database messaging simplifies the architecture for the simple reason that most client/server architectures already include database software. Using that software for messaging allows developers to solve a new problem with a familiar tool. It allows system administrators to support a smaller set of software, while still enabling use of fat-client, thin-client, and three-tiered applications. It also allows us to use the statistics-gathering capabilities of modern DBMSs to begin managing our client/server environment.

### Transaction Process Monitoring

On the other hand, if we really want to manage our client/server environment, we need software that was specifically designed to do the job, not some jury-rigged middleware solution. The form of middleware that, far and away, provides the best management capabilities consists of products known as transaction process (TP) monitors.

Using a TP monitor is significantly different from using other forms of middleware. For starters, a TP monitor is a separate piece of software, typically running on a separate piece of hardware. With other forms of middleware, a client computer communicates across the network to an *application server* computer, which eventually communicates back. Using a TP monitor, the client communicates with a special computer known as a *transaction server*, which then passes the information on to the application server. Upon finishing its task, the application server communicates back to the transaction server, which finally responds to the originating client (see Figure 4.8).

Thus, using a TP monitor (the software that runs on the application server) adds another set of steps to every middleware process. It adds another piece of hardware to the network environment; it creates another potential bottleneck; it doubles at least a portion of network traffic; and it's not cheap—TP monitors can easily cost five figures to purchase, and the transaction servers they run on are often nonstop redundant processors because of the fatal consequences of server outage.

So why would anyone use a TP monitor? Well, consider the advantages of having a central point of control, a central management capability, in the design of all your client/server applications and in the operation of your client/server environment. Think of a TP monitor as a particularly intelligent traffic cop.

A TP monitor adds value by collecting statistics, making those statistics available, and acting on the information contained in the statistics. It logs and tracks each client-to-server transaction

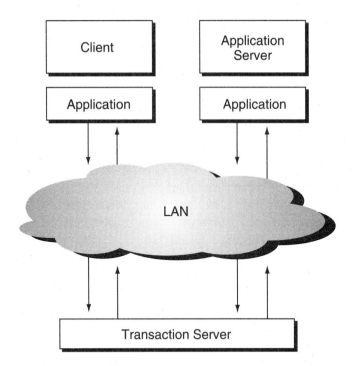

Transaction Process (TP) monitoring uses a dedicated server
on the LAN to provide centralized management and control.

**Figure 4.8:**   Transaction Process Monitoring

that it handles. Therefore, it can keep track of transactions in
process, which clients are interacting with which servers, server
response patterns, which clients have been waiting for server
response and how long, what the mix of transactions is, what
the chronological or other pattern of transactions is, and so on.

A TP monitor can notify a client if a particular server has
stopped responding. It can allocate the load of a certain type of
transaction across a number of application servers, based on the
total processing demand on each of those servers or even the
recent response times exhibited by those servers. If multiple
transaction servers are available, it can reassign a transaction
from a failed server to one that is still responding. In short, it
can manage your transaction process dynamically, at the same
time providing useful statistics about how your client/server
applications are performing—not as experienced by the server,
or the network, but as experienced by the user at the transaction
level.

## Choosing Module-to-Module Middleware

Why is it necessary to standardize the Presentation layer interface? Why must you select at the architectural level a standard way for your user interface modules running on client PCs to communicate with application logic running on a server?

To answer this question, think of the system developers who must learn to use these tools. Given the major differences in philosophy and technology between the approaches, how many different forms of middleware can they really become expert in using?

Now think of the user support people. How many different forms of communication across the network can they reasonably be expected to troubleshoot? To know well enough not just to make them work properly, but to recognize (often with a user screaming in one ear) what went wrong?

Finally, consider the network personnel. The more high-level protocols, such as middleware, there are in use, the more difficult designing, implementing, and supporting a reliable, well-performing network becomes. Optimizing and tuning a network to support one form of interaction between clients and servers (such as database middleware) is challenging but relatively straightforward. Designing and operating the same network so that it will efficiently support two forms of interaction (database middleware and one of the forms of module-to-module middleware) is a pretty good trick, but doable. Trying to get a single network environment to give good support to four or five wholly differing forms of interaction, each with its own application-level software and protocol requirements, requires a support staff with leotards, capes, the letter S emblazoned on their chests, and a big infrastructure budget.

Proof of the wisdom of standardizing architectural interfaces lies in the experience of companies, particularly large companies, which adopted client/server computing and failed to establish standards. Typically, within 2 to 4 years, their network and application support problems have become enormous. A common refrain starts out "If we had only known...."

Which form of module-to-module middleware should you choose? If you're a large organization with plans to put a large number of production, professionally developed, enterprise or mission-critical client/server applications on your network, look at TP monitors very closely. They're expensive, they virtually double your network traffic, their benefits are typically experienced only after multiple applications have been implemented, and they can be hard to sell to senior management, but they give you a level of control and auditability that cannot otherwise be achieved.

If you're an organization that has managed (or is actively planning) to standardize on a single database management system, particularly if your choice is one of the industry leaders and has good distributed database and stored procedure capabilities, then consider database messaging.

If your programming language of choice is C or C++, look hard at remote procedure calls. If your programmers have some C capability, but don't really prefer it, then still look at RPCs, but not as hard.

If you don't fit into any of these categories, look at simple messaging. If you're pretty much a single-vendor shop, at least in terms of server hardware, then consider any proprietary messaging-oriented middleware offered by your hardware supplier. Otherwise, stick to standards-based middleware, which at this point means sticking to e-mail software, but may soon include open messaging middleware products.

Are standards for network interfaces the only architectural decisions that must be made? Not at all. Client and server hardware must be selected. Network technology must be implemented. Network capacity must be modeled, network demand predicted, and network management enabled. Redundancy and recovery issues must be addressed, but each of those subjects can, and will, be revisited. If your network doesn't have enough capacity, you can reconfigure it. If you experience application outages for lack of server redundancy, you can add it later. Even if your network has enough capacity and enough redundancy at the start, you're likely to have to add some of each down the road anyway. What makes interface/middleware standardization critical is that, once missed, the opportunity does not present itself again. The payback from standardization is enormous, and the only good time to do it is up front.

What if you've already missed the opportunity? To start with, *stop making the problem worse*. Take a step back, look at how your organization is using and will be using the network and client/server computing, and make a standardization choice for the future. The immediate benefit will be mitigated by any newly nonstandard applications you have up and running (see how long it takes your people to start calling them "legacy" systems), but that's unavoidable. Over time, you may have the opportunity to reengineer those applications, bringing them into conformance with your standard. Remember, failing to standardize is just ignoring the problem. As an industry, we tried that with the "Year 2000" situation. The problem didn't conveniently go away.

## Designing Client/Server Applications

Once your company or organization has established a client/server architecture, you can begin designing and implementing individual applications. This effort can take many forms; each of the following decisions will affect the nature and duration of your systems development effort and the formality of the design process within it.

- End user versus professional development, implementation, and support
- Information retrieval versus information maintenance systems
- Purchased software versus developed software versus developed software with major purchased elements
- High-volume versus low-volume processing loads

### End User–Supported Systems

If the application being created is in the top half of our categorization matrix, it will most likely be developed or purchased, implemented, and to whatever extent necessary, supported by end users rather than systems professionals. This likelihood brings both benefits and costs, but one predictable outcome is that there will be little or no actual design activity performed, and almost certainly no design information written down.

End-user-supported systems tend to be smaller and less complex than professionally supported systems. Their design need not be as formal, because there simply isn't as much to formally design, and the risks of not having a formal design are reduced, because there isn't as much that can go wrong. Moreover, when end-user-supported systems fail, the user community is very forgiving. The systems belongs to them; they feel ownership of it; they are the primary line of defense. Users will typically take whatever steps are necessary, not only to fix a broken system, but to recover from any impact of the system outage.

For all these reasons and more, it is generally OK that end-user-supported client/server systems tend not to be bulletproof. That's not to say that end user developers shouldn't be trained in the gentle art of systems development, so that their products are as reliable and as easy to use as possible, but it is to say that, past a certain point, trying to turn end users into professional developers is counterproductive.

### Information Retrieval Systems

A large proportion of client/server applications capture and maintain no data. They are strictly information retrieval, analysis, and display systems. We've already identified some of the acronyms that apply here: EIS, DSS, and OLAP. Regardless of the name applied, the business function or user community supported, the type of information accessed, or the automated analysis capabilities provided, all these systems share certain design characteristics and are best created with certain design emphases.

By definition, information retrieval systems perform some fairly basic functions:

- Understanding precisely the nature of the user's inquiry
- Finding the information necessary to answer the user's inquiry
- Summarizing or otherwise manipulating the information, to facilitate analysis and presentation
- Analyzing the information according to a set of rules
- Presenting the information on either a monitor or a printed report

Design of information retrieval systems, then, consists of determining just how to perform each of these basic tasks in an orderly and efficient manner, but the design task is both complicated and simplified by the change in information retrieval patterns inherent in the shift to client/server computing.

When we discuss information retrieval systems with typical mainframe or other host-based programmers and designers, we can see them struggling with the concept of ad hoc retrieval. Host-based designers want to analyze what the retrieval patterns will be so that they can design a system that will efficiently retrieve just the right information, in just the right quantities and just the right manner. This assumption about system design is understandable, because for years it has been the designer's job to understand and anticipate usage patterns in order to support and facilitate them.

In the client/server arena, however, it is no longer sufficient to identify the top number of likely inquiries and design a system that supports each of them. Users now expect to be able to ask any question of the system and, if the data exists, to get an appropriate answer. As a result, it is no longer possible, nor necessary, to determine the inquiries that will constitute 80%, or 90%, of a system's workload. Our major task is to provide an access capability that will support 100% of future inquiries even though the precise questions are not yet known. The initial design task, then, for information retrieval systems, is the identification and design of appropriate data; the data is most often stored in one or more relational databases.

## WHAT IS DATA NORMALIZATION?

For client/server applications, particularly suites or collections of client/server applications, to provide the greatest possible utility, they must use a common set of databases. They must all update the same data, and they must all report and inquire against the same data. No other arrangement guarantees consistency of processing or of results.

By implication, then, the databases used cannot be designed to support the processing needs of any single application. They must be designed to support all applications, both those now known and those coming in the future.

The only way in which databases designed and implemented in the present can reasonably hope to support applications that aren't even conceived yet is by being fully *normalized*. Data normalization is a process by which specific patterns and characteristics are removed from databases or file layouts. As normally described and practiced, it is a rather dry, mathematical process. However, the end result is to store all data elements (fields, columns, and variables) in records that correspond to the real-world entities to which the data elements themselves actually pertain.

To allow some examples, recall the personnel database that we described in Chapter 2 when we defined relational database management systems: employee, position, work location, department, and division information. In a normalized database, an employee record will hold only information about the employee proper, not the employee's position (except to list a coded identification of position), work location (again, except for a code), department (except to give a number), or division (no information at all, as division is determined by department).

Going further, there would be a record for a particular employee, a separate record (in a separate table) to describe the job position to which the employee is assigned, and a third record (in a third table) to record information about the chronology and conditions of the assignment. These would, typically, be called the Employee, Position and Employee-Position tables.

The general pattern of normalization is to go from large collections of data in single records (e.g., some pertaining to the employee, but some pertaining to department, some to position, and some to position assignment) to a number of smaller, more focused records, each pertaining to a distinct entity. To the extent that a normalized database is structured according to objective reality, rather than any subjective view of that reality, it can't fail to support future applications as they come along. Future applications may require the addition of more types of entities, more tables, and more data elements, but they shouldn't require any change to the entities, tables, and data elements that already exist, and that previous applications are already using.

Formally, data normalization is a process of stepwise refinement, from unnormalized to fully normalized data.

- Unnormalized data consists of any collection of data elements, usually at least loosely related to a common entity.

- Data in *first normal form* has no repeating groups. That is, no data element in the record occurs more than once. A repeating group, for instance, might consist of monthly employee performance ratings—the same fields could be listed for January, February, March, ... through December. To place data in first normal form, the repeating group must be pulled out of the larger record and made into a number of smaller, independent records (such as one record per month, each carrying the employee performance rating information and each also carrying the employee ID number as an identifying field).

- Data in *second normal form* all pertains directly to the entity identified by the primary record key. Thus, the employee performance rating information wouldn't contain employee name or position, just the employee ID number, the rating period (month), and the actual rating information.

- Data in *third normal form* doesn't need any nonkey fields to identify its relevance. For instance, an employee record might not even contain a job position code, rather job position might be stored in a separate record keyed to employee number and date in position.

- Finally, *fourth normal form* requires that no conditional fields (fields that sometimes have a value and sometimes don't) be stored in the same records with unconditional fields. As a result, name of spouse would not be stored in the employee's primary record, as some employees aren't married.

If the necessary data resides in databases that were designed to support multiple applications, then the databases are probably well normalized (see "What Is Data Normalization?"). On the other hand, if a database was created to serve only a single application, it will often not be normalized. In that case, a redundant, fully normalized, database should be created to support information retrieval applications. This normalized database can be part of a data warehouse.

If all appropriate data is available and fully normalized, then the information retrieval system will be able to access it in whatever combination is necessary to answer any business problem. The need to predict specific inquiries vanishes. It becomes sufficient to be able to predict classes of inquiry, or the types of information that must be available.

One common mistake in the determination of what data is necessary, understandable in a host-based programmer or systems analyst, is to limit the scope of the inquiry to information in databases that are maintained internal to the company or organization. The tacit assumption is that all important questions can be answered from existing databases; however, for modern information retrieval systems this is often not the case. More and more, managers and employees with marketing responsibility or with direct customer contact need answers to questions about how a company's products, services, prices or activities compare and relate to the world outside the company's walls. To answer questions like these, many information retrieval systems must provide access to data that resides in the outside world. A useful information retrieval system design will identify not only what and where these external data sources are, but how users will access them. System designers must define what communications technologies will be used, what chronological patterns will be exhibited, whether an internal copy of outside data will be created, what volume of data will be retrieved, and under what circumstances.

Once access to sufficient and appropriate data has been assured, most of the functionality of an information retrieval system can and should be provided by commercial software. Off-the-shelf tools provide reliable, flexible support for all manner of inquiry, efficient access to databases, and far more effective graphical display capabilities than most custom-developed systems. Because information retrieval systems typically serve only a single user, there is little reason to force standardization of software here; each department might very well be allowed to choose the package that suits its users best, as long as the necessary support resources exist.

However, if users require more than just data identification, retrieval, and display (e.g., if there are needs for substantive mathematical analysis of the data), then a second tool (or set of tools) may be required. Statistical and other standard mathematical analyses are provided by many commercial products. Again, there is little reason to force standardization to a single toolset across the entire enterprise; concerns of accuracy and consistency are addressed by making sure that sufficient data is available, clearly structured, and fully understood by the user.

## Custom Information Maintenance Systems

Information maintenance systems—applications that capture and collect data as well as retrieve and display it—account for most of the time of business systems developers. Some of these applications perform standard business functions in standard ways, but many embody processes or business logic that are truly unique to a single company. The standard processes can, and usually should, be supported by commercially available packaged software (which we will discuss next). Automation of unique processing, however, must be addressed on a custom basis, either by in-house developers or via contract.

Custom application development should be conducted according to the standards and guidelines established by your client/server architecture. Any reasonable architecture will leave many options open to accommodate different system sizes, types and complexities. The first step in designing a custom client/server application is to categorize it according to our matrix.

- Is the system likely to be used in combination with other applications or to share data with other applications, or is it really addressing an isolated, standalone sort of function?

- Is transaction volume, data volume, or the number of simultaneous users likely to overburden your infrastructure?

- Is the performance of critical transactions a driving requirement?

- How large is the user community? Does it extend beyond your company's employees?

- What is the robustness requirement?

- If the application goes down for a period of time, is one of your company's profit centers out of business (even temporarily)?

Answering these and similar questions will allow us to categorize the system as standalone, integrated, or high volume; and as departmental, enterprise, or mission-critical. This categorization is more than an academic exercise. Where a particular application falls on the matrix helps us to determine whether it should be two- or three-tiered, for example.

## Deployment Patterns

As we said earlier, the largest and most important applications—the mission-critical integrated, enterprise high-volume, and mission-critical high-volume systems—tend to be implemented using a three-tiered architecture. Mission-critical standalone, enterprise integrated, and departmental high-volume systems often exhibit a three-tiered design, although it's by no means universal. Applications in other categories may be two tiered (either fat client or thin client) or three tiered, depending on a number of circumstances and conditions.

How should you decide whether a particular application should be two tiered or three tiered? Fat client or thin client? How do you know when a complex information system needs to go beyond the three basic deployment patterns and split processing or data, placing some on the client and some on the server?

The key to addressing issues of deployment pattern is to remember that it has no effect on the functionality provided to the user. The only impacts of fat-client versus thin-client applications are in the areas of performance, reliability, security, and ease of management. The proper deployment pattern for any application, therefore, is the one that gives the best mix of these features. Indeed, the reason that truly large client/server systems are most often implemented as three tiered is that this approach allows them better performance, reliability, and manageability, and to a degree also enhances security.

To determine what sort of deployment will enhance your system's performance, consider how much data must travel between your Presentation (user interface) layer and your business logic. Don't concern yourself with system overhead, just identify the application data—the input transaction that must be captured and processed, the data that is passed to the presentation layer in response to a query. Quantify the data in terms of bytes per day, week, or month.

Compare the amount of data that crosses the presentation interface with the amount of data that must be passed between your database and your business logic. Consider database updates (adds, changes, deletions) and database inquiries. For inquiries, don't limit your calculations to simple single-record displays, but also consider situations in which the business logic will have to examine large quantities of data in order to present summarized output to the user. If your application requires that each transaction be interpreted in terms of large quantities of data already on the database, factor in the records that must be retrieved for interpretation, as well as the record(s) that will be added.

The pattern of data movement may help you determine what deployment makes most sense, because data movement across a network is the most common performance bottleneck in a client/server system. Computing technologies, both on the client and on the server, have advanced rapidly. Desktop clients commonly have twice the computing power that was found only two or three years ago. Server platforms offer faster processors, more processors, and more memory, all at dramatically lower prices, but networking technologies have, over the last few years, advanced more slowly. The most common LAN technology, known as 10Base-T, was standardized in 1990, and the IEEE 802.3 standard of which it is a part has been around for much longer. The 10 in 10Base-T refers to a theoretical maximum capacity of 10 Mbps (megabits per second)—a standard speed that has been in use since the 1970s!

If your LAN was installed in 1995 or later, or has been completely refurbished in that time, it probably operates at 100 Mbps. This "Fast Ethernet" comes in a number of different flavors (100Base-T, 100Base-TX, 100Base-VG), but all offer the same basic advantage—ten times the communication capacity of earlier Ethernets. However, even in this instance, moving data across the network presents the most likely performance bottleneck for your client/server applications. With more people running more applications simultaneously, with many applications being run unattended or "in the background," with the advent of graphics, audio, and other forms of multimedia data, even 100-megabit performance is merely adequate. We'll go into discussions of performance in more detail in Chapter 5, but the simple fact is that choosing a form of client/server deployment (fat client, thin client or three tiered) that minimizes the need for data to cross the network is a powerful technique for maximizing system performance.

If markedly more data passes between your user interface and your business logic than ever makes it to the database, then a fat-client deployment should be your clear preference. On the other hand, if a lot of data goes from the database to the business logic, without ever making the trip to the presentation layer, then thin-client deployment is preferred. In each case, we speak of "preference" rather than "imperative," because there are other considerations than just performance, and other decision factors than just network demand versus available capacity.

Factors that might mitigate in favor of a fat-client deployment include:

- A desire to maximize use of desktop hardware while minimizing investment in centralized servers
- A large number of remote or mobile users who must perform complex systems interactions
- Many (or complex) data validation rules that can be enforced without constant reference to database contents
- A limited need to scale system operations (transaction volumes, number of users) upward
- An established investment in, and preference for, one of the commonly used application development tools, which typically support fat-client deployment only

On the other hand, a number of factors might increase the likelihood of a thin-client deployment:

- Concerns about the security of business logic code if it is executed on the desktop platform

- The need to support a wide range of client hardware or software platforms
- A desire to minimize configuration management problems by having fewer copies of business logic software
- An organizational culture that still emphasizes control rather than creativity and wishes to enforce common ways of system interaction

There is one common situation in which three-tiered deployment is a logical choice, even when application size and complexity really don't require it. If a client/server application is being developed to replace a host-based application, and if the business logic already programmed into the host is complex, then a three-tiered deployment may significantly decrease the amount of programming and testing necessary to produce the new system.

The three-tiered approach allows the business logic to be executed on a computer that doesn't have to worry about the Presentation layer, nor about the database. Thus, the second-tier computer (application server) can be chosen based on its ability to support the same programming language in which the host-based system is written. This being the case, it becomes possible for the key business processing algorithms—those key decisions or data manipulations upon which the application depends—to be "cut and pasted" out of the predecessor system. It's generally not possible to salvage whole programs by this technique, but major sections of code can be reused in their entirety, and every line of code that doesn't have to be written is one that shouldn't cause problems during testing. After all, the key code in your long-term production applications is probably the most tested code your organization owns!

As mentioned earlier, there are other possible deployments than just the three mentioned here, but anything more complex than a three-tiered design should be avoided if possible. Some applications, such as those that must provide full functionality to mobile users even when they can't communicate with the database server, will require a local database on the client as well as a central database (and, perhaps, some associated business logic) on the server; see Figures 4.9 and 4.10. However, industry experience shows that these systems are harder and more expensive to develop, manage, tune, and maintain than applications that stick to the three basic design patterns.

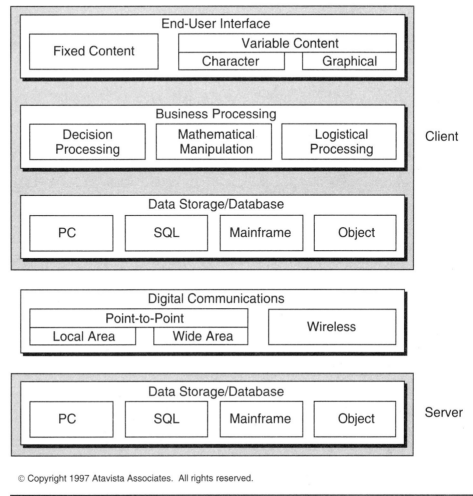

**Figure 4.9:**   A Split-Data Client/Server Architecture

## Designing Application Logic

Regardless of how your application will be deployed, the question remains, "How should your application logic be designed?" We have found that design of application logic is a major factor in determining the "bulletproofness" of client/server systems. Application logic encompasses everything from a graphical user interface element to a piece of data in a database. Application logic design determines how the components are formed, what each piece contains, how the elements are arranged, and how they interact.

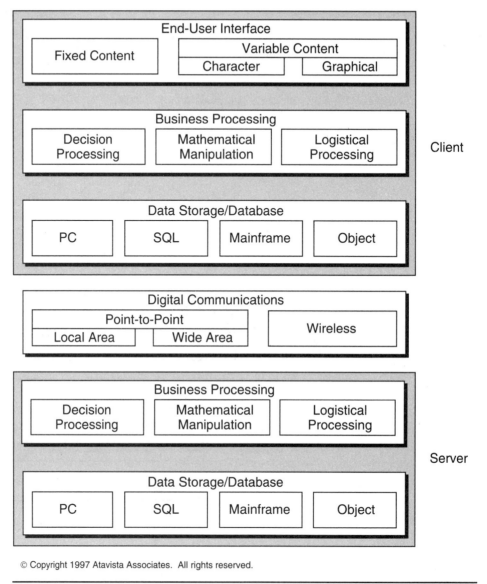

**Figure 4.10:**   A Split-Processing Client/Server Architecture

Client/server applications are most bulletproof when they are cleanly designed to be *event-driven*, that is, when they have the flexibility to respond to real-world events in whatever order those occur, and when they don't try to force the user through a predetermined path of interaction or hierarchy of menu selections. One general pattern of application design has proven itself most amenable to event-driven processing.

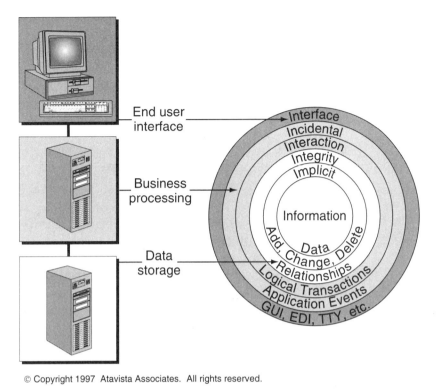

**Figure 4.11:**   Application Design Rings

The six-ring architecture shown in Figure 4.11 is one way of depicting event-driven application design. The rings in the diagram are separate and independent layers. Every component of the application logic fits into exactly one of the layers; no component is allowed to span the dividing line between two adjacent rings.

Starting from the center of the diagram, the main characteristics of each ring are

- **Information.** The center of the architecture consists of all the data that is retained and maintained about real-world objects (people, places, things, events) that concern the application. Most of this data is persistent; that is, it stays around even if the computer is turned off—it's in the database. However, some of it is volatile or temporary; volatile data should be explicitly designed and contained within the Information layer any time it's available to two or more application functions (typically, at the Interaction layer).

- **Implicit.** Surrounding the Information layer is a layer of services (procedural logic) that exist because the data itself exists. Implicit services provide such low-level functionality as adding, inserting, deleting, and updating records. If the Information layer contents are contained within a database management system, then the Implicit layer is supplied by the database engine, but any central data that is not contained in a DBMS must still have Implicit services surrounding it; no access to the Information layer contents are allowed, except through the Implicit layer.

- **Integrity.** The Integrity layer consists of program code that enforces rules and protects data integrity. *Referential* integrity rules make certain that no data record references another record that doesn't exist, such as adding an employee to a personnel file, but using an invalid department number. *Entity* integrity concerns making sure that only complete entities are added, such as requiring all "car" records to be associated with four "wheel" records. *Logical* integrity rules enforce business requirements, such as making sure that the sum of debits equals the sum of credits. No change to data is allowed if it would violate production integrity rules.

- **Interaction.** The fourth ring of the architecture consists of processing modules that implement atomic business functionality. Interaction modules each perform one fundamental business function; they may be invoked in response to a number of different business events. An example might be the processing to remove an employee from the active payroll. A number of low-level database changes might be required to accurately reflect this change, but the module itself might be invoked under a number of circumstances: An employee is fired, quits, retires, goes on disability, dies, etc.). Every action that a client/server application might take and that can end up being reflected in the central data must take place in an Interaction module.

- **Incidental.** One module in this level of the architecture exists for each business event to which the system must respond. Incidental modules control which Interaction modules are to be invoked, and in what order. Extending the example of removing someone from the active payroll, separate Incidental modules would exist to handle firing, quitting, retiring, disability, death, and so on. Each such Incidental module would invoke the same

Interaction-level module, but none of them would stop there. The retirement logic would remove the employee from the active payroll and add her to the active pension list. The firing process would remove the employee from the active payroll and call Security to escort him out of the building. Incidental modules may contain decision logic to allow them to call different combinations of Interaction-level modules, but Incidental modules should not do any direct actions themselves.

- **Interface.** Modules of code at the Interface level communicate to the system what business event has occurred and what data pertains to the event. For instance, an Interface module might capture the information that Mary Smith (employee number 12345) has retired on a specific date and has elected certain options with regard to her pension. Each Interface module should call a single Incidental module, or it should call multiple Incidental modules only at the explicit direction of the system user. Interface modules may contain basic semantic data validation logic, but should leave substantive business processing to the lower layers of the architecture.

Multiple Interface modules may call the same Incidental module, as there may be a number of technical or business circumstances that result in the same business event. For instance, there may be a PC graphical interface, a Macintosh graphical interface, and maybe even a character-based interface for users whose hardware is limited. Additionally, the same business event may be invoked under different circumstances, such as

*external* circumstances, where an event happens outside the control of the system and must be communicated to the system;

*chronological* circumstances, where processing is triggered by the passage of time, or by the arrival of a predefined time; or

*conditional* circumstances, where processing is triggered by a particular condition in the data.

A simple example of multiple circumstances triggering a single business event might be the cutting of checks out of an accounts payable system. Under normal circumstances, bills might be marked for payment with checks to be created in batch mode on a certain date (chronological event), but in an emergency single checks might be created based on information entered at a graphical user interface (external event). In each case, however, each check created would be the result of invoking the same Incidental module, with all its attendant Interaction and lower-level processes.

This application architecture provides client/server systems with a high level of "bulletproofness" because it leads to high levels of code reuse; consistent processing under all circumstances; a clear differentiation between control and process logic; a clear differentiation between Presentation layer, business logic, and data storage; and a system that is both flexible and easily maintained or enhanced. The six-ring architecture also creates systems that deploy well regardless of client/server design approach.

- For fat-client systems, the Interface, Incidental, and Interaction rings go on the client; the Integrity, Implicit, and Information rings go on the server.
- In thin-client systems, only the Interface ring goes on the client; all other rings go on the server.
- In three-tiered systems, the Interface goes on the client, the Incidental and Interaction rings go on the application server, and the Integrity, Implicit, and Information rings go on the database server.

## Application Design in the Organizational Context

The preceding discussion has concentrated on technical aspects of client/server system design, but it's crucial to recognize that the design process takes place in the context of an organization with multiple constituencies, changing business needs, and time and cost constraints. That organizational context can either frustrate or facilitate effective design. Bulletproofing the design process, then, also involves the following steps:

- Providing for the contributions and ideas of those who will authorize, support, and use the system, in a way that emphasizes cooperation without permitting democratic paralysis
- Creating an interactive and iterative design process that can react to changing priorities and business environments
- Preventing "runaway" projects by establishing schedules and checkpoints

Although we can only mention these organizational issues briefly in these pages and many of us are more highly trained in making technical decisions than political ones, their importance should not be underestimated.

### Involving the Constituencies

Any computer system design project that doesn't involve the eventual users all along the process is almost guaranteed to fail. The literature is full of examples wherein IT departments don't consider the people who will be using the system daily. After all, they're not experts, right?

Actually, they *are* experts—not in design, surely, but in business problems and system usage. We saw in the previous chapter that a poorly thought through, or inconsistent, user interface can torpedo a system's business effectiveness. Boeing would not design a new jet without consulting with the pilots who will fly it. The organization can often reduce client/server project costs significantly by identifying point-of-use problems early in the project instead of after it's completed.

Another important constituency is the management staff who will evaluate, authorize, and support the new system. Designers must therefore dedicate time and energy toward educating management about the proposed benefits of the new system, the anticipated costs, and how the two relate. Such education can be challenging in that senior managers may not have a technical background, so design issues must be presented without off-putting jargon and excessive detail. Our experience has shown that managers who don't adequately understand a new information system project are not likely to fight for its establishment in the first place or its continuance in the second.

The third constituency to consider, and to involve in at least selected design discussions, is the group who will be charged with supporting the new system. Whether such individuals make up a formal help desk or an informal support network, their enthusiasm about the project will be important to its success during and after the implementation phase. They will also have to invest time learning and understanding the new system in order to effectively provide user technical support. (We'll explore support issues further in Chapter 8.)

The danger in involving these three groups in client/server design is that the project will be discussed to death and never move ahead—the paralysis of democracy. It's true that the design process will probably take longer if managers, users, and support staff have the opportunity to comment and contribute. However, the implementation process will probably proceed faster with the support of these constituencies. If they are left out of the loop, they're certain to criticize the new system; if included, they're likely to look for ways to make the system succeed. The time that is given up on the front end will be more than made up on the back end, and the results will be more useful to everyone involved.

Having said that, it makes sense to begin design discussions with some reasonable ground rules for moving ahead even without unanimous agreement on every idea. Such rules are easier to agree on if all the constituencies have a clear understanding of how the new system can make their lives easier or more productive, so that it will be in no one's interest to delay the project unnecessarily. Lipnack and Stamps write (in *The TeamNet Factor*) that "In practice, a consensus decision is one without significant opposition, one members can support, or at least tolerate."

### Iterative vs. Static Design Procedures

Creating a one-time, static set of functional requirements for a client/server system is a very risky way of proceeding in a world where business needs have a way of changing with markets, and where managers, users, and support staff don't stop thinking once the functional requirements document is written. We've seen cases where a design document is created, the design experts go off for 6 months and create a system, and the constituencies then see it and say, "Great, now can we do X, Y, and Z?" The designers may at that point have to say, "No, that wasn't part of the design," which then frustrates everyone.

Discussing an information system in the abstract is one thing; seeing it in action is entirely different. When managers, users, and support staff begin to see a system take shape, they're likely to think of enhancements they didn't think of earlier in the process. It therefore makes great sense to apprise constituencies of design milestones as they occur and provide them the opportunity to comment. On larger projects, it may be wise to build small-scale demonstration systems in parallel with the actual systems and to encourage an iterative design review process that makes it possible for designers to fold in at least some good ideas along the way—instead of summarily dismissing them as being past the deadline.

The technologies used to create new client/server systems may determine the extent to which the design can remain flexible under development. Systems that use objects, controls, forms, or other types of modular code are far more amenable to change than monolithic systems written in rigid procedural languages. Smaller, simpler systems may take longer to create this way, but they will permit the inclusion of good ideas that come along after the functional specification document is drafted, and they can adapt better to changing demands over the system's lifetime. Further, they will be easier to maintain, which is no small advantage considering that maintenance typically comprises 90% of a system's life-cycle cost whereas initial development makes up only 10%. Larger, more complex client/server systems (those in the bottom-right corner of the application categorization matrix) actually cost less and take less time to develop incrementally, because of a reduced level of reworking as business requirements and technologies change.

## Project Management Safeguards

After the start of a client/server project, designers become so immersed in it that they run the risk of losing perspective—specifically, time and cost perspective. We've already established that client/server design is riddled with complexities, and complex projects can easily become runaways that bust both budgets and schedules. Part of bulletproofing design projects, then, is establishing checkpoints and contingency plans.

*Checkpoints* associate demonstrable design progress with target dates. Project management tools (GANTT and PERT charts and their variants) can help designers track their own progress relative to checkpoints agreed upon early in the project. Just as the functional requirements document should not be perceived as a rigid and inflexible guide, so should the checkpoints be "slippable" to some degree if new ideas come along during the system's development. If the slippage is likely to be significant, a design board should evaluate whether the benefits of the change order are likely to exceed the pain of the delay.

*Contingency plans* are ideas for what to do if things get really bogged down. Fred Brooks has eloquently articulated (in *The Mythical Man-Month*) that it's often faster to scrap a runaway project entirely, and start over, than to try fixing it. He also suggests that it may be better to reduce a project's scope or lengthen its schedule than to put more people on the job, as the latter course tends to make late projects later.

By establishing architectural guidelines, picking appropriate middleware, selecting an efficient and effective deployment approach, properly creating application logic architecture, and considering the design process in the context of multiple organizational constituencies, changing business needs, and time and cost constraints, you can build client/server systems that provide efficient and reliable service both initially and over time. That's not to say that specific challenges and requirements won't need your attention form one application to the next. They will. It's to address the majority of those specific challenges and requirements that we've written the rest of this book. We'll look at performance issues in Chapter 5, then get to the topics of security, fault tolerance, and support.

# 5

# Bulletproofing
# Client/Server Performance

For years, Sue had managed the data-entry operations for a large university. She supervised eight data-entry operators who used electronic key-to-tape and key-verification equipment. On any batch of input (forms to be key-entered), one of Sue's operators would key the data for original entry and a second operator would rekey the same data, for comparison purposes. If both operators keyed the same characters, the input was presumed to be valid.

With this arrangement, tried and tested over the years, Sue's people experienced about a 10% error rate. That is, about 10% of the forms were initially keyed incorrectly, and the errors were caught the by second keying and the automatic comparison. A month's data, all filled out and batched for processing, took about 20 hours to enter and verify.

Recently, a modern client/server data entry subsystem was created to replace the legacy data entry process. A graphical user interface provides full editing capabilities on original entry, forcing many of the field values to be selected from prevalidated lists. Operators receive the same forms as previously, in the same month-end batches as previously, and enter data as much as possible as they did before. The process that used to take 20 hours a month now takes over ten times that long.

Around the world, broadcasters use satellites to send television programs from one continent to another. The programs are transmitted up to the satellites, where they are received, amplified, and retransmitted down to earth on another frequency. Broadcasters reserve satellite capacity, defined in terms of frequency and time slot (and a number of other parameters) minutes, hours, days, months or years before they actually use it.

Many of the programs transmitted via satellite recur periodically. A regular news program may be transmitted every day, Monday through Friday, every week of the year. Other programs are transmitted at the same time, on the same day, every week or every month. For years, broadcasters had requested satellite capacity to handle these programs by sending international telegrams listing the specific dates and times they wanted, with a more general description of the satellite(s) they wanted to use and the transmission characteristics they could support.

A new client/server system was developed to replace the telegrams and resulting data entry. Broadcasters anywhere in the world were given the ability to download portions of the schedule established for a particular satellite, to determine for themselves what time slots, frequencies, and other transmission characteristics were still available for reservation. Powerful programs, running on PC clients, would allow broadcasters to merely generate the patterns for periodic transmissions, allowing the client program to actually request 10, 20, or 200 specific transmissions.

Broadcaster personnel were trained and equipped to take advantage of their new capabilities and looked forward to taking control of their own scheduling requests, but when the system was implemented, complaints were rampant. The downloads of existing schedule information, which would allow viable new scheduling requests to be generated, took anywhere from 3 to 30 minutes. The logic that would accept a recurring transmission pattern definition and generate from it the necessary population of individual transmission scheduling requests sometimes took as much as an hour to execute. The new system did in fact deliver all the new capabilities promised, but it performed so slowly that no one wanted to use them.

## Performance Concepts and Terminology

In Chapter 4, we talked about the design of client/server systems. The subject of performance came up, as achieving good performance is one of the critical objectives of system design. In this chapter, we will concentrate solely on the subject of performance. Although it is widely discussed, it is not generally well understood. In fact, even the terminology systems people use to discuss system performance reveals the narrow view most take on the subject.

When most programmers, analysts, or project managers speak of "system performance," what they're generally discussing is system *response time*, that is, the amount of time it takes a system to respond to some definitive action taken by the human user and to display the first screen or window of information which shows the results of that action.

This definition of system performance is limited in two regards. First, it presumes that the relevant measurement of client/server system performance is transaction response time, as was the measurement of performance in host-based online transaction processing (OLTP) systems. Second, it ignores the many dimensions and variables of system performance that exist outside of any computer.

### Response Time vs. Throughput

Before there were online transaction processing systems, there were batch transaction processing systems. System performance was still an issue, but no one thought of performance in terms of response time because there was no visible response to any individual transaction. Instead, system performance was measured in terms of *throughput*. Rather than the amount of time a system took to process a single transaction, performance was measured in terms of the number of transactions the system could process in a unit of time.

The two approaches are but mathematical inverses of each other in the minds of typical programmers and managers, and in many host-based (including PC-based) processing environments. However, in the client/server world there is a key difference. The *form* of the interaction between clients and servers can make response time and throughput two effectively independent variables.

System response time and system throughput are closely linked for a given number of users, if coordination between clients and servers is synchronous. As we mentioned before, in the synchronous model, the human operator waits until processing of a first transaction is complete before starting to process a second transaction. An alternative, asynchronous, approach allows the human operator to begin (and perhaps finish) process a second transaction while processing of the first transaction is still underway. Using asynchronous client/server coordination, system throughput may be high even though the amount of time it takes the system to process any individual transaction may still be considerable.

### Measuring Performance

Whether you're more concerned with response time or throughput, it is important to compare mainframe to client/server performance in a fair and reasonable manner. After all, the reason companies purchase computers is to allow a particular job to be done better, faster, and cheaper—not just one small part of a job, but the whole job. Because client/server systems often deliver their greatest value by changing the way a job is done, it simply isn't reasonable to compare the time a mainframe takes to perform one small part of a series of tasks—especially when the entire series was originally designed to make optimal use of the mainframe itself—to the time it takes a client/server system to perform the same small activity. In a properly designed client/server process, that particular task might not ever be done!

> A recent *Reader's Digest* included a joke about someone taking a government job qualification test. Upon turning in his marked answer sheet, he was given a form stating, in part, "Your test will be scored by high-speed computer. Results will be available in four to six weeks."

In terms of simple machine efficiency, the test-scoring software might be an absolute marvel. (Probably not, but let's be kind!) Presumably, only a small fraction of a second was required to actually calculate the test score of a single individual. However, the organization and procedures that have accumulated around the test scoring process cause the output to be unavailable to a key user, the job applicant, for up to six weeks!

In this case, a client/server system wouldn't have to be terribly machine efficient to provide better response time (and, who knows, perhaps better throughput as well) than the mainframe system. Merely allowing results to be calculated and communicated on a same-day basis would constitute an order-of-magnitude improvement in the eye of the user.

This example, although extreme, points up a key truth. The only meaningful comparison between host- or mainframe-based system performance and client/server system performance is one based on *all the time and effort required to completely perform a job function*—not just the portion of the process performed by the machine, not just the last manual process (data entry?) before the machine takes over and the first manual process (inquiry or report examination) after it's done.

For example, in the government test-scoring situation, a respectable client/server system would eliminate the following procedural subtasks:

- Batching of the completed answer sheets
- Transportation of the answer sheets to the national processing center
- Batch input (mark-sensing) of the answer sheets
- Batch input (optical character recognition)
- Quality control of the batch input processes
- Sorting and tabulating of the scored answer sheets
- Generation of form letters conveying results to job applicants
- Quality control of the form letter generation
- Stuffing and mailing of the form letters
- Delivery of the form letters through the U.S. Mail

None of these subtasks adds any benefit for the job applicant; each of them is necessary only as part of a process designed to make optimal use of a mainframe computer for actually scoring the test. A well-designed client/server system probably wouldn't include any of them (with the possible exception of form letter generation).

Compared on the basis of how long it takes to score a single form, already scanned into the system, a client/server application might perform a couple of hundred percent slower. Compared on the basis of how long it takes to get the critical output to the job applicant, however, the same client/server system might prove to be over 99% faster! (See Figure 5.1.)

## Designing for Performance

None of this is meant to say that traditional measures of system performance are useless in the client/server world. Even when viewed and evaluated as part of a fully reengineered business process, many client/server applications exhibit less than ster-

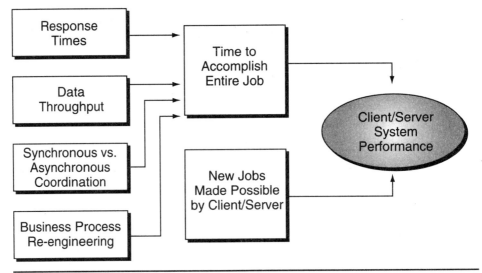

**Figure 5.1:**    Measuring Client/Server System Performance

ling performance. In fact, slow system performance is one of the most common complaints about client/server systems.

Slow system performance results when a client/server system is not well designed for the load it experiences. "Load," in this sense, means demand for resources. If any resource (client computing power, client disk response, client graphics response, network communication capability, server computing power, server disk response, and many others) is available in less quantity than the system demands, then performance will suffer. To design a system for good performance, then, it is necessary to predict what resources will be required and then supply those resources (with an adequate safety margin). This means not only looking at what the system will do, but *how* the system will do it.

At present, there are no reliable methods or algorithms for predetermining the optimal design of a client/server system. The guidelines that exist were discussed in Chapter 4 when we talked about choosing among fat-client, thin-client, and three-tiered deployment approaches. However, there are ways of evaluating a proposed design to determine whether it is likely to support a specific load on the system.

## User Actions and Frequencies

The first step in estimating system load is to quantify just what functions each user will perform, and how many times per unit

| User Category Description | | |
|---|---|---|

| 1) User Category Name | |
|---|---|
| 2) Approximate Number of Users | |

| 3) Business Event or Transaction Name | Number of Events per Unit of Time | Unit of Time |
|---|---|---|
| | | |
| | | |
| | | |
| | | |
| | | |

| 4) CPU Requirements | |
|---|---|
| Class | |
| Speed (MHz) | |
| 5) Hard Disk Requirements (MB) | |
| 6) RAM Requirements (MB) | |
| 7) Communication Requirements (bps) | |

**Figure 5.2:**   User Category Description

of time (hour, day, week, month) the user will perform each function. For large user communities, the obvious way to do this is to group users into categories, so that each user in a category exhibits basically the same usage pattern. The typical usage pattern for a user in a category can be multiplied by the number of users in that category. Adding up the demand levels for each category, then, will give an estimate of total system load.

For each identified category of user, we might fill out a form similar to that shown in Figure 5.2. We would assign a descriptive name to the category and note the number of users who are anticipated to exhibit that pattern of activity. We would then

| Event Client Requirements | | | | | |
|---|---|---|---|---|---|
| 1) Business Event or Transaction Name | | | | | |
| 2) Transaction Input Size (bytes) | | | | | |
| 3) Complexity of Processing (5= Very High) | 1 | 2 | 3 | 4 | 5 |
| 4) Data to or from Hard Disk (bytes) | | | | | |
| 5) Data to or from Network (bytes) | | | | | |
| 6) Error Rate (%) | | | | | |
| 7) Client Application RAM Requirements (MB) | | | | | |
| 8) Number of Other Applications Executing Simultaneously | | | | | |

Note:  Version shown is appropriate for fat-client systems.
Form may be adjusted for other development patterns.

**Figure 5.3:**   Event Client Requirements

identify each business event or transaction that users in the category would likely initiate, as well as the number of such transactions per time period and the length (typically hour, day, week, month) of the time period in question. The remaining fields on the form we leave blank, for the moment.

### Transaction-Specific Data

For each identified business transaction or event, we typically fill out a set of forms such as those shown in Figures 5.3 through 5.5.

The first transaction-specific form helps us to estimate the requirements that processing of the business event will place on the client platform. After identifying the event by name, we enter a number of estimates, including

- The number of bytes (characters) of input that we anticipate a user to enter in initiating the event
- The relative complexity of the transaction process logic associated with the event (initially Very High, High, Medium, Low, Very Low; later a numeric value generally expressed in milliseconds)

| Event Server Requirements | |
|---|---|
| 1) Business Event or Transaction Name | |
| 2) Number of Simultaneous Users (90% level) | |
| 3) Data from Database (bytes) | |
| 4) Average Number of Relational Joins | |
| 5) Data to Database (bytes) | |
| 6) Number of Tables Updated | |
| 7) Data to or from Network (bytes) | |
| 8) Desired Cache Hit Rate (%) | |

Note:  Version shown is appropriate for fat-client systems.
Form may be adjusted for other development patterns.

**Figure 5.4:**   Event Server Requirements

- The average amount of data to be transferred to or from the client's hard disk during event processing
- The average amount of data to be transferred to or from the network during event processing
- The average error rate expected of the user community, expressed as a percentage
- The anticipated RAM requirements for client application programs
- The number of other business applications that users initiating this particular transaction will simultaneously be executing

The next transaction form addresses server-side requirements, such as

- The likely maximum number of simultaneous users executing this transaction (should cover at least 90% of observations)
- The average number of bytes of data to be retrieved from the database in response to each transaction
- The average number of relational joins required to retrieve data in response to this transaction

| Event Network Requirements | |
|---|---|
| 1) Business Event or Transaction Name | |
| 2) Number of Network Messages | |
| 3) Data across Network (bytes) | |
| 4) Maximum Frame or Packet Size (bytes) | |
| 5) Number of Frames of Packets Generated | |
| 6) Maximum Transactions/Hour (99% level) | |
| 7) Network Demand (#6 X #5 X #4 / 450) (bps) | |

**Figure 5.5:**  Event Network Requirements

- The average number of data bytes to be inserted or updated on the database in response to each transaction
- The average number of relational tables to receive new or updated data in response to this transaction
- The average amount of data to be transferred to or from the network in processing this transaction
- The desired or anticipated percentage of "cache hits" (transaction activity against database records already resident in RAM) for this transaction

The last form that captures transaction-identified information relates to the amount of network traffic that each business event will generate. Estimates include

- The number of messages (client-to-server or server-to-client) that each event will cause
- The average total number of data bytes to traverse the network as a result of each event
- The anticipated maximum frame or packet size on the network in question (consult your network administrator)
- The number of frames or packets to be generated for each transaction (total number of bytes divided by maximum packet size, plus number of messages)

| System Server Requirements (derived from the Event Server Requirements datasheets) | | |
|---|---|---|
| 1) CPU Requirements | | |
| Class | | |
| Speed (MHz) | | |
| 2) I/O Channel Requirements (bps) | | |
| | Initial | In 2 Years |
| 3) Total Database Data Size (MB) | | |
| 4) Total Database Index Size (MB) | | |
| 5) Total Hard Disk Requirements | | |
| Size (MB) | | |
| Speed (average access time, ms) | | |
| Number | | |
| 6) RAM Requirements | | |
| Programs (MB) | | |
| Cache (MB) | | |
| 7) Communications Requirements (bps) | | |

**Figure 5.6:**   System Server Requirements

- The number of transactions or events per hour (should cover at least 99% of observations)
- The resulting network demand in bits per second (events per hour times packets per event times maximum packet size, times 8, divided by 3600)

Once sets of forms have been filled out for each identified business transaction or event, then a final form (Figure 5.6) is filled out to estimate total server demand and the remaining columns on the form in Figure 5.2 are completed.

To estimate server demand, use the information on all the forms shown in Figure 5.4 to estimate

- Processor requirements on the server, based on the number of simultaneous users and the total number of transactions/events anticipated per hour (your hardware vendor(s) will have reference charts or formulas)
- The amount of data that will have to traverse the input/output channel and hard disk controllers per second
- The total amount of data contained in the necessary database files
- The total amount of data required to index the various database files (10 to 20% for update-intensive applications, 25 to 50% for retrieval-intensive applications)
- The size, speed, and number of hard disks necessary to store the database files for efficient retrieval and update (consult your database administrator or vendor)
- The amount of RAM required on the server (must support database programs plus file and communications cache)
- The total number of data bits per second that must be communicated from or to the network (should cover at least 99% of observations)

For each category of user, estimate client demand by looking at total

- CPU requirements, based on complexity of process logic, number of simultaneous applications, anticipated operating system, etc.
- Hard disk and controller requirements, based on size of local data files, speed of required data transfer, etc.
- RAM requirements, based on anticipated program size, number of simultaneous applications, anticipated operating system, etc.
- The total number of bits of data per second that must be communicated from or to the network (should cover at least 95% of observations)

Finally, estimate total network demand for this application by adding the network demands (expressed in bits per second) for every identified business event or transaction, and allow a safety margin—perhaps 50% early in the project, down to 20% later on. A typical form to present this information is shown in Figure 5.7.

Throughout, we have spoken about "typical" forms, as the columns and calculations should be adapted to best correspond

| **System Network Requirements**<br>(derived from the Event Network Requirements datasheets) | |
| --- | --- |

| 1) Business Event or Transaction Name | Network Demand (bps) |
| --- | --- |
|  |  |
|  |  |
|  |  |
|  |  |
| 2) TOTAL |  |

| 3) Safety Margin (%) |  |
| --- | --- |
| 4) Total Network Demand (#2 X (1 + #3)) |  |

**Figure 5.7:**   System Network Requirements

to the nature and "shape" of the design. If two alternative designs are being evaluated, a full set of estimates should be prepared for each. Some of the information, clearly, can be shared from one set of estimates to the other. Comparison, and evaluation of which design will offer better performance, should take place based on total client demand, total server demand, and (especially) total network demand estimated for each.

### Minimizing Use of Least Available Resource

In any managerial economics course, one of the basic messages is to achieve efficiency by minimizing use of the least available resource. Client/server systems are no different.

- If your estimates indicate that you're going to run out of server capacity first, then you should design your system to minimize use of the server.
- If you seem likely to run out of client capacity before anything else, you should design your system to make less demand on the client.
- If your database engine is going to run out of gas, find a way to use less in the way of database services.

With the technology commonly in use today, you're most likely to run out of network capacity first, so let's start there.

**Minimizing Use of Network Capacity**    There's nothing magic about our supposition that you're likely to find network capacity your least available resource. Almost everyone does. For years, the most commonly used local area network speeds have been 10 Mbps (megabits per second) for Ethernet and 16 Mbps for token-ring. Since those standards were established—most recently, 16-MBps token-ring in the early 1990s—client PCs have gotten faster and cheaper, server boxes have gotten faster and cheaper, and the shift to client/server computing has greatly increased the volume of data clients and servers move across the network. Of course, network capacity is in short supply.

The good news is that, since 1995, 100-Mbps Ethernet has become economically viable and so, for the first time in years, LAN speeds are going up. The bad news is that there are still a lot of 10- and 16-Mbps LANs out there; they will continue to dominate the installed base for several years; and for longer-than-LAN distances (figure anything over about 2 miles), transmission speeds are slower yet.

To accommodate this universal bottleneck, the first step in client/server system design is often to estimate the volumes of data that would cross the network first in a fat-client deployment, and next in a thin-client deployment, and then pick whichever gives less network traffic (see Figure 5.8). (Note that three-tiered applications never minimize total network traffic, and minimize localized network traffic only when the three tiers—client, application server, and database server—are spread across two physically separate networks.)

- Fat-client applications often minimize network traffic by performing all processing up to but not including the actual insertion of a record into the database on the client platform. All data validation, interpretation, and application processing is performed on the desktop workstation (usually a PC). Any files or other information that might be necessary to validate data are downloaded from a server to the PC only once and are then available to process an entire day's worth of transactions. In large networks that support complex data validation requirements, the reference data may even be downloaded in stages, overnight from a central server to local network servers, and

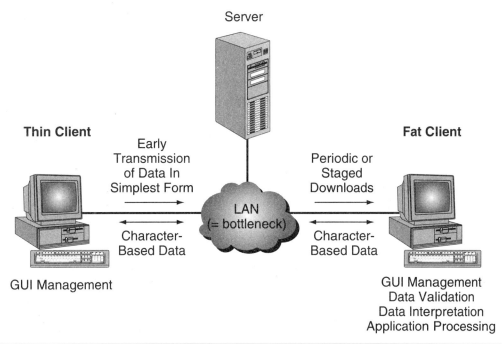

**Figure 5.8:**   Minimizing Network Traffic

on an as-needed basis from the local servers to whatever clients have need.

- Thin-client applications typically minimize network traffic by getting the data to the application or database server as soon as possible, before validation or application logic expands it or makes it more complex. Character transaction data is generally of low volume, and not likely to overload a network. Once all application processing is done on the server, then a relatively short return message (also character data) will often suffice.

- Regardless of whether your system turns out to be fat-client or thin-client, avoiding the transmission of graphics over the wire decreases load on the network. It may be true that a picture is worth a thousand words, but on a network we can transmit the thousand words a lot faster and less expensively!

**Minimizing Use of Server or Database Resources**   If your system seems likely to run out of server processing capacity before anything else, you're probably not building a fat-client system.

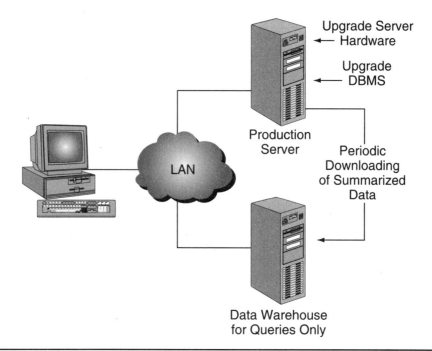

**Figure 5.9:**    Improving Server/Database Performance

Network capacity may have forced you to keep much of your processing near the database, but there are still solutions (see Figure 5.9).

The first and most obvious possible solution is to simply upgrade the server. Whether that means adding hardware components into an existing platform or replacing the existing hardware with a larger model, this is not a solution to ignore. In the mainframe world, any suggestion of buying a bigger computer just to meet the performance needs of a single application was typically ignored; only the largest mission-critical applications could justify the expenditure of large chunks of hardware money.

In the client/server world, the chunks of money don't have to be anywhere near as large. In some cases, spending capital on increased server capacity can solve a performance bottleneck problem quickly, cheaply, and reliably. If a bottleneck truly exists on the server, we estimate that each dollar spent on hardware can save five to ten dollars in software engineering during system development, and twice that amount over the life of a typical client/server application.

A variant on that theme is to add redundant servers to the design. This works best in inquiry-intensive systems (where database inquiries can be directed to a database server separate from the "master" database, where updates are managed) and in three-tiered systems (where multiple, redundant application servers can update a single, centralized master database). As a matter of fact, the two patterns can be combined in the case of three-tiered applications that are also inquiry intensive.

The particular database management system used can also affect use of server resources. The clearest example of this involves the way in which the various DBMSs handle contention among multiple competing requests. Some DBMS products establish a separate process or program, running on the server platform, for each client user who is accessing the data. They then use the multitasking capabilities of the server operating system to manage the multiple programs. Other products establish only a single process to handle as many simultaneous users as required; they then manage contention via internal multithreading, which is by its nature far more efficient than multitasking.

Since the bulk of your application logic is probably executing on a server, there is an opportunity to reduce server demand by making the application logic more efficient. Some of this might be done by redesigning the application logic, but there's often a trade-off: efficiency versus flexibility or efficiency versus robustness. Examine such trade-offs, but don't allow yourself to be forced into a short-term compromise with excessive long-term costs. Demand for server resources is more successfully managed by changing the implementation technology (as we will see) or by simply supplying more server capacity.

**Minimizing Use of Client Resources**   On the client side of the equation, a similar situation faces us. Minimizing use of client resources is most often of concern in fat-client applications, but otherwise the circumstances are very similar.

The first question to be addressed in decreasing client demand is implementation technology. Some popular database front-end development tools generate extremely inefficient code, as we will discuss in the next section. Presuming, however, that you have picked a tool that generates relatively efficient code, or that your tool selection is driven by considerations other than the efficiency of the code generated, there are still some things you can do to decrease client demand.

Although it won't be popular with the users, the first step in a logical process of simplifying client-side processing (and thus reducing demand) is to rank-order the various bits of functionality that the system will provide in terms of the amount of processing resources necessary to support each. Simply dividing system transactions, functions, and business events into five categories based on the relative complexity of processing (Very High, High, Medium, Low, Very Low) as estimated on the form in Figure 5.3 will generally suffice.

The purpose of the rank-ordering, or sorting by category, is to highlight those transactions or business functions with High or Very High complexity processing, and to question the necessity of each one—not the benefit or utility of each, not whether each is useful or desirable, but whether each is truly *necessary*.

Often, the most complex processing logic is associated with a transaction that will be used only rarely, or only under special circumstances, or only by one or two specific users, or that could just as successfully (if not as conveniently) be handled by a combination of simpler transactions.

- If the complex logic will be used only rarely or under special circumstances, consider putting it in an application or module of its own. Segmenting system functionality makes it more difficult to use but can also reduce the client-side demand for resources if the two segments don't have to be executed simultaneously.

- If the complex logic will only be used by a small number of operators, then design the system so that it has to be deployed only to those operators. This won't reduce worst-case demand for client resources, but it can reduce the *number* of worst-case situations considerably. If you then decide to upgrade client hardware to resolve the difficulty, the number of computers you will require can be significantly reduced.

- If the complex logic can be handled by a combination of simpler transactions, the question becomes, "Why not do it that way?" The typical answer is that it would be too complex, or too time-consuming, for the user to manage each of the individual transactions separately, so the system needs to do the job automatically. Sometimes that's true, and sometimes it's not. It's certainly not a statement that should be taken on faith—the amount of difficulty involved in requiring the user to execute multiple system transactions instead of one can be reduced by creative graphical user interface design. Coordination between multiple logical transactions can often be implemented more efficiently at the graphical user interface than in process logic (although implementing it in process logic is the first impulse of many programmers who learned their craft on the mainframe). Useful GUI integration is most often achieved using the Object Linking and Embedding (OLE) standard promulgated by Microsoft Corporation.

**Minimizing Use of Human Resources**   Often, the least available resource is the human operator sitting in front of the client computer. Almost certainly, when factored for cost, this is a resource that good system design should use sparingly. Any time spent waiting by human beings is, and is immediately perceived as, less than ideal system performance.

Historians of technology have pointed out that this human-centered approach is diametrically opposed to that of the early Industrial Revolution engineers and managers, who dictated that human beings adapt to their machinery rather than vice versa. Nowadays, of course, human labor in the developed world is a little more expensive than it was then, but the more compelling point is that humans are capable of much more complex activity than the most sophisticated information processing systems. In large part, then, bulletproofing client/server systems means making them nearly invisible, so that the human users can concentrate less on wrestling with the tools they use and more on the jobs that the tools are supposed to help them perform.

As mentioned earlier, one way of optimizing use of the human resource is to decouple human performance from automated system performance, by using asynchronous communication between clients and servers. With synchronous communication, the human operator must wait for transaction #1 to be completely processed before he or she can start entering transaction #2. As IBM researcher Arvind Thadhani discovered in a series of 1981 tests, human productivity drops significantly if this delay increases as slightly as from half a second to a full second. Part of the reason is that experienced computer users don't think in terms of doing one step at a time: They have several steps in mind at the outset of a task, and even slight delays can derail their train of thought and increase the chances for both frustration and mistakes. With asynchronous communication, the entry of transaction #2 can begin (and, perhaps, finish) while transaction #1 is still being processed. Asynchronous communication, then, allows the human being to work faster even if the computer or network can't, but asynchronous communication can create difficulties as well, most often in the interaction between humans and computers.

- If you're entering a group of transactions, presented to you on a stack of forms, and you've worked your way down to the seventh form in the stack when an error message relating to the second form in the stack appears on your computer, what do you do? Do you stop work on the seventh form, flip back to the second form, correct the error, return to the seventh form and resume your work? How do you know when it's safe to send the stack of forms back where they came from, or to destroy them?

- Consider an application, such as an office supply requisitioning system, that you use only occasionally. Say you use it to request a specific type of pencil and then exit the application. Later, the asynchronous processing runs into an error. How do you learn of the problem?

Issues like these can be dealt with by rethinking the human/machine dialogue. Error correction can take place in a second GUI window, or at a later time, or by another person. Error (or success) notification can take place via e-mail or some other inherently asynchronous feedback mechanism. The application may be designed so that all asynchronous processing must complete before the user is allowed to exit. Some fundamental rethinking of how people interact with machines may be required, but for high-volume data entry situations, asynchronous linkage can pay big performance benefits.

## Implementing for Performance

Presuming that the basic system design is fundamentally sound, the greatest impact on system performance is achieved during construction (formerly known as *programming* or *coding*) and implementation. These phases involve building an application system that conforms to the design and fulfills all business requirements, both functional and performance related.

If you're concerned about system performance throughout the construction stage—if simply picking the proper deployment pattern and avoiding a grossly inefficient design isn't going to be enough—then you're working on an application in the far-right column ("High Volume Transaction Processing") of our categorization matrix (Figure 4.2). If this is your first or second client/server application project, this is a clear sign to back off, get some additional experience, and readdress this project in a few months. (This is not always politically possible, but it is a very good idea nonetheless.) A key bulletproofing technique is to explicitly manage the construction process to achieve the necessary transaction performance, very much as you would manage the process to achieve a programmatic requirement such as meeting a schedule or staying within a budget.

High-volume processing systems often must provide a wide range of transaction services—various types of information that can be added, or changed, or displayed, or deleted. Not all transactions in a system will have the same performance requirements or the same difficulty in meeting those performance requirements. Transaction performance may be a key success criterion for your project and may need to be explicitly managed, but it's often neither necessary nor possible to manage the performance of every set of transaction logic being implemented in a large project.

Happily, efficient system construction can almost always be achieved by identifying the most performance-critical transactions, explicitly managing the performance that they will provide, and extending the techniques that prove successful to the rest of the application. Identifying the most performance-critical transactions requires looking at a number of characteristics:

- How many of each transaction will be processed in a typical business day? On the busiest business day? (Much of this information should already be available on the forms shown in Figure 5.2.)
- Are there transactions likely to be processed under external time pressure, such as while a customer is speaking to the system operator over the phone or before some other critical process (not part of this application) is executing?
- How complex is the business logic for each transaction? How much database activity is it going to generate? How much traffic will it cause on the network?

▪ At what time of day/week/month/year is each transaction likely to be executed? Are there any transactions that typically get invoked when the system or network is most heavily loaded?

Transactions that are executed most frequently can be performance critical by their sheer numbers. If you can implement a system to save a quarter-second on a transaction that is executed a half-million times a year, that's 125,000 seconds, or over 34 hours of system resources freed up annually.

Transactions that are executed while someone is waiting, or in a hurry, have a large psychological impact on user satisfaction levels. Even if they are executed relatively infrequently (a few times per day, perhaps), they may be considered performance critical. If the person who is waiting, and maybe also in a hurry, is a major customer, then these transactions are almost certainly performance critical.

Transactions that involve complex business logic, or cause large quantities of data to be manipulated in the database, or move lots of data across the network may not be performance critical, but any performance requirements that apply to them can be particularly difficult to achieve.

Finally, transactions that often are executed when the network environment is already most heavily loaded have an unusual potential: They can bring your entire network to a screeching halt—not just a single user, not just users of your application, but everyone who's using a particular network (local area or larger) for any purpose whatever. As a result, these transactions create an unusually large vulnerability. Their performance may need to be explicitly managed, regardless of application criticality or relative complexity.

The trick to successfully managing transaction performance during construction is to select one to three transactions for detailed, explicit management, and then apply the techniques and lessons resulting from that management to the other transactions in the system. The transactions selected should ideally be ones that are performance critical (because of either volume or external time pressure) and complex or time-consuming in their processing. If necessary, a transaction that typically is executed under peak load conditions can be added to the set, to help focus attention on network vulnerability.

That phrase—"focus attention"—is key. To a large extent, that's one of the most important effects of explicit performance management, to focus the attention of system developers on transaction performance. Whatever is measured typically improves, so part of the purpose of performance management is to be seen measuring, paying attention to, and publishing, system performance data.

How do you manage system performance during the construction phase? As indicated earlier, it's kind of like managing a project schedule. In each case, there's a complex, interrelated set of activities that have to reach completion within a set amount of time. In the case of the transaction, the activities are automated rather than manual, and the time frame may be expressed in seconds rather than months, but the situations are still analogous.

Because the transactions we explicitly manage for performance are most likely to be those where performance will be a problem, the first step is often to produce not so much a performance *estimate*—how long we think each task will take—but a performance *budget*—how long we can afford for each task to take. In more familiar parlance, we "back into" our initial performance model (or schedule). What tasks need to be estimated/budgeted? Anything that needs to execute successfully in order for the transaction to be processed.

- The application-specific graphical user interface modules that capture the definition of what transaction is desired
- The graphical environment (e.g., Microsoft Windows) modules that intercept events at the graphical user interface and invoke the appropriate application processing modules
- The application processes that apply the appropriate business logic
- The application-level, transport-level, and media-level protocols necessary to communicate between the client-based application logic and the database on the server
- The database-specific user management modules on the server that deal with contention among multiple requests from multiple clients
- The SQL interpretation, indexing, and scheduling modules of the database engine
- Database retrieval activities, including logical and physical joins, data transfer, and filtering
- Communications protocol processing to get the data back to the client

- Any postdatabase application processing necessary
- Display of results (retrieved data, confirmation of success, indication of error)

Unlike system development project schedules, transaction performance models often put almost all activities on the critical path. Database processing often performs several tasks in parallel through multithreading, but most application logic and communications processing are generally performed sequentially. If your choice of programming tool allows it, performance can be improved by identifying sequences of processes that can be performed in parallel and multithreading them; your transaction performance model should reflect this parallelism. Using a simple project management tool to create, track, and manage transaction performance will help you deal with locating the minimum critical path, with parallel activities, and with the impact of slippage (longer-than-scheduled execution times).

As we said, your initial performance models will be budgets rather than estimates. Much of the task of performance management during construction consists in transforming these models from allowance budgets into empirical studies of demonstrated performance. During the construction process, the component tasks listed in your performance model will be automated. Some of the tasks will be fulfilled with commercially available software; others will be created on a custom basis. As each logical component becomes a physical entity (module or set of modules), its real-world performance can be measured.

How do you measure the execution time of a single module that performs only part of a larger task? How do you know how long it takes to complete a string of modules that doesn't start at a graphical user interface, and doesn't end at any specific measurable event? The answer is that someone on your team will need to create a set of driver modules that will be used only in testing, perhaps only in *performance* testing.

If a module is to be tested as a unit, the developer or integrator of the module often will create a driver program that can be used to execute the module, supplying it input, and capturing the output to detect instances of incorrect processing. If string testing is to occur, someone will typically create a similar driver program that invokes not just a single module but a sequence of modules. These drivers, used to test functional correctness, usually trigger only a single execution of their subject module or modules, but they can easily be modified to cause the repetitive execution necessary for low-level performance testing.

To test the performance of a module at the lowest level, it is necessary to invoke that module not once, but a large number of times. If module processing will vary depending upon the inputs supplied to the module, then a number of performance tests reflecting different input mixes should be performed, but the basic pattern always remains:

- Capture the system time (as precisely as possible, down to hundredths of a second).
- Invoke the subject module a fixed number of times (1000 and 10,000 are typical).
- Capture the system time again.
- Calculate the amount of time used for all the executions.
- Divide by the number of module executions in the test.
- Display the calculated average time per single module (or module string) execution.

Performance test results of alternative commercially available software, or of alternative custom implementations of an application-specific algorithm, can allow system developers and integrators to select the fastest, best-performing solutions to every part of the application problem.

Using simple tests such as these, a project team can derive empirical measurements of the best time necessary to execute individual tasks within the performance model of any transaction. These empirical measurements can be compared to the initial budget estimates, and the remaining budget numbers adjusted accordingly. In this manner, the project team always knows how actual and budgeted performance are comparing—in other words, whether the system will meet key performance requirements or not. If most of the empirical numbers come in below their respective component budgets, that tells one story. If all of the actual performance measures are longer than the time allowed, then corrective action (reprogramming or faster hardware or communications) may be indicated. On the other hand, if the actual execution times of the various components are far longer than the time budgeted, then a fundamental rethinking of the design approach may be necessary.

During the construction process, having driver programs that do timing measurements on module execution is generally sufficient, but in production these driver programs will not be used. As a result, *instrumentation* is often added to client/server applications. "Instrumentation" refers to code that is not necessary for performing the business function, but that records data about the performance of the application program itself.

In production, instrumentation code will generally be "turned off," that is, resident in the program but not executed because of some sort of system switch or parameter. Instrumentation code, like any code, takes time to execute. Keeping the instrumentation turned off most of the time keeps the code from affecting system performance. (Heisenberg's uncertainty principle of client/server systems: Measuring system performance affects system performance.) Periodically, or in case of notably degraded performance, the instrumentation can be turned on, and performance data collected.

Instrumentation code most often collects timestamps each time it is executed, stores the timestamps in some sort of array in memory, and periodically writes them out to a data file. The physical I/O to the file is generally performed in parallel with the capturing of timestamps so that the impact on system performance is minimized. After a period of data collection, the statistics stored in the data file can be analyzed to create a picture of system performance.

Because of the impact of active instrumentation on system performance, however, statistics gathered via instrumentation often indicate response times slightly longer than users experience when the instrumentation is turned off. For this reason, some companies transform the empirical performance numbers calculated into "estimates," subtracting a small amount of time to allow for the instrumentation code execution itself. Other companies publish not specific performance numbers ("transaction x currently completes in y seconds at least z percent of the time") but performance *indices* indicating the percentage of change in the system speed since some baseline (usually production implementation).

## Managing for Performance

### Network Performance

As implied by the preceding discussion on instrumentation, system performance concerns don't stop the day an application goes into production status. In the network environment, continual attention must be paid to the performance levels system users experience. System performance will be affected over time (Murphy's law tells us, usually for the worse) by any number of factors:

- An increase in the transaction or event volume
- An increase in the number of primary system users
- An increase in the number of secondary users (those with jobs in other parts of the company, who find the system a useful source of information)
- An increase in the number of computers on the network, whether or not they use your application
- An increase in network traffic, whether or not it's related to your application
- Changes in the location of application users
- Growth in the network's scope and configuration
- An increase in the number or complexity of other networked applications
- Tuning or performance improvements in another application, which result in that application consuming a larger portion of total network capacity

For all these reasons and many others, users may experience degraded system performance. It's not helpful to tell them that nothing in your application has caused the slowdown; they don't care whether it's your fault or not. They just want the system to perform like it used to.

If you're responsible for an application in the eyes of the user (whether or not your management thinks you're responsible for performance of production applications), it's a good idea to take regular measurements of the performance of your application in production. Instrumentation code, and some basic capability to analyze time-series data, are very useful tools.

Similarly, you may want to start paying attention to the regular status reports published by your network support group. (If there are no regular status reports, you might want to suggest initiating them.) The unfortunate truth is that the availability of the network as a whole will factor into the satisfaction level your application users feel for your system. It may also be a factor in determining whether your system's performance is adequate on a more objective basis:

- If your application must process 2000 transactions in an 8-hour shift, and if testing proved that the system, as delivered, can process 2000 transaction in 7 hours, but twice a week the whole network is down for an average of an hour and a half at a time, the users may argue that your system doesn't allow them to do their job, and they would be right.

When network performance/availability as a whole becomes a problem for specific applications, there is no single best way to solve the problem. Network performance may (and doubtless should) be improved, but an equally valid approach is to say that key applications must meet performance requirements even in the case of a certain level of network outages. Indeed, such an approach probably protects system users best.

In terms of improving network performance, network administrators have a number of techniques at their disposal. The most common, known as segmenting or "subnetting," involves taking one large local area network and breaking it into two or more smaller ones; network speed as seen by any particular user will typically increase by an order of magnitude.

Subnetting will only take you so far before the approach no longer makes sense. The ultimate result of splitting and resplitting the net—making more and more local networks, each with fewer and fewer users—would be that each individual PC would be on its own LAN. Because traffic from one LAN must cross a specialized computer (bridge or router) to get to another network, too many small LANs becomes worse than too few big ones. As a result, network administrators stop subnetting at a minimum LAN size (often 25–30 users), and instead add LAN capacity.

The speed of local area networks can usually be improved by

- Replacing passive network hubs with switching hubs, intelligent devices that establish dedicated real-time connections between individual computers on a LAN rather than forcing all computers on the LAN to share a single connection
- Increasing the speed of all the network adapters on the network (e.g., from 10 to 100 Mbps in the Ethernet environment) and of the cabling and hubs if necessary

Both techniques are described more fully in "Fast Ethernet and Switched Ethernet."

## FAST ETHERNET AND SWITCHED ETHERNET

Fast Ethernet is a 100 Mbps to 200 Mbps implementation of the CSMA/CD shared medium network standard that has become the most popular networking technology. It's backward-compatible with regular 10 Mbps Ethernet and retains the 100-meter PC-to-hub distance limitation. It uses the same LAN card connections and wiring types, and will work with existing Ethernet protocol analyzers and network management software. The network cards are inexpensive, on the order of $150 at this writing, making Fast Ethernet a much less expensive speed upgrade than FDDI, where adapters still cost around $1000.

There are three variations on the theme:

- 100Base-T4 can use 4-pair Category 3 twisted-pair cable, or 2-pair Category 5 cable. It cannot perform duplexing and is therefore limited to 100 Mbps.

- 100Base-TX requires 2-pair Category 5 cable, but supports duplexing for a top speed of 200 Mbps.

- 100Base-FX uses fiber optic cable.

The quick fix for network peak load or non-timing-critical performance problems is to put Fast Ethernet cards in LAN servers and buy Fast Ethernet hubs where traffic problems are most severe.

Even though your organization may not immediately replace its hubs with Fast Ethernet models, you can save a lot of time and money by using combo cards for all new workstations and to replace old cards when they die. The combo cards will run at 10 Mbps unless they detect a Fast Ethernet hub port, when they'll shift into 100 Mbps mode. This way, when you do move to the faster hubs, you won't have nearly as many components to replace.

PCs with fast bus designs will get better use out of Fast Ethernet's speed. Buy PCs with PCI slots for LAN cards and graphics boards; they'll outperform ISA, EISA, MCA, and VL boards.

ATM, or Asynchronous Transfer Mode, will ultimately probably replace Fast Ethernet, but it's still expensive, somewhat immature, and lacking in network management support. Bulletproofers will follow the technology so that when the time is right, your organization can begin testing ATM with knowledge of who the leading vendors are and what the relevant standards mean.

Another type of speed need may not be met well by shared-medium, non-deterministic technologies such as Fast Ethernet or FDDI. Users running multimedia, digital video, or videoconferencing applications need speed, but they also need consistency: a high sustained transfer rate. For these applications, the industry has provided two near-term solutions: switched Ethernet and 100VG-AnyLAN.

Ethernet switches typically provide ad hoc, dedicated 10 Mbps channels to workstations that need them. As long as the switch channel remains allocated, the workstation can communicate at the maximum LAN speed. The switch is constantly reconfiguring the cross-point links based on traffic needs. Ethernet switches may not be as good as Fast Ethernet for general LAN workloads, because they tend to load up server utilization, but they're good for sustained-rate needs and are easy to implement because they use existing LAN wiring. By replacing bridges with switching hubs, you can realize substantial improvements in sustained data transfer performance

Hewlett-Packard's 100VG-AnyLAN standard runs on Ethernet and token-ring and is capable of speeds from 100 Mbps up to (eventually) the Gbps range. It uses a non-collision-oriented access method called DPP (Demand Priority Protocol). DPP is really a two-tiered protocol: One level of priority is for data and the other is for multimedia. A real-time video request would get priority over a simple data request. This network standard can run on 4-pair Category 3 twisted-pair cable, but with Category 5 it permits runs of 200 meters instead of 100.

Organizations should think carefully before upgrading to 100VG-AnyLAN for two reasons: It has very limited vendor support at this time (just HP and Thomas-Conrad, plus halfhearted support by IBM), and it seems to be declining in popularity compared to Fast Ethernet, raising doubts about its longevity. Protocol analyzer manufacturers haven't yet committed to building 100VG-AnyLAN products, thinking that it may be a temporary technology even by computer industry standards.

As we mentioned earlier, most observers agree that ATM is the best long-term bet for high-speed networking, though whether it will find its way to the desktop will depend on how quickly those $900 LAN cards drop in price. ATM currently runs at 100 Mbps or 155 Mbps, and many organizations are implementing it on LAN backbones for now. It requires new adapters, new hubs, and new training, but bulletproofers will want to track its progress and prepare for ATM tomorrow by becoming literate on the subject today.

Substandard network performance can also be improved by eliminating sources of undue electrical noise (interference from electric equipment not physically connected to the LAN) or optimizing the network design to reduce the number of bridges and/or routers a typical message has to traverse (the "hop count").

## Platform Performance

**Configuration Tuning**  Unless your network is significantly over-loaded, however, truly large performance problems (such as taking a minute to process a transaction with a 3-second response target) are generally caused by inadequate program design or a poorly configured client or server platform. Program design was discussed in Chapter 4, so let's now look at how and why computers become badly configured.

When we speak of "configuration," we mean setting switches and choosing options that will allow a computer platform, consisting of both the hardware and the software, to operate at maximum efficiency for its intended use. Given the wide range of hardware and software products, the lack of industrywide standards and design guidelines, and the fact that installation software that comes with each bit of add-on hardware or commercial program attempts to reconfigure the computer to its own best advantage, the prevalence of poor configuration is not surprising. In fact, the application of copyright law to system software and microcode (BIOS, etc.) virtually assures that incompatibilities, or at least inefficiencies, will occur and cause configuration problems.

System configuration is a large enough subject for a book of its own, and in fact some of the other titles in the "Bulletproofing" series address just that issue in the context of popular environments such as NetWare and Windows 95, so let us just say here that bulletproofing requires that compatibility and consistency issues be addressed at all levels:

- Network hardware
- Network adapters
- Network software
- Network addressing
- Server hardware
- Server software
- Server integration (hardware to software)
- Client hardware
- Client software
- Client integration

Particular attention should be paid to the movement of data from one piece of hardware to another—how many packets of data, in what order, at what size(s), and under what circumstances. Hardware interactions exist to allow data to move from one piece of equipment to another, so inefficient data movement is the common symptom of configuration problems.

**Caching and Bus-Mastering**    Platform performance is often degraded by hardware components that are forced to do more work than necessary. Bottlenecks can be eliminated if processing tasks can be off-loaded from overworked components, or performed outside of the critical process sequence. Two tuning techniques that help in this area are *caching* and *bus-mastering*.

Caching is the general technique of establishing memory areas where useful data can be stored in anticipation of being used. Disk caching can allow an entire file to be read into memory, anticipating that because one record was used, the rest may well be. If a second record request *does* come for the same file, no time-consuming reading of the disk is required—the response is instantaneous.

There are three caveats on caching, though:

- Expensive hard drive controllers that have their own cache memory are not necessarily faster than establishing an area of the system's RAM to be used as a cache, for instance with the DOS SmartDrive utility or Windows 95's VCACHE, and two levels of caching (hardware plus SmartDrive) are almost always slower than one.

- Caching on a read operation is almost always a good idea, but caching on a write operation can cause problems. Caching on a write means that the application program thinks a record has been written to the hard disk, but in reality it has only been stored in memory, to be written to the hard disk at a later time. If the computer is turned off before the record is actually written, data will be lost (and the application and user will be unaware of the loss). Microsoft DOS 6.0 was notorious for data loss this way; the problem was fixed with version 6.2. Some database applications also require that physical writes be performed in the exact sequence they are handed off to the cache; here again, SmartDrive could introduce problems. *Write-back* caching can give better performance, but expose you to data loss; *write-through* caching (direct write, caching only on the read operation) gives less of a performance improvement, but protects the data.

- For every system, be it a workstation or network server, there is a point of diminishing returns beyond which additional RAM cache provides negligible performance improvement. Too much cache memory could actually degrade performance by siphoning RAM away from application and data space.

In the same way that caching can perform physical reads before they're required, thus taking them outside of the critical path, bus-mastering can allow system components to deliver blocks of data to or from system memory without imposing on the CPU to manage the system bus. Bus-mastering is generally used by disk controllers, network adapters, and video cards.

Using bus-mastering, a disk controller can read a number of records from system memory, move them to the disk, and write them, without requiring the CPU to do any work. Similarly, the controller can retrieve a file from a disk and place its contents in system memory, again without imposing on the CPU to manage data movement.

A bus-mastering network adapter can be instructed to send a large amount of data across the network and then be left to its own devices to achieve the task. The CPU will not be required to move progressive chunks of data across the bus; the network adapter can do that while the CPU is otherwise engaged.

- Just because a disk controller or network interface card supports bus-mastering does not mean a PC will use it. For example, in most EISA-bus machines, which have been popular in the LAN server role, only a few of the total slots in the machine offer bus-mastering capability—and they're not always adjacent slots, either.

**Increasing Processor Speed**   Within limits, PC performance can be improved by upgrading slow processors within a particular model line with faster ones. Many PC motherboards can accommodate a full line of processors (such as the Intel 486, Pentium, and Pentium Pro processor lines); the motherboard will often automatically detect the processor speed and adapt itself. Some newer operating systems for both workstations and servers also support Symmetric Multiprocessing (SMP), which provides for performance gains by adding processors to the one already in the box—particularly if the applications your system runs have been written to take advantage of SMP by being multithreaded.

Upgrading processors is relatively easy and often inexpensive. If there is reason to believe that all other system components are more than adequate, if the motherboard makes the processor upgrade easy (e.g., with a Zero Insertion Force socket), and if your current processor is toward the bottom of its model line, then replacing your old processor with a faster one can make sense. That's a lot of ifs.

- If your processor is already toward the top end of its model line (such as a 486DX2 running at 66 MHz), the performance improvement achieved by switching to a faster processor (such as a 486DX4 running at 100 MHz) will be minimal.

- If your motherboard doesn't readily (automatically or with the setting of a few switches) adapt to a new processor speed, it may need to be replaced along with the processor. Cost and difficulty, not to mention risk, go up considerably.

- If your other system components are marginally adequate with your slow processor, they will be inadequate with a newer one. Indeed, a slow hard drive or graphics adapter can totally negate any benefit that a fast processor might bring.

One lesson to be learned and applied in this context is that when you are specifying the hardware for your new client/server system, you should consider the ease of upgrading the processor along with other functional, performance, and cost requirements. The ease of processor upgrades may be particularly relevant for organizations using budgeting procedures that permit upgrading existing hardware in favor of replacing it.

**Tuning Hard Disks**    Often, improving hard disk performance achieves more increase in client/server throughput than a faster CPU does. Hard disk performance can be improved in a number of ways:

- Slower (IDE, ESDI, MFM, etc.) hard drives can be replaced by faster (EIDE, SCSI, SCSI-2, Fast/Wide SCSI) ones.

- Slower (ISA) disk controllers can be replaced by faster (PCI, SCSI) ones if the motherboard will accommodate them.

- Chained SCSI drives (multiple drives or other devices connected to a single controller) can be connected with individual controllers. Single large SCSI hard drives can replace multiple smaller ones, reducing contention at the controller.

- File block size, read-ahead record buffering, and disk-to-memory transfer block size can all be adjusted (using commonly available utility programs) to improve disk access times.

- Hard disks can be defragmented to move all the records in any file closer to one another and make free space contiguous. Depending on users to perform defragmentation has proven iffy at best, and expecting IS staff to run the utilities regularly on every workstation is unreasonable, but newer environments such as Windows 95 provide for automatic scheduled background disk optimization.

- RAID (Redundant Arrays of Inexpensive Disks) uses disk array technology to speed performance while improving fault tolerance (see "RAID").

## RAID

RAID, or Redundant Array of Inexpensive Disks, defines an approach to disk drive management that combines reliability, fault tolerance, and high performance. Manufacturers have implemented RAID in hardware as well as software.

Although RAID is rarely used on client-side workstations, it may be appropriate for certain types of power users, such as graphics professionals working with digital video or computer-based animation. More commonly, RAID is used with network servers to help prevent the disk subsystem from being the bottleneck it has so often been in the past.

In RAID arrays, data is spread out over multiple hard drives, sometimes with extra parity information for rebuilding data that becomes damaged. RAID is lightly standardized, with many vendors providing proprietary solutions whose pieces aren't always interchangeable.

Hardware-based RAID solutions use proprietary hardware components to constantly perform advanced error checking and rebuild failed drives while the system continues operation, without burdening the server. Software-based RAID relies heavily upon server resources to accomplish the same goals.

There are five commonly used subsets or variants of the RAID approach:

- RAID Level 0 stripes data across multiple drives, writing the first segment of a data file to Disk 1, the next segment to Disk 2, etc. This can be fast, but it isn't a fault-tolerant design, being susceptible to both disk and controller failure and having no data redundancy.

- RAID Level 1 is essentially the same as mirroring and duplexing. Mirroring is a simple system using a single controller to serve dual, redundant disk drives or drive chains; duplexing, on the other hand, uses dual controllers and redundant disk drives or drive chains to protect against controller failure as well as disk failure. RAID 1 can provide an improvement in disk read performance, as the system can issue simultaneous read requests to two disks and use whichever one responds first. Duplexed RAID 1 systems provide better write performance than mirrored RAID 1 systems, because concurrent writes can be handled by multiple controllers rather than by a single controller.

- RAID Level 2 uses data striping and parity interleaving across multiple drives, but isn't much used in LANs because many extra drives are needed (for example, three drives may be required to store parity data for eight data drives).

- RAID 3 and 4 store all parity data on a dedicated drive, so dual writes are needed, both to the data drives and to the parity drive. RAID 3 specifies parallel writes, while RAID 4 specifies independent writes. These levels aren't often used.

- RAID 5 does not store parity information on a dedicated drive; instead, it spreads parity data over the entire array. This design permits multiple concurrent reads and writes for high performance, though it can still be slow for write-intensive applications. It also provides fault tolerance; if one drive (but not two!) fails in a RAID 5 array, it can be replaced (even "hot swapped" in some systems) and the controller can rebuild the drive from the data and parity information on the remaining drives.

- RAID 6 is basically RAID 5 but with two sets of parity data instead of one, so that the disk subsystem can tolerate the simultaneous failure of two drives, not just one.

RAID is not without its drawbacks. RAID systems can be more difficult to install, configure, and expand than simple duplexed systems. One's choice of drives and controllers may be limited by proprietary approaches; this should be an evaluation criterion when shopping for RAID solutions. Also, the dollar cost of RAID belies the "Inexpensive" in the acronym. It may be necessary to bring a disk subsystem down to perform microcode updates or to add RAM cache. Finally, although RAID systems can often recover from the failure of a single drive in the array, performance may degrade noticeably while they are doing so.

Having said that, a good hardware-based RAID 5 array can provide fast performance, reliability, and a very quick time-to-repair. Many companies have found RAID to be a necessity to deliver fast response times to end users in client/server systems.

**Tuning Application Software**   If your company runs a large number of custom programs, either created in house or built by a contractor, then you have an opportunity to improve performance by optimizing and tuning the application software. Sections of program code that are particularly inefficient, or sections that are executed often and are even a little inefficient, can be identified and examined for possible improvement. Some development tools and programming languages provide utilities called "profilers," which will identify programs and portions of programs that account for the largest percentages of execution time; these are the portions of the application where efficiency efforts will pay the biggest benefits.

Specific tuning techniques, of course, depend on the programming language you're using and the particular application being tuned. The only universal statements about application tuning are that it requires a certain level of expertise (if not in the language, then in programming in general), and it's often best done by some person(s) other than the original programmer. Tuning often requires bringing a different perspective, a different view of the problem, to find a more efficient approach to programming a solution. The best tuning is often done in open meetings, where a group of experienced programmers review the output of a profiler (if available) and offer suggestions about alternative ways of solving the problems addressed by the highlighted sections of code.

Of course, no tuning of code is possible if the program in question is part of a purchased commercial application. Typically, when your company purchases software you buy the rights to execute the program, but not the source code that would allow you to modify or enhance the program. If you can't even see the source code, you can't make any improvements in how it runs, except to ensure that the underlying operating system provides the application with suitable amounts of resources such as disk and communications buffers

One performance factor that can often be improved, even for purchased applications, relates to the question of where the program files reside. This decision is always based on a trade-off between mutually exclusive benefits, and the initial decision is not always the best one in the long term. Program files (sometimes referred to as program libraries) are images of executable programs that are stored on hard disk. When an operating system is told to run the program, the image on the hard disk is loaded into RAM and executed.

In a network environment, the hard disk on which the program file resides and the RAM in which it will execute are not always on the same computer. Program files can be stored on individual desktop computers, on network servers, on distributed file servers, or on a centralized program server. Storing program files on each individual desktop computer gives the fastest performance to users of the program, and is necessary, for example, for mobile users linking to the LAN via "remote node" access. The file can be copied from the hard disk into memory rapidly whenever needed, and network delays never impact program loading, but storing individual images of the program on each of a large number of desktop PCs is a lot of work for your network administrators and raises the likelihood over time that some user on some computer will end up with an incorrect version of a program. Keeping track of each individual copy of a program, which successive version each represents, and when each was last updated can become a major administrative task known as "configuration management."

The most common solution to the configuration management problem is to avoid storing individual copies of the program on each PC, but rather to store a smaller number of copies on one or more servers. In this approach, each time a user wants to execute a particular program, the program image must travel across some portion of the network to get to the computer on which it will execute. Storing programs on servers reduces the number of individual copies and thus simplifies the configuration management task, but it also increases network traffic (sending large program files across the network each time a user clicks on the program icon), makes the act of executing a program subject to network delay or outage, and slows down network performance for everyone.

If system performance is your only consideration, then the best approach is often to store individual program copies on each desktop and use an automated configuration management tool to help you keep track of them. However, bulletproofing is concerned with making sure each user has a correct version of each program as much as with performance—don't trade away accuracy in the interests of speed.

**Video Performance**  We've made the point elsewhere in this book that "client/server" usually means "Windows/server," and it's well known that Windows (as with any GUI) places more demands on a PC's video subsystem than text-mode interfaces. This fact is a key element in the common user complaint that

"Windows is slow," a complaint that is more common among users who had become accustomed to the nearly instantaneous response of text-based applications in the first few years of PC deployment. It follows, then, that one effective way to boost client PC performance is to use high-performance video controllers that offload display tasks from the primary CPU.

A key to improving client-side video performance is to understand what sorts of tasks a particular PC user, or class of users, typically performs. Video cards that accelerate Windows drawing engine functions may be the best bet for most client/server application front ends. However, if a class of users will be running multimedia applications, Computer-Based Training (CBT), or databases that include digital video clips as data objects, then graphics cards specifically designed for improving digital video may be required. Graphics cards that take advantage of newer display methodologies, such as Windows 95's DirectDraw, allow PCs to bypass some of the Windows code layers for lower overhead and improved performance, especially in digital video applications. Display technologies such as Intel's 3DR provide very specific performance enhancements, such as boosting the speed of 3D object rendering in CAD applications.

Client-side video configuration options can have a big impact on performance, as well as the video card that one chooses for the standard desktop. Most business users will enjoy faster speeds with their PCs set to 8-bit color, for example, than with their PCs set to 15-, 16-, or even 24-bit color. The display resolution may also affect video subsystem speed, and 1024 x 768 displays may run noticeably slower than 800 x 600 displays. It behooves any company to perform benchmark testing with the particular graphics boards in common use to determine which configuration settings provide the best performance while also providing a color depth appropriate for the applications users are running.

System performance usually ranks right up there with usefulness and usability in the minds of the users. However, security may be even more important than performance in the minds of the IS staff, who may feel responsible for providing a mainframelike level of access control in the distributed processing model of client/server systems. The risk of compromising security has held back many a client/server system deployment, and security remains a prime concern of those charged with implementing distributed processing environments. Therefore, it's the subject of our next chapter.

# 6

# Bulletproofing Client/Server Security

## The Need for Security

The business press has been full of stories about how insecure modern information technology is. Netscape's stock price fell when its premiere products proved to be less secure than intended. A lack of security is hindering the ability of the Internet to become a major commercial channel. Standards covering World Wide Web security are only beginning to emerge.

Client/server technology, although new and volatile, appears almost staid when compared to the rapidly changing technologies associated with the Web, but is client/server mature enough, secure enough, and standardized enough to meet your needs? As a recent sales brochure asked, would you bet your business on your current client/server security?

Before you answer a question obviously designed to bring out all your professional insecurities, let's take a look at the issue of client/server security—what the risks are, what solutions are available, and how costs and benefits compare. "Security" can be defined as freedom from danger and risk, that is, from significant concern that something will, or might, go wrong and cause loss to you or your organization. With today's use of client/server technology, what might go wrong? How badly might it go wrong? What could it cost you?

### Unauthorized Use and Resource Consumption

For starters, having an insecure client/server system can throw all your painstaking plans—all your performance and capacity estimates, all your models of network traffic—into a cocked hat. An insecure system can be used by users you don't know for purposes you didn't expect, and all that unauthorized activity draws down the level of resources available to your intended users.

When you migrate to client/server computing, you justify the investment in hardware based on a set of assumptions about how it will be used. Your assumptions in all likelihood don't include setting aside a percentage of the hardware's capacity for the use of unauthorized individuals who somehow gain access to your system. Your long-term hardware projections will be thrown off if you have to upgrade hardware or network capacity sooner than would otherwise be required.

The cost of supplying hardware capacity to support the demand of unauthorized users is a cost of security (or rather, of lack of security). Any savings that your company can realize by limiting system access to authorized users only will be a clear benefit of bulletproofing your security.

### Fraudulent Activity and Financial Loss

Unauthorized users don't just consume system resources—they trigger potentially fraudulent system activity. Anyone who gains access to your system will start by looking around, by taking a peek at the information stored in your databases and files. Unauthorized users don't have to stop there. If they can access the programs that generate transactions within your system, then they can cause your computers to work to their advantage— they can generate fraudulent transactions within any application or function that has financial or operational implications.

- Unauthorized users of a payroll system can put fictitious individuals on your payroll, so that your system will create and send out seemingly legitimate checks or direct deposits.

- Unauthorized users of an accounts payable system can create fictitious bills, all approved and ready for payment, which will cause another set of unearned payments to be made.

- Illegitimate users of your purchasing system can generate their own purchase orders, allowing them (perhaps) to deliver and bill for overpriced goods for which your company has no use.

- Malicious users of your order-entry system can generate phony orders, causing your company to invest resources in producing goods that aren't really sold, or they can create phony cancellation transactions, causing you to not produce (or at least delay producing) the goods that your most important customers have ordered. Finally, malicious users can generate spurious change transactions, causing your company to produce the wrong good, the wrong size, or the wrong color.

Any monies that your company sends out as a result of fraudulent transactions are lost because of lack of security. So are dollars spent creating products that no one ordered and dollars of income lost because a manufacturing order was fraudulently canceled. Any reduction in such losses can be counted as a security bulletproofing benefit.

### Confidentiality, Competitive Advantage, and Customer Confidence

Increasingly, companies are using client/server information systems to help them compete. Faster order processing, better customer service, and more flexible manufacturing operations are all of value because they set one company apart from its competition, but any system that will allow these important functions to be performed in a superior manner must contain, or have access to, some very sensitive information—information about customers, orders, operations, products, problems—information that competitors would very much like to see.

Unless your client/server security is bulletproof, the very mechanism that was intended to make this critical and sensitive information available to your employees and managers can also make it available to your competitors, and hackers, and the press, and the financial community, and, indirectly, your most important customers.

Losing control over information that should remain confidential may or may not be fatal, but it's always serious. Would you want your competitors to know exactly what your biggest customer service problems are or where your manufacturing operations are experiencing the highest error rates? Do you want the financial press to learn that your orders are up (or down) in real time—before you have an opportunity to make an appropriate announcement and help them interpret the data?

To the extent that client/server systems can provide competitive advantage, that advantage is eroded or destroyed by lack of information security. Unauthorized users of your information systems can see not only *that* you're beating your competition in a particular area, but exactly *how* you're accomplishing it. Given this information, your competitors can duplicate your advantage faster, often for less money than it cost you to originate the new techniques.

Information is power. More information is more power. Inside information about your company and its operations can give outsiders the power to manipulate your stock, steal your customers, advertise your weaknesses, and offset your strengths. Companies that invest in client/server applications are paying good money to make information available to their employees and allies. Without bulletproof security, the competitive advantage that that information was intended to create will simply vanish.

Worst of all, a loss of confidentiality is similar to a conflict of interest—an apparent instance can do as much damage as an actual problem. If it appears to your customers that your company cannot keep sensitive data secure, their confidence in you—their willingness to have you as a supplier—can quickly erode. If customers see you apparently unable to manage your own information securely, why should they entrust you with their orders, their information? If they feel that anything they tell you might be communicated to their competitors, they're less likely to tell you anything important. They'd rather do business with someone who knows how to keep a secret.

### Vandalism

So far, our discussion about the need for security has centered on protecting you from people who are involved in, interested in, or knowledgeable about your business and your industry. These are people who have an understandable (if not always legitimate or honorable) reason to want to know more about your company, its products, its operations; people who might be in a position to take advantage of information or of your weaknesses. Unfortunately, in today's world, it seems that even people with no such clear interest in you or your well-being are willing to spend time and, occasionally, money to breach your information systems. In some cases, they know who their target is; in others, they don't.

The rapid spread of information technology has led to the rise of cybervandals—people who attack information systems for the sheer joy of the attack, who destroy something simply because they can. Sociopaths with computers will try to gain access to your network and your databases to see if they're smarter than you are and to do damage and prove their superiority. The people who create computer viruses and worms are even worse. They don't even do it for the thrill of twisted victory, because they typically don't see the fruits of their work. They wreak untold damage to systems, companies, and individuals they'll never meet, nor even know of. They harbor no specific malice and experience only the most abstract thrill. They're so wrapped up in their own abilities that they simply don't care about anyone else. In an old and simple word, they are evil.

## Security Challenges

Unfortunately, the matter of security in a client/server environment goes deeper than the fact that breaches and unauthorized use can cause serious damage. Risk is measured in terms of both potential damage and likelihood of loss. We have seen that the potential for damage is considerable. The bad news is, so is the likelihood of problems.

A number of aspects of client/server architecture make it easier to penetrate, for whatever motive, than typical host processing or make the consequences of such penetration more severe. These aspects include

- Distribution of hardware and access
- Anonymity
- Global connectivity
- Increased user control
- Increasingly important data
- The "klutz" factor

Let's look at each of these in more detail.

### Distribution of Hardware and Access

To begin with, the hardware in a typical client/server system is distributed over at least some physical area. As a result, access to the system can be achieved, by authorized or unauthorized users, more easily than would be the case with closely centralized hardware.

The easiest way for an unauthorized user to access your client/server system may be to gain physical control over equipment (typically, client computers) that is an authorized component of that system. In the host-based processing environment, this was often the only way to gain unauthorized access; in the client/server world, it's still a simple and effective one.

Client/server systems often support widely distributed user communities, not just the clerks in some centralized department, each of whom works in an office on the same floor of a given office building, but

- Sales representatives, who work in small offices all over the country, or all over the world

- Customer service operators, who provide telephonic support to callers while working from their homes all over town

- Troubleshooters and repair personnel, who interact with the system from various locations (restaurants, vehicles, customers' premises), perhaps via cellular phone and modem

Because these intended users of client/server systems are widely distributed, the client hardware components of the systems must be equally widely distributed. The more locations, and the more informal the locations, in which system hardware is available, the more likely that hardware is to come under the control of an unauthorized user.

- Smaller offices, often in older or mixed-use (retail and office) buildings, typically lack the security provisions of large, dedicated office facilities. A company may provide 24-hour guards, alarm systems, and even closed-circuit surveillance of its central office buildings, but that company is unlikely to be able to provide the same level of protection at each of the small offices of its sales representatives nationwide.

- Client computers, supplied by a company to customer service operators or representatives who work from home, can come under the control of family members, visitors, neighbors, tradespeople, and all sorts of potentially unauthorized users.

- Mobile equipment, such as notebook computers and cellular phones/modems, can become convenient not only for the intended users, but for anyone with whom they come into contact. Unfortunately, mobile equipment can easily be targeted by anyone who wishes to gain access to your client/server system. Your mobile personnel are visible and vulnerable elements of your business operation; industrial spies have been known to target and steal specific computers from briefcases, vehicles, hotel rooms, even airport security checkpoints!

If the hardware component of your client/server system is physically distributed, it may be difficult or impossible to secure physically. Under these circumstances, an element of software security will also be required. We'll look at the various means of accomplishing it later in this chapter, but bulletproof client/server software must make certain that, should your client hardware fall into the wrong hands, the system will still prevent unauthorized use.

Physical distribution makes hardware difficult to monitor and makes physical security (lock and key to restrict access) much harder to accomplish effectively. It also means that the network, whether computers are permanently connected or dial-up, has a certain geographic spread and is itself vulnerable to attack.

In a host-based computing environment, the host operating system has complete visibility over everything—every user, every program—that is operating on that machine. However, in a network environment, no such all-seeing entity exists. It's therefore possible for unauthorized persons to gain access to a network even if they don't have direct access to one of your networked computers.

For instance, if a technically knowledgeable individual can gain access to any portion of the cabling of your network, he or she can tap into your network—connecting a computer of which you and your network managers are totally unaware—and start participating in the activity of your systems. The unauthorized computer can read messages, generate messages, intercept data, and cause your system to perform unnecessary or unauthorized work. All of this can be achieved without ever cutting your cable or interrupting your network flow, whether the cable is copper or glass fiber. It's even easier if you've gone to the trouble and expense of installing a wireless LAN, or some other form of radio communications. If your network extends outside of space that you physically control, it is vulnerable to being "tapped" by outsiders.

### Anonymity

In a network computing environment, computers must cooperate; client/server computing is a specific form of cooperative processing. The difficulty that arises is that, to cooperate in a network environment, computers must exchange information. Regardless of the form of middleware in use, cooperation is achieved by communication. Communication on a digital network is, in the final analysis, always anonymous.

When a server receives a message to process a particular transaction, the message contains some form of identification indicating which client computer originally sent it. Ideally, this identification will be on two levels: the transport level and the application level.

*Transport-level identification* is accomplished (using the terminology of the OSI model) by the Network layer, which places "to" and "from" addresses on each data packet crossing the network. These addresses are physical network addresses, intended to cause each message to be delivered to, and recognized by, a particular physical computer (or, more technically, the network adapter card in a physical computer).

The address of the sending computer is saved within the communications protocol stack, to allow the receiving computer to respond in the proper time, but this physical address is not generally available to (and would not have meaning to) the application program. A transport-level address has no significance except in terms of a particular network configuration. It says nothing about the program that was running on the computer when the message was sent or about the human operator who initiated the program.

Application-level processing must depend on *application-level identification* of what computer, and what human operator, sent the message. That is, a server application can only know what computer, and what human being, originated a message if the client application passes along that information, and the server program can only take information passed on face value: In most cases there is no physical way for the server to independently verify the identification passed along.

## Global Connectivity, Hackers, and Viruses

If your network connects to the Internet (or any other large-scale information service), you're vulnerable to attack by users who gain access via pathways that were established for your employees, but that are available to any other individual user of the larger-scale network.

The Internet is notorious for being insecure. As a result, any network that is connected to the Internet has to be considered insecure until proven otherwise. Certain netizens take great joy in searching information bases connected to the Internet; if your corporate network is connected to the larger Net, protecting its security becomes your job.

Even if you can prove that no user outside your company can even possibly gain access to your system, but your network is Net-connected, your worries aren't over. Your own employees can, unknowingly and with the best intentions in the world, import trouble from the Internet any time they download any Internet data file.

Programs that have been downloaded from the Net are notorious for containing viruses. For years, savvy companies have made rules that no program downloaded from the Net (or otherwise acquired outside normal company purchase procedures) may be run on their computers. Other companies, somewhat less risk averse, have rules that such programs must be scanned for viruses before being run. Unfortunately, simply banning or scanning programs files is no longer sufficient. Files that many individuals think of as "data" can, in fact, contain viruses as well.

Files that contain word processing documents or spreadsheet data can easily contain embedded programs (often known as "macros"). These embedded macros can themselves be infected with viruses. If you open the word processing document (only to read it), or load up the spreadsheet (just to see what it contains), these embedded macros can be triggered and the viruses they contain can infect your system, for example by redefining commonly executed commands such as "File" - "Save."

The only reasonable approach to security in an Internet-connected environment is to scan *every* file and message coming into your network. Effective virus-detection programs exist, but they only work if they're used. Every time. All the time. No exceptions. We'll go even further and say that effective network virus detection requires both server and client components, and that both components must be updated regularly (e.g., every month) with the latest virus signature tables.

## Increased User Control

Ironically, one of the greatest advantages of client/server systems leads to one of the greatest vulnerabilities. Client/server systems are effective because they allow people to do things in ways they've never before been able, but client/server systems are vulnerable because they encourage people to do things in ways they've never before been able.

Security, in the past, has often depended on safeguards built into rigid procedures. The safeguards were effective because no one could easily avoid invoking them. That's no longer the case. In a client/server environment, part of the plan is to allow people to create their own work processes, solving ever-changing business problems in ever-changing ways. However, if nothing ever stays the same, where do you put the safeguards? How can you be sure they'll be effective?

Users are taking control not only of formal "production" applications (into which traditional security provisions could, in theory, be implemented), using those in flexible and unpredictable ways, they are also creating their own applications, by using ad hoc retrieval capabilities, by doing simple programming, and by combining pieces of various applications to solve business problems that are otherwise difficult to address.

As described in Chapter 4, creation of ad hoc, single-user and workgroup applications is most often performed by end users, especially in organizations that have been using client/server for more than about a year. As a result, a wide variety of system development tools and patterns, reflecting a wide variety of programming styles, is typically evident in these smaller information systems. Many users, freed from their traditional role as passive consumers of information technology, warm to the task of creating application systems that truly and evidently reflect the way people choose to do business. This increased creativity, and the feeling of comfort and control that goes along with it, create an atmosphere in which traditional, restrictive security approaches simply will not work. Looking at it another way, an insistence on maintaining restrictive security can preclude your organization from achieving one of the major benefits of client/server computing.

## Increasingly Important Data

As we saw in Chapter 3, many organizations shift to client/server computing out of a need to automate more than traditional, bureaucratic, administrative applications. They now use client/server systems as key components in marketing, sales, product development, engineering, manufacturing, operations, distribution, and customer service processes. As a result, ever more critical business data is being stored in computer-readable format, and the damage to the business, should this data be lost or destroyed, can be far greater in the client/server environment.

That's not to say that administrative data isn't important—it is. Losing track of your purchasing, accounting, or personnel data can make it extremely difficult to do business. However, consider the consequences of losing all your engineering or manufacturing data: It's no longer a question of the business being difficult to administer, there will be no business left that's worth administering!

### The "Klutz" Factor: Distribution Invites Exposure

To make matters worse, a move to client/server computing is often concomitant with a move to smaller, decentralized computers. Because many servers are physically small, relatively inexpensive, and have no special environmental requirements, there is often a push to locate servers physically in the workspace of their primary users.

Placing even the server, the shared central component of a client/server application, into the users' work area strongly amplifies the feeling of user control and ownership, and can produce significant psychological benefits that result in increased user satisfaction and more productive system use. However, putting critical computer hardware into an uncontrolled workspace rather than an isolated "clean room" environment also creates a number of unfortunate results.

- Dust and dirt are far more prevalent, and tend to collect on electronic components inside the computer's casing.
- Smoke and smog enter the computer through unfiltered air.
- Humidity and temperature vary far more widely.
- Electrical power is often subject to fluctuations, and even outages.
- Boxes, papers, file cabinets, desks, and other business paraphernalia are placed near (or even on top of) the computer, resulting in restricted ventilation and decreased cooling of internal components.
- The computer may be jostled in the normal activity of the office.

- Switches, power cords, network connections, etc., may accidentally be bumped, resulting in system interruptions.
- Heaven help you if the sprinkler system goes off, or if some klutz spills a cup of coffee into the server!

## Security Approaches

We started this chapter by defining security as freedom from danger and risk. It is now apparent that, in the client/server environment, danger and risk can take many forms. It's unrealistic to think that a wide range of dangers and risks can be eliminated by any single countermeasure. Security, in the client/server environment, is the result of a number of different actions or techniques, planned and conducted in such a manner as to complement one another.

There are four basic steps by which security can be established and maintained:

1. Discouraging or precluding unauthorized access
2. Preventing loss or corruption of data in the event of unauthorized access
3. Detection of unauthorized access
4. Detection of the results of unauthorized access

We will explore each of these in turn.

### Discourage, Prevent, and Preclude

The most obvious place to implement security measures is where unauthorized users most often gain access to a system—using the interface designed and provided for authorized users. The logic of this is especially apparent to builders and designers of host-based (minicomputer or mainframe) systems, as it is in this location that online host-based systems effect their security.

Host systems, working through "dumb" terminals, generally require that a person supply a valid user ID and password combination before allowing that person to use the system. No data may be added, updated, or deleted unless a valid user ID and password are first supplied.

In the client/server world, similar security measures are often used. User authentication may be required whenever a client platform (generally, a PC) is turned on, connected to a network, or used to access an application or database residing on a server. Authentication may even be required in order to use specific transactions within an application, even after access to the application as a whole has already been established.

However, these measures solve only part of the problem. User authentication measures are sensibly invoked only at the location within a system where authorized users are intended to gain access. That is, the system only asks, "Who is it?" when there's a knock at the door. What if someone quietly slips in through a window or takes advantage of you not being at home, and cuts a big hole in one of your walls?

Precluding unauthorized access means not only screening people who come in the front door, but also making it difficult or impossible for anyone to gain access in any other manner. Key system components (programs, databases, operating system parameters) must be made unavailable by any means other than "entry through the door." Not only must the system's functionality operate correctly when accessed through the defined methods, but it must fail to operate if accessed any other way. For instance,

- Programs that are intended to be accessed only via specific system components must refuse execution if accessed by any other components, either recognized or unrecognized.

- Files and databases that contain sensitive data must refuse to be accessed unless by intended and authorized system programs.

- System messages, communicated over a network, should accept routing to and from only authorized system components.

- System documentation and "help" should be available only to authorized users of the system.

### Encrypt

What if an unauthorized user were to breach your access security? What if someone were able to get into your system, perhaps accessing system files or network messages through a means other than the released production programs that contain user authentication features?

A second opportunity to avoid danger and risk, at least of unauthorized data access or modification, exists in the form of *data encryption*. Data encryption is the mathematical manipulation of data characters in such a manner as to make them unintelligible to unauthorized viewers. Even if an encrypted message were to be intercepted or an encrypted record extracted from a data file, no information could be discerned nor extracted. In theory, you could give an encrypted file containing your most sensitive data to your most aggressive competitor and that competitor would not be able to learn anything at all about your business. In practice, however, encryption is not quite all it's cracked up to be. It's close, and it's very useful, but it's not perfect.

Any successful encryption implementation consists of two major parts: a set of *algorithms*, and one or more *keys*. At least one of the keys is secret; the algorithms are not. In fact, if some salesman ever tries to sell you encryption technology based on "secret" algorithms, run (don't walk) out of the presentation. Successful, reliable, and industrial-strength encryption is based on mathematical formulas that are well known and well understood. Only when it has been well publicized for a period of time can an algorithm be considered thoroughly proven. "Proven," in terms of data encryption, means that a message that has been encrypted according to the algorithm cannot be decrypted unless you know the key.

Given a strong encryption algorithm, the degree of security it provides depends entirely on the key. More precisely, security depends on the effective length of the key. The longer the key, the more secure the encryption (with one significant exception). Any particular encryption depends on both the algorithm and the key, but the algorithm is well known, so if someone can figure out or guess your key then that person can decrypt your message. All encryption is subject to "brute force" decryption, that is, to a trial decryption with all possible values for a key of a given length. The reason that encryption still works is that, if the key is long enough, there are so many possible values that even if you know *how* to decrypt by brute force, and have a supercomputer dedicated to the process, it takes too long (and so, costs too much money) to be worthwhile. Anything over about 10 years is generally considered adequate.

Rendering encryption effectively unbreakable generally requires a randomly generated key of at least 128 bits. A number of commercially available technologies (based on the Data Encryption Standard (DES), Pretty Good Privacy (PGP), or the Blowfish algorithms) can use keys of up to 448 bits in length. The problem is that the U.S. government considers unbreakable data encryption to be a military technology and subject to the International Treaty on Arms Reduction (ITAR). As a result, encryption technology using keys longer than 40 bits may not legally be exported beyond the United States and Canada. (Please note that PGP is, and other products soon will be, available throughout the world. The legal restriction doesn't mean that foreign governments, companies, and individuals can't use strong data encryption, it only means that U.S. companies can't sell strong data encryption products outside North America.)

In cases where the key is not randomly generated, its effective length (determined by the number of possible values and calculated according to binary exponents) may be less than its physical length. For example, if I have a key of 40 bits, but the only two values I ever choose are the ASCII representations of "BROWN" and "BLACK," then the effective length of my key is one. The difference between physical key length and effective key length is not moot. The problem Netscape experienced with a version of Navigator was caused by a less than fully random key generator that decreased the effective length of the key by about one-third (and the number of possible key values by a factor of about 4000).

Encryption technologies come in two basic flavors: *symmetric* and *asymmetric*.

- Symmetric encryption programs use one key to both encrypt and decrypt a message (similar to the classic book code used in Ken Follett's novel *The Key to Rebecca*). If you use symmetric encryption and someone has the key to send you an encrypted message, they can also decrypt any message intended for you (see Figure 6.1). As a result, symmetric encryption keys are always kept secret, which poses its own security problem.
- Asymmetric encryption programs use one key (the "public" key) to encrypt the message, and another key (the "private" key) to decrypt it (see Figure 6.2). As a result, the public key may be widely distributed without the same risk that would attach in a symmetric encryption environment. Asymmetric encryption is, understandably, becoming the de facto standard for data security purposes.

For commercial purposes, asymmetric encryption with a random key of 128 bits or more is generally considered sufficient. As we said earlier, products are now available in North America that use keys of up to 448 bits and still provide speedy perfor-

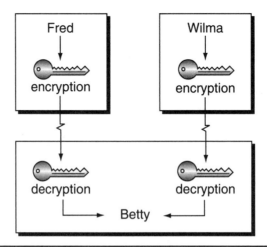

**Figure 6.1:**    Symmetric Encryption

mance. (As a rule, the longer the key, the more computing power or time is necessary to encrypt or decrypt each message. One of the advantages of the newest algorithms, such as Blowfish, is that they are relatively fast to compute for any length of key.) However, even if your business needs to transmit data securely to or from a foreign country, do not be satisfied with encryption using keys of 40 or fewer bits—recent studies have shown that such encryption is simply too easy to crack.

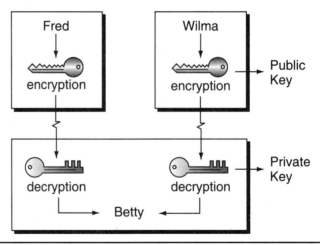

**Figure 6.2:**    Asymmetric Encryption

### Detect/Alarm/Trap

Even if all your production data and all your network messages are encoded, it makes sense to keep your eyes open to possible security attacks. How safe can you feel if someone's actively trying to break in? How safe *should* you feel if you don't know whether anyone's actively trying to break in?

Depending on the network operating system, the various server operating systems, and the database management system you use, there may be software packages you can run that will alert your network administrators, in real time, of a detected security attack. Security attacks can be detected under a number of different circumstances. Typical ones are repeated unsuccessful signon attempts (for instance, more than two successive incorrect passwords), rapidly occurring signon requests (which often signal an automated attempt to guess a password), and attempts to copy (usually via FTP) your master password file to get valid user IDs and passwords for subsequent use.

Some of these programs do a pretty decent job of capturing information about the identity, or at least the apparent location, of the attacker. If your system is connected to the Internet, attackers (known on the Net as *crackers*) probably won't attempt to access your system directly; they tend to sign on through a chain of computers around the world, to complicate attempts to identify them. Nevertheless, crackers can be traced with sufficient effort and diligence, so it makes sense to capture any information possible about apparent attacks. These programs are not 100% effective, and a questions remains: Even if you know someone is trying to break in, what can you do about it? At very least, keeping track of the obvious security attacks, even when they're defeated by current countermeasures, can give you a feel for just how serious your security situation is. It can also help you identify specific security weaknesses.

### Audit

OK, the doors are all locked, the data's encrypted, you're keeping track of all detectable security attacks. Can you relax about client/server security now? Well, almost.

There's just one more thing you might want to do to make your client/server environment more secure. Unfortunately, it's kind of a pain, but it will let you sleep at night better than anything else you can do. If you're really concerned about the security of your system and your data, you can install a comprehensive audit capability. This will not prevent unauthorized access to your network or your data, but it can detect (admittedly, after the fact) any unauthorized access.

The best-known case of computer security violation is the one described in Cliff Stoll's popular book, *The Cuckoo's Egg*. It starts on the left coast of North America and ends somewhere in Eastern Europe, and it was all triggered by a minor accounting discrepancy. The amount of resources that the operating system said had been used was slightly more than the total of resources for which various users of the computer were being billed. Rather than a simple rounding error, the problem turned out to be an unauthorized, and therefore unbilled, system user.

Stoll stumbled upon his system's cracker only because his university's computer was subject to "charge-back"—the billing of various internal customers for their proportional use of the machine, but the basic technique that highlighted the attack is applicable whether or not your organization charges customers (users) money for computer use. Keeping track of all known or authorized system activity, on any level, allows us to determine whether unknown and unauthorized activity has taken place and, if so, how much.

If your organization has not implemented some form of charge-back, the record keeping necessary to allow comprehensive system audit can seem more trouble (and more costly) than it's worth. However, if you're truly concerned about the security of your system or your data, only comprehensive auditability will allow you to determine

- What portion of network messages originate from no known and authorized system user? Which ones? What do they look like? What do they attempt to do?

- What portion of network messages originate from a known and authorized system user who was not signed on to the network at the time the message appeared? Which ones?

- What portion of database update activity is the result of known "production" transactions initiated by authorized users? Over a period of time, were any database changes made that cannot be traced to a specific application transaction? If so, why?

- What portion of database inquiry activity is the result of known "production" inquiries, and what portion of it is ad hoc? What time of day does the ad hoc activity occur?

- What portion of system activity is attributable to "root" or other irregular user IDs (which crackers just love to use)? Is any of this apparently the work of employees (which may indicate a procedural problem if not an intentional security violation)? Is any of it inappropriate for authorized "root" users?

All of these questions can be answered if your organization keeps track of every network message, every network session, every production application transaction, and every database activity (including inquiries). Collecting all that information can be a lot of work, analyzing it can be even more laborious, but at the end of the day, there's no other way of knowing just how effective your security measures have been.

## Security Venues

So, in a client/server environment, security is important (because a lot's at stake) and challenging (because cooperative processing in a networked environment is vulnerable). Even so, there are some approaches that, used in combination, can do an effective job of reducing or eliminating danger and risk. Where should you implement security technology, and what types of security technologies should you implement? Figure 6.3 suggests the answers. First, you must secure against unknown computers that may try to act as if they were legitimate users of your system. They're unknown, so presumably they're located outside your offices.

### Remote Access Security

One of the most important aspects of client/server security is security for, and from, client platforms that are located remotely—that is, away from the facility where your main server or network is situated. For security purposes, distant users who communicate via permanent dedicated connections, such as a leased line or T1 line, are considered local to the network. Remote platforms communicate with your application according to two basic patterns: via dial-up connection, or via a network such as the Internet. Each communication pattern has its own form of commonly used security.

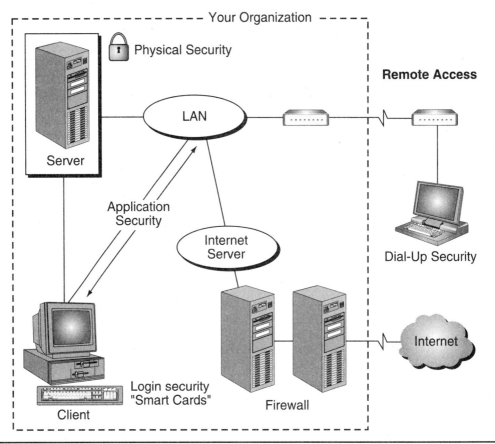

**Figure 6.3:**   Security Venues

**Dial-Up Security**   The most commonly used, and probably the most effective, security measure for dial-up connections is known as "prearranged call-back" or simply "call-back." In a system with such a feature, a remote user cannot just dial in to a central modem, establish a connection, and start using an application program. Rather, when the user dials in to the central modem, he or she gives an identifying code and immediately hangs up. The system waits a few seconds and then dials a prearranged number, determined by the specific code that the user entered. The user's client computer answers the call with its modem, a connection is established, the user enters a user ID and password, and application use may begin.

The call from a network to a remote user may seem sort of backward, but the arrangement has a definite advantage. The main reason dial-up connections are insecure is that callers are often anonymous (even in these days of caller ID). By placing the ultimate call from the network to the user, the system can be certain that the user (or at least the user's phone number) is on an approved list.

Prearranged call-back was useful for remote users who were in fixed or at least predictable locations. However, it could not be used for remote users who were truly, that is to say unpredictably, mobile: for example, traveling users who dial in to a network from hotel telephones. Recently, the advent of reliable high-speed cellular modems to go with now ubiquitous cellular phones means that a truly mobile user can still have a predictable call-back number, so this security measure is now universally applicable.

**Internet Security/Firewalls**   Any organization thinking of connecting its client/server systems to the Internet (or any other widely accessible network) almost immediately begins considering something called *firewalls*. Unfortunately, there is a great deal of confusion about just what a firewall will do for your systems, what it won't do, what it is, and how it operates.

Much of the confusion stems from a typical source—technology salespeople who attempt to sell their product as if it were the best of its kind (a time-honored and noble concept), and as if its kind were the only kind in existence (usually a prevarication, at best). A firewall is not a particular type of computer hardware. In fact, it may not be one computer at all. A firewall is simply any system or group of systems that implements and enforces any sort of access control policy between any two networks. That is, a firewall is any arrangement, consisting of one or more computers, that connects two networks but limits the form (and sometimes the quantity) of interaction between them. The nature of the limitation varies widely.

Internet firewalls have become popular because the Internet has become the common denominator of data communications, used as a transport mechanism for information flowing between individuals, between companies, and even within companies or organizations. Before the Internet became so widely popular, it was populated primarily by scientists and students, many of them devotees of the Unix denomination within the computer science religion. Many of these original residents seem to believe that technology is its own justification, and some of them greatly resent the invasion of their formerly exclusive domain by businesses, average civilians, and other "newbies." The worst cases of resentment lead to sociopathic behavior that can, unless prevented, trash your client/server system. Internet firewalls are sold to keep this behavior on the Internet, where it cannot be precluded, and out of your system, where, we hope, it can.

Internet firewalls come with a variety of capabilities. Some of the simplest generic products allow only e-mail traffic between your network and the Internet, thus protecting all of your business applications (although exposing your e-mail system). Other generic firewalls filter out specific types of messages and services that are known to present security problems, such as remote logins. These messages and services may be blocked selectively (only if they originate outside your organization) or completely, regardless of their point of origin. Custom firewalls, often consisting of multiple computers, can filter out all traffic except very specific transaction types and formats, providing a terminus where all outside traffic must stop and only certain carefully selected messages will be passed on inside your organization.

The specific level and nature of security that you want from a particular firewall will depend on many factors—the sensitivity of data and systems located within your network, your organization's intended use of the Internet, your degree of paranoia, your budget, and so on. All of these factors determine your access control policy, which you can then select or design a firewall to implement and enforce.

Many organizations have decided to provide Internet access for ad hoc information retrieval and for the occasional Internet e-mail but not for purposes of application computing. These companies often support Internet connectivity only on one or more standalone (that is, nonnetworked or separately networked) dedicated PCs. The computer(s) with access to the Internet simply are not connected to any computers used for normal operational computing. The physical and electronic gap between the two types of computers is the most effective firewall (or firebreak?) of all. However, if your internal e-mail and your internal applications are to make use of the Internet, or if you want Internet

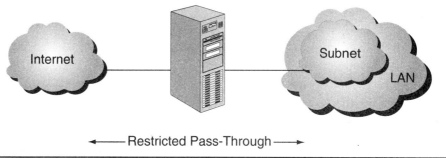

**Figure 6.4:**  A Routing Firewall

access to be available to more than a few of your employees, then you need to provide connectivity through your local area network(s) and you will require a firewall that consists of a physical presence rather than a physical absence.

Some firewalls are really nothing but routers, passing traffic directly between an internal network and the Internet (see Figure 6.4). These may provide no real security themselves, relying on the network and its applications to be themselves secure, or they may allow traffic between the Internet and selected portions of the private network while precluding such traffic with other subnets or platforms.

At the other end of the spectrum, we have what are sometimes known as proxy servers. These typically permit no direct traffic between one network and another. Instead, all messages terminate at the firewall, where they are captured, stored, logged, and examined. Some of these proxy servers will, upon successful screening of an incoming message, forward it to an appropriate application within the private network, but in the most secure proxy servers, a message originating outside an organization cannot go any farther than the firewall unless it passes all the inspection criteria implemented at the firewall *and* an independent application, running within the organization's network, selects the message from a storage area on the proxy server and consciously brings it inside the protected network (see Figure 6.5).

For a truly bulletproof client/server system to be connected to the Internet, or to any widely accessible information network (such as CompuServe, America Online, etc.), a firewall in the form of a proxy server built to limit access to specific transaction types, formats, and contents is required. As a general rule,

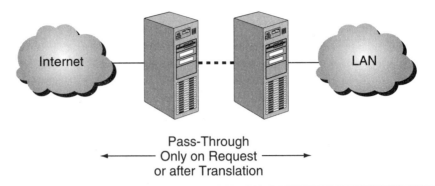

**Figure 6.5:**   A Proxy Server Firewall

this firewall consists physically of at least two general-purpose computers. For high-volume or fault-tolerant network connections, more computers may well be required. In a very real sense, the firewall becomes a client/server application unto itself, charged with protecting the network and the other systems running on it.

### Platform Security

Beyond securing your client/server systems from remote access, you must also take steps to secure the client workstations and other computers that *are* authorized to participate in your system, to prevent them being used by human operators who have no such authorization. We now look at two aspects of platform security: physical security, and user/platform authorization.

**Physical Security**   Physical security is achieved by protecting the physical equipment and the physical premises associated with a system. Most often, this is thought of in terms of restricting access by unauthorized individuals: locking doors, locking windows, having guards, employing motion sensors or other alarm equipment.

With client/server technology, the challenge of providing physical security is increased because of the increased number and variety of hardware platforms, and thus physical locations, that must be controlled. Even without reference to mobile or distant users, a client/server system often is vulnerable wherever certain types of equipment are located.

*Client Workstations*   Client workstations are the pieces of equipment that most invite security violations. A client workstation whose user has departed but left running, connected to a system and displaying sensitive data, is the very definition of an "attractive nuisance." The thing is almost impossible to walk by without looking at, perhaps closely! Not only can client workstations, left logged into a system, make system output available to the wrong people, they can also accept system input from the wrong people. Fraudulent or otherwise spurious transactions may be entered and accepted, and will most likely be attributed to the user who logged on and then walked away—there is usually no way to identify the real offender.

Normal procedures for client workstation security include area access control—restricting physical access to the work area in which the computer is located—and requiring users to log out of the system whenever they leave their computer, even for a minute. Many networks use add-on "watchdog" programs that forcibly log users off the LAN after a specified period of inactivity. Before using such programs, however, make sure that they don't cause data corruption if the user left applications or files open.

An additional security measure that has often proved its worth is to make certain that client workstation use is readily observable and that all users are aware that such monitoring technology is in use. The mere knowledge that unauthorized use of someone else's computer can easily be *seen* has proven to be an effective deterrent—not 100% effective, and easier to do with computers assigned to clerical staff than to those for executives, but a good idea wherever practicable.

*Database and File Servers*   Database and file servers are both easier and more critical to secure than client workstations. An unauthorized user at a client workstation can create a fraudulent transaction or find out sensitive information, but an unauthorized user at a server can make off with an entire database or critical set of files!

The good news about servers is that they are few (unlike client computers) and often need not be located in exposed areas. Servers can be locked up in special rooms or closets where physical access is more easily controlled than in a regular office, and even if a particular server needs to be located where anyone can walk up to it, it can still be enclosed in, and protected by, a specially made casing or "safe," perhaps provided with ventilation, cooling and even fire-resistant capabilities.

Physical security for data servers is especially important if those servers are equipped with removable media (hard disks, etc.). Removable hard disks or CD-ROMs make it simple for anyone to steal an entire database, so special precautions are doubly necessary. Again, an observable location is better than one that is difficult to see; miniature "glass houses," although reminiscent of mainframe technology, combine the virtues of access control and observability.

The method of disposal of server data backup sets is another element of server security. It does little good to lock up server rooms and put in a lot of windows if old tapes or optical disks go out in the trash. The data on such discarded backups may not be absolutely current, but it may be current enough for competitors or professional industrial spies to glean valuable information about your organization's operations.

*Printers and Print Servers*    Printers and print servers deserve as much security attention as does the data that will appear on them. If all data likely to be printed is nonsensitive, then printers and print servers may be located wherever is most convenient for the user group. However, if data may be printed that is sensitive, or valuable to competitors, then printers and print servers should be controlled to reflect that sensitivity or value. Reports and printouts that are uncontrolled may be picked up, or merely observed, by unauthorized individuals. And it is all too easy to attach a second printer, configured just like the first, to a print server; in such a case, all the data output on one printer would be duplicated in the output of the second!

*Network Hubs*    Network hubs offer particularly easy access to all the traffic, and all the data, that is carried on your LAN. For this reason, they should be located in a controlled area, typically referred to as a *wiring closet*. Wiring closets should always be locked, and in security-sensitive organizations they are also alarmed. If the hubs are in the same wiring closet as telephone punchdown blocks or switching equipment, telephone service personnel may also gain access to your network hubs.

Alternatively, network hubs can be located in a centralized, controlled area. Companies that are concerned about both security and customer service sometimes locate all network hubs in a glass house physically adjacent to their help desk operation. In this manner, the hubs are both controlled and quickly accessible to technicians diagnosing or repairing a network problem.

**User/Platform Authorization**   After physical security, the second aspect of platform security we examine is user/platform authorization.

*Networks*   Physical security can rarely be 100% effective, as the previous section indicated, and for systems with remote or (worse) mobile clients, it can never suffice. Fortunately, there are other means of achieving client/server system security. The first of these relates to the platforms upon which our client/server systems operate. That is, to the computers and the networks through which people execute particular client/server applications. Each of these allows us the opportunity to preclude unauthorized system use.

Network operating systems are often installed so as to require a user ID and password before allowing network use. This security is only marginally effective, for all the reasons any user ID/password scheme is of limited value:

- People's user IDs are widely known.
- People tend to pick passwords that are easy to remember.
- Even so, people often write their passwords down (generally in a pretty obvious place).
- People often tell co-workers their passwords.
- Even if not told, co-workers often learn each other's passwords.
- Outside contractors, such as consultants and vendor technical support analysts, may have user ID's and passwords that must provide privileged security levels.
- When contracts are terminated, contractor accounts may not be.
- People will log into a system or network, and then leave their computers turned on.
- When people leave a company, their user IDs/passwords are often valid for a period of time.
- When people leave a company, the co-workers' passwords they have learned are still valid.

That's not to say that software developers and system administrators don't do their best to make user ID/password security of some value. They often force passwords to be of at least a minimum length, to include a numeric or special character, or to be changed regularly. They can even require a new password to be significantly dissimilar to previous passwords, but, regardless of the efforts expended, user ID/password security is not sufficient in the network environment, so it is not sufficient for client/server systems.

*Client Workstations*  Client workstation (that is to say, PC) hardware often comes with password protection features, usually built into the BIOS (basic input/output system). However, BIOS password protection is subject to all the same shortcomings of any password protection (listed above), plus an additional one. In most PCs, BIOS passwords can be disabled simply by opening the case of the computer, then disconnecting and reconnecting the battery. Fortunately, better PC hardware security options exist.

Internal security cards, which fit into a slot on the motherboard and look similar to video cards or disk controller cards, can be added to PCs to control who may use the equipment, and what portions of the equipment (hard disk, floppy drive, serial and parallel ports) each person may use. Although they still (in some cases) operate by means of passwords, these cards are more sophisticated than simple BIOS protection and harder to defeat. For instance, a security card can encrypt the boot sector and partition information on a hard disk so that, if the card is removed in an attempt to disable password protection, all the information on the hard disk becomes unusable.

Internal security cards, then, can provide reliable protection, if some alternative to simple user ID/password authentication can be found. A number of such alternatives exist, each with advantages and disadvantages.

- Automatic password generators (sometimes called "token generators") are physical devices, about as large as a credit-card-sized calculator. They display a new and different password in an LCD window, often every minute. Each password generator operates on a different algorithm or a different schedule, so each one will display a different password at any time. Using one of these time-synchronized token generators, the user first identifies herself to the system by means of a PIN (personal identification number), similar to ones used with automated teller machines. This PIN tells the system which individual token generator is assigned to the individual. The user then keys in the password shown in the LED window, and the machine continues booting.

- An alternative to the time-synchronized token generator is the transaction-synchronized password generator. Rather than password matching based upon time of day, these devices generate a new password each time they are used. That is, the correct password will be a function of the previous password, rather than of the wall-clock time. To learn the new password, a user simply pushes a button on the device. Inadvertent pushing of the button can put the generator and the computer out of sync with each other, but this can readily be remedied.
- Perhaps the most secure form of automatic password generation is the challenge-response token generator. Using one of these cards (which looks even more like a credit-card sized calculator, having not only an LCD window but a numeric keypad as well), the user begins by turning on the PC. As part of the boot process, the PC monitor will display a numeric value known as the "challenge." The user must key this numeric value into the token generator card, at which time the card will calculate and display another value known as the "response." The user then keys this response into the PC, and booting may continue.

Password, or token, generators provide improved security because any user must have physical control of the device, rather than simple knowledge of a password. You receive no warning when someone learns your password, but a missing physical security device is, by its absence, more noticeable.

Theoretically better than any form of password is biometric technology, recently available for commercial systems. The most common form of biometric security involves identity verification by fingerprint. At the time that a PC is booted, or when connecting to a network, the user is required to place a finger on a special sensor pad. This pad records the fingerprint of the user, compares it to a database of authorized fingerprints, and determines specifically which user (with what authorization) is at the computer. The major advantage of a fingerprint is that you never forget it and, if someone were to borrow or steal it, you'd be very likely to notice!

However, any security measure that is invoked upon initiation of computer use, and not thereafter, is still vulnerable to a common problem—legitimate users signing on to the system and then going to get a cup of coffee (or lunch, or to speak to a coworker, or to use the rest room, or...). To provide reliable security in all but the most carefully controlled environments, a device must authenticate the presence of an authorized user throughout the session of computer use, not only at initiation.

A number of such devices exist. Typically based on "smart card" technology, these devices embed a microprocessor chip into a convenient artifact such as a card or button. The card or other artifact must be placed into a slot in the computer's keyboard for the computer to function. Astute security-sensitive organizations have embedded these microprocessors into identification badges that their employees must carry to be able to move around the building. In this manner, they have guaranteed that the card will not be left in the computer when the authorized user departs.

No single technology, no single approach, can guarantee system security by operating at the client workstation. However, taken in combination, these technologies can make a significant contribution to the security of your client/server system.

### Application Security

So far in our discussion of security venues, we've considered remote access security—both dial-up and Internet—and platform security, in its three forms of physical, network, and workstation security. Our discussion of all these issues has focused on hardware, and system-level software. However, the *applications* that run on the network and client workstation platforms offer additional security options—or, if the glass is half empty, additional ways security can be breached! Application security, then, is the third and last security venue that this chapter will consider.

**Kerberos**  Kerberos, currently the most widely used authentication technology, was developed at the Massachusetts Institute of Technology. Kerberos allows client and server programs, running on different computers, to prove their identity to each other. Additionally, Kerberos can prevent eavesdropping by unauthorized users and the commonly used hacking technique of replaying or regenerating an earlier transaction, perhaps slightly modified. Finally, Kerberos can detect interruptions in the stream of data from one computer to another (a common indication that the data stream has been intercepted and, perhaps, modified) and can provide for maintenance of data secrecy by using data encryption techniques.

Kerberos works by providing system users and services with *tickets* that those users and services then use to identify themselves to other system components. These tickets, each several hundred bytes long, are passed between system components using standard network communication protocols. Each ticket has a defined lifetime (minutes or hours) and contains within itself an encrypted number indicating the number of times it has been used. This *use count* must be incremented with each message, so replayed messages that copy the key from a previous message will be detected as invalid.

In effect, Kerberos manufactures secret keys as requested and transmits these keys safely across even an open, unsafe network. Thus, Kerberos provides the capability for client programs and server programs to authenticate each other. Kerberos encrypts its own secret keys before transmitting them, but does not provide encryption for data passed after authentication has been achieved. However, by using the secret keys as part of another independent encryption scheme (often based on DES), systems can still use Kerberos' capabilities to ensure secure data communication.

Most often, Kerberos tickets are passed between protocols at the application level (OSI Level 7) or, less frequently, at the presentation level (OSI Level 6). Application-level usage is sufficient to provide component (client or server) authentication, but the lower-level usage, most often in remote procedure call environments, also allows data stream integrity assurance.

Kerberos is widely used because it is effective, and because it is free. The basic key distribution model at the heart of Kerberos was first published in 1978, and is still eminently viable. The latest version of the product is available from MIT, although enhanced and extended implementations of it are available commercially (not free!) from such companies as Transarc and Digital Equipment, and as part of the Distributed Computing Environment (DCE) from the Open Software Foundation (OSF).

At present, two separate versions of Kerberos technology are in use. Unfortunately, they are incompatible. Version 4 (available in final form) and version 5 (still undergoing beta testing) are based upon completely different protocols, and cannot be used in combination. Commercially available implementations of Kerberos, such as those from Digital and Transarc, are based on version 4, although each adds its own unique characteristics. DCE security, available from the OSF, is based on version 5, although it is not fully compliant with version 5 specifications.

One problem with security technologies such as Kerberos is that they take a lot of testing, and a lot of time to move from the drawing board to a final production release. Companies that want to take advantage of the latest security technology advances often end up working with an incomplete specification; they often develop products that incorporate technologies not yet fully standardized, as they feel they cannot wait for the standardization process.

However, even with all the testing that goes on, Kerberos authentication is not foolproof. The *Wall Street Journal* recently reported that a glitch in the random key generation formula used in Kerberos version 4 made those keys significantly less random, and so less secure, than intended. This was discovered some 4 years after version 4 was released in final form! (Version 5 keys are generated using a different formula, and are unaffected.)

**Database Security**  Modern relational databases provide much of the commonly used client/server security. Database management systems have, from their infancy, provided means of ensuring that only authorized individuals can update or retrieve secured data. Modern relational DBMSs go the extra mile to make sure that the same level of security (and perhaps a little more) is available in the client/server world.

Each database management system installation comes with a *superuser* account ID. Anyone logged into the DBMS using this ID has complete privileges to create other users, create databases, maintain and access data, administer the database, or perform any other available function. Good database administrators typically use this ID only rarely, and create other, slightly less powerful account IDs for their day-to-day use.

Database security is based on the account ID, or user ID, which each user or program must supply to the DBMS. The database uses this account ID to access a table of user authorities or capabilities to determine precisely which data an individual or program may access or update, as well as whether the individual has the authority to create new databases, delete old databases, or even create new user account IDs.

In a typical DBMS security administration setup, each user must be explicitly authorized for each database, each relational table, and sometimes each column or data element that the user can access. Each user must also be granted authority to read, add, update, and delete information as appropriate. Failing explicit authority to perform a particular database operation, the user's request for that operation will be rejected by the DBMS. Like network user IDs, database account IDs are typically associated with passwords. Many of the DBMS security enhancements to deal with the client/server environment have come in the area of password generation and user authentication.

DBMS security now includes many of the types of enhanced technology we spoke of in terms of network security. Complete datastream verification and encryption, comprehensive administration of access to individual servers, integration with mainframe and other legacy security administration technologies, fingerprint verification, and automated password/token generation are available to authenticate database user identity, depending of course on the specific DBMS you choose to use. Secured data access is made more convenient by provision of single-signon protocols, so that once user identity is established it can be shared by one database server with another as necessary.

Relational DBMSs provide reasonable assurance that only authorized users can access stored data. The files in which DBMSs store their data are not easily readable without going through the database engine, which enforces user restrictions. Unlike many PC-derived "database" systems, fully relational databases add several levels of information administration beyond the file structure of the operating system, so even a complete printout of a particular DBMS data file will yield little in the way of legible information. In cases where truly sensitive or classified data is to be stored, modern DBMSs offer data encryption to make certain any "stolen" data is illegible and therefore useless. The most popular relational DBMSs even offer encryption for data as it flows from a database server to a client machine. Using this technology, a fat-client application can be assured that all network traffic (which, in the fat-client model, is equivalent to saying "all database traffic") is illegible to unauthorized recipients.

So, we have ways of preventing unauthorized access, whether through a known, authorized computer or from somewhere "outside the system." We can make it virtually impossible for a "cracker" to pretend to be an authorized user, or for him (and in the case of crackers, it usually *is* a "him") to extract meaningful information through any means whatever, but how do we know that's enough? What standards exist to which we can compare a set of security capabilities, to understand whether (and to what extent) they're sufficient? How can we benchmark the effectiveness of our security scheme?

The best-known and most thorough available standards for system security come from the U.S. military. Their language may be different from what you're used to, and their assumptions about information processing differ somewhat from those of a typical company, but the security thinking they embody is sound. A security scheme that evaluates well according to military standards can be expected to be pretty well bulletproof (no pun intended). To conclude our discussion of client/server security, then, we'll take a look at the relevant military standards, and make some recommendations for how to assemble your particular security technologies.

**DoD Security Levels**   The U.S. Department of Defense (DoD) has, since the early 1970s, spent a lot of time and money on the problem of application security. Before most corporations, DoD worried about how "trusted" their computer systems were. For years, the government has used networks of geographically distributed computers to automate mission-critical (indeed, often literally life-and-death) applications. Most companies that use client/server systems don't need the same degree of security that some of DoD's systems require, but the approach DoD has taken, and the framework it has worked out, are none the less instructive. Like any business, DoD has some systems that need strict security, and others where far less security is required.

Under the imposing title of Trusted Computer System Evaluation Criteria, DoD's National Computer Security Center has established a hierarchy of seven levels of trust, arranged into four basic divisions. Associated with each level or *class* are specific security requirements and, typically, common techniques for meeting those requirements. DoD's experience can be applied to commercial systems that exhibit similar security needs. However, for commercial purposes, the degree of specificity provided by four divisions is probably adequate, and it is on the differences among those divisions that we shall concentrate our attention. They are:

D    Minimal Protection
C    Discretionary Protection
B    Mandatory Protection
A    Verified Protection

In typical government fashion, DoD has documented the four divisions in mind-numbing specificity:

> The hierarchical classification component...shall be equal to the greatest hierarchical classification of any of the information in the output...; the non-hierarchical component shall include all of the non-hierarchical categories of the information in the output...but no other non-hierarchical categories.

For the sakes of brevity and clarity, however, we offer capsule summaries of the four divisions, and the security requirements applicable to each.

*Division D, Minimal Protection* contains all applications that meet no particular security requirements. "Minimal protection" is as close as the military is allowed to come to saying "no security." Many commercial applications, and (truth be told) many military systems operate with no particular reference to security requirements. Because security is costly, both in time and in money, there needs to be a category for systems without security requirements; this is it.

*Division C, Discretionary Protection* contains all systems that must restrict information to individuals on a "need to know" basis. That is, they provide facilities for declining information requests, for restricting information output, and for tracking system users and the transactions they initiate.

Discretionary protection generally requires:

- That data not be stored where the user can gain direct physical access to it. (Separating users from data allows the interjection of logic to protect the data from unauthorized access and to track access to, and modification of, the data.)
- Allowing users who create data to protect it from modification or deletion, and even accidental observation, by unauthorized users.

- Protecting the program code, system data, and user access authorities from unauthorized modification.
- Providing some way of checking the system in production to see that all elements are as they should be.

Optionally, discretionary security may also require the ability to control access to specific programs or bits of data based on the individual user, and to audit precisely which user made each access to, or modification of, system data, programs, user authorities, etc.

*Division B, Mandatory Protection* differs from discretionary protection primarily in that while division C systems contain data that *may be* subject to security restrictions, division B systems contain only data that *is* subject to restriction. As a result, all data created in, or imported into, an application with mandatory protection must be labeled with a particular security level (or set of restrictions), and must carry that labeling with it wherever it goes. Systems with mandatory protection contain code that prevents sensitive data from being passed to any other application that might not respect the security labeling or its implications.

Systems that provide mandatory protection typically

- Categorize system components, down to the level of input-output devices and communications channels, by their level of security.
- Mark all human-readable outputs (reports, inquiry screens, etc.) with information about the security level of the information displayed, so that users can determine whether they are authorized to view particular information.
- Preclude access to secure information by less-secure programs or users, both in terms of security level and subject matter or content. (That is, a person or program can access data only to the level, and within the subject areas, for which that person or program is authorized.)

Additionally, many systems with mandatory protection have features that are specifically designed to defeat covert, intentional attacks. Some such systems are intentionally simplified to reduce the likelihood of an attacker being able to use a less-known feature of the application in a manner not originally intended. Testing of systems that require mandatory protection, and the criteria for passing such tests, are specified to be extremely stringent.

Finally, *Division A, Verified Protection* is applied to only the most security-sensitive applications. The programs, data, parameters, and other components of a verified system may be no different from those in a system with mandatory protection (particularly one that has been intentionally simplified to prevent error), but the process of developing and accepting a verified system is far more stringent.

Verified systems

- Have formally modeled security policies and mathematical proofs that the model provides sufficient security.

- Have formal specifications not only of what functions will be performed, but also of how those functions will be partitioned and controlled for security purposes; this specification must be formally reconciled with the security model.

- Have mathematical proofs of the correctness of their *implementations*, both in software and in hardware, in terms of both application function and system security.

What does the Department of Defense have to tell us about client/server security? Realizing that DoD's Trusted Computer System Evaluation Criteria have their origin in the 1970s, and that the current DoD Standard was published in 1985, it's obvious that this information is not specifically targeted at client/server technology. However, there are some lessons we can learn from DoD's experience.

- As with the user community/robustness spectrum, the database usage variations, and the fat-client/thin-client/three-tiered deployments we spoke of earlier, there is a range of system security requirements—from none at all through intense and exacting. For client/server computing to deliver its maximum value to your organization, systems fitting in any and all of these security categories must be accessible at the same time, on the same platform, to any appropriate user.

- The variations in security requirements do not in themselves necessitate different security technologies. Rather, they can best be handled by utilizing common security technologies in differing ways and to differing extents.

- Providing system security involves securing data, programs, and physical and logical access. But all of these, to be useful, must complement one another. They cannot successfully be addressed in isolation.

The most demanding security standards in the automation industry, then, point out how important it is, not so much which security technologies we use—after all, security technologies are continually evolving—but how we plan, coordinate and manage the use of those technologies.

## Recap and Recommendations

Bulletproof client/server security can be achieved, but it takes a significant investment of both effort and money. It's not something you can buy, one size fits all, off the shelf, and it's not something you can build on the basis of "ready, fire, aim!"

Client/server security requires planning. It requires policy decisions. It requires a thorough understanding—not so much of what business problem each of your applications is going to address, but of how business applications as a whole are intended to operate, be used, and interact. In short, if you really need bulletproof client/server security, the requirements for that security must be included in your architectural design efforts.

A client/server architecture with bulletproof security will include effective provisions for making certain that

- System data cannot be accessed except through approved applications (typically, through data encryption).
- System messages cannot be accessed and interpreted except by their intended recipients (typically, through network traffic encryption).
- Clients and servers always authenticate the other platform's identity before performing any application cooperation (typically, through Kerberos version 5).
- Client platforms are always attended by an authorized employee whenever they're participating in the system (typically, through "smart card" or "button" technology).
- Client platforms are safe from unauthorized users and unobserved use (through some form of physical security).

- Seemingly inappropriate system actions are flagged to the attention of a responsible person in real time.

- Inexplicable system actions are detected in reasonable order after they have occurred, and are analyzed to determine how they were allowed to happen.

A secure client/server architecture will typically combine these elements, such as using the same "smart card" for physical access and client workstation access, and it may involve making changes to aspects of your organization not normally thought of as system related, such as controlling access to work areas and installation of controlled enclosures for servers within the work area.

Can such an architecture provide 100.0% security for your client/server system? No. For instance, if you have mobile users with cellular modems, or if your mission-critical application serves users within your customer's organization, it may be impossible to provide meaningful physical security, but the alarms and audit capabilities built in should detect any minor vulnerabilities before they become major disasters.

In client/server computing, as in any form of security, skepticism is a critical survival skill. "Crackers" are continually innovating. Technological advances constantly introduce new capabilities, but new vulnerabilities as well. In words attributed to one system security expert,

> The only system which is totally secure is one which is switched off and unplugged, locked in a titanium lined safe, buried in a concrete bunker, surrounded by nerve gas and highly paid armed guards. Even then, I wouldn't bet my life on it.

# 7

# Bulletproofing
# Client/Server Fault Tolerance

In the previous chapters, we've discussed bulletproofing client/server design, performance, and security. However, even if you follow all our suggestions in these areas, faults will still occur. A bulletproofed client/server system can, at least to a reasonable extent, "tolerate" such faults. Therefore, in this chapter we turn our attention to *fault tolerance*, and we begin by defining just what we mean by the term.

## What Is Fault Tolerance?

Fault tolerance is the characteristic of certain automated systems that allows them to continue performing even in the event of hardware failures and certain fundamental software problems. Fault *resilience*, on the other hand, is commonly used to mean that a fault may create downtime, but that downtime is short—measured in seconds or minutes. The concept of fault tolerance is closely related to the concepts of reliability, availability, performance, and security. Indeed, it is difficult to say that a system is reliable, available, high-performance, or secure unless it is also fault tolerant.

### What Is a Fault?

"Fault" is merely another word for "failure," although "fault" has, perhaps, a less permanent connotation.

A hardware fault is the failure of some physical device, typically the complete failure of a particular component. If you experience a memory error, or a hard disk crash, or a processor overheating, that's a hardware fault.

A software fault is a similar failure, although more common and (typically) less absolute. A program that aborts, or that "locks up," or that creates the wrong output has committed a software fault. (We're excluding software faults that are part of a computer system's design, such as page faults, which are part of the intended functioning of a virtual memory system.)

Data communications can also experience faults—for example, a message that, for any reason, fails to be delivered as intended can be described as having experienced a communications fault. Significantly, communications systems are expected and designed to experience a certain level of faults and to tolerate (or survive, or rectify, or correct) them. Every commonly used communications technology exhibits some level of fault tolerance, which is not necessarily true of every commonly used hardware or software technology.

### What Types of Faults Occur?

As you can already observe, not all faults are of a single flavor or type. Any fault can, if unrecoverable, cause your client/server application to become unavailable or unreliable, but different faults have different characteristics and are subject to differing resolutions.

One common categorization of faults into *crashes, omissions, timing* faults, and *Byzantine* faults comes originally from the system integration field, in which different components must be made to interoperate predictably and reliably without necessarily understanding each others' purpose, much less internal operation. Because client/server systems operate on much the same principle (and are often the result of system integration efforts), this set of categories can prove useful to your fault-tolerance efforts.

**Crashes** The simplest faults to describe are hardware, software, or communications crashes. A *crash* is said to occur whenever any component of a system suddenly, immediately, and irrevocably stops working.

The term "crash" has been around at least since the advent of the hard disk drive. The earliest hard drives, made to connect to powerful mainframe computers, were about the size of a kitchen appliance. (Not a can opener—a refrigerator!) They had, within them, a number of circular platters on which data was recorded. The platters spun at high speed, only microns away from the read/write heads that wrote and retrieved data. If anything went wrong with the rotation of the platters—if they got the least little bit wobbly—the disk experienced a "head crash." The noise was tremendous, the fireworks were impressive, and the smoke often set off the building's sprinkler system which caused even more damage!

Today's crashes are typically smaller and quieter. No noise, no sparks, no smoke, no fire department pulling up to your front door, but if a piece of hardware or software or a communications link upon which your application depends crashes, your system can be just as much "off the air" as in days of yore.

**Omission Faults**   Other failures occur in the form of a hardware or software component failing to respond to a command or some other input. That is, a SQL command may be delivered to a database server, yet the server may fail to respond, or a server may return a string of data to a client and that client may fail to recognize the server's response, remaining in "wait" mode.

In the broad context of client/server systems, omission faults include such problems as data unavailability, where all the hardware operates properly and all the software programs perform as specified, but the server responds to any request with some version of "data not found" because the data that should be on disk simply isn't. Omission faults can also involve software omission or absence, such as occur when one program goes to execute or invoke another and the second program is nowhere to be found, or hardware omission, in which some necessary hardware component isn't installed (or, perhaps more commonly, isn't installed properly).

**Timing Faults**   In the case of *timing faults*, the appropriate component (be it software, hardware, or communications) is present, is installed correctly, and produces the proper output result for the input in question, but produces that result at such a time that the output is not usable. Typically, timing faults involve a component, or set of components, taking too much time in the production of their output. However, in come cases taking too *little* time is equally erroneous.

As we saw in Chapter 5, client/server systems often operate under strict performance requirements. Transaction-based systems must respond within a certain number of seconds. Continuous processing systems must handle a certain volume of activity, such as external events or internally triggered observations, per day. Real-time systems must be synchronize their internal processing with some occurrence in the outside world. Given the cooperative processing necessary for client/server systems, even the most rudimentary of them is subject to timing faults:

Each time one computer communicates with another, it may set a timer (often called a *timeout*) to indicate how long it will wait for an acknowledgment of its message. If the timer expires with no acknowledgment received, the sending computer must presume that the message was not delivered successfully and retransmit. If the receiving computer properly receives the message but cannot acknowledge receipt within the allowed time period, then retransmission will occur as the result of a timing fault. Because many communication protocols handle timing faults automatically in this manner, timing faults may be occurring frequently without generating any alerts or alarms, using up bandwidth and reducing performance.

With most middleware, a client application that calls a server application has no direct knowledge of the operation, or even the location, of that server component. As a result, the client application must also set a timer. If the server does not respond before the timer expires, the client must presume that the server program has failed to execute, perhaps because the server platform is down. What action the client program takes next is a matter of system design, but when such alternative action is taken there is a risk of a timing fault. Perhaps the server program is processing properly and will produce the appropriate response, but is simply taking longer than anticipated for some reason.

Another type of timing fault involves a process or device that performs too fast for other interdependent processes or devices to handle. A simple example is a modem that attempts to dial a number immediately upon going "on-hook," before the telephone network can provide a dial tone.

**Byzantine Faults**   Finally, there is the category of faults in which the major symptom is that something inappropriate and unexpected occurs. The observable problem may be in the portion of the system that is responsible for the fault, or it may be somewhere else entirely. A *Byzantine fault* is typically created when one component of the system (hardware or software) alters a condition, intentionally or otherwise, that another component assumes to be true. For instance, one program may change the contents of a particular memory location, accidentally overlaying a variable that was stored in that same location and will soon be relied upon by a second program. When the second program attempts to retrieve its previously stored variable and attempts to act upon its contents, results are unpredictable—a Byzantine fault has occurred. Byzantine faults (as their name implies) are more complex than other types of faults, and so more difficult to resolve or tolerate. Automatic resolution of Byzantine faults is often not possible.

## Where Do Faults Occur?

To expose a system to the possibility of faults occurring, the only thing you have to do is turn it on. Any time something is happening, something can go wrong, and unfortunately, any *place* something is happening, something can go wrong. As a result, faults can occur in any portion of the system (see Figure 7.1):

- *Client hardware* can experience failure of its processor, memory, disk controller, disk, video adapter, monitor, network adapter or modem, power supply, and even the on/off switch.
- *Client software* application programs, GUI environments (e.g., Microsoft Windows), operating systems, and device drivers can all fail.
- *Client data* in the form of databases, data files, parameter files, and even executable files (inactive programs stored on hard disk) can be deleted or corrupted by any activity that is authorized to write to the PC's hard disk. ("Format c:"!)
- *Network communications* may fail to deliver a packet of information, or it may deliver the packet's contents incorrectly, or to the wrong recipient, or in the wrong order, or so slowly as to be useless.

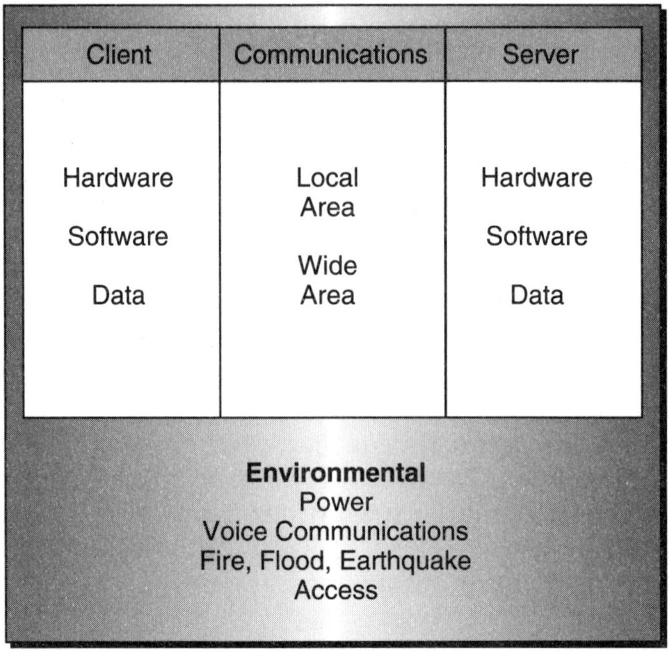

| Client | Communications | Server |
|--------|----------------|--------|
| Hardware | Local Area | Hardware |
| Software | | Software |
| Data | Wide Area | Data |

**Environmental**
Power
Voice Communications
Fire, Flood, Earthquake
Access

**Figure 7.1:**   Client/Server Fault Venues

- *Server hardware* can fail in its processor(s), memory, disk controller(s), disk(s), video adapter, monitor, communications interface, or power supply, just like client hardware. However, because there are more "moving parts" in a server (the hardware is more complex), occurrence of faults is more likely, and because many clients interact with (and are dependent upon) the same server, any failure is just that much more serious.

- *Server software* can fail in its application component or its operating system and device drivers. Indeed, server software, because of its need to support many simultaneous users and, typically, keep track of what each of them is doing individually, is a frequent cause (or at least, location) of system faults.

- *Server data* constitutes the long-term memory of the system, not just in terms of application data (personnel records, accounting figures, production control information) but also in terms of system programs and parameters. Any corruption of this data can easily create a system fault, often of the Byzantine variety.

- The computer system *environment* can also be a source of faults: power interruptions, voice communication problems, fires, floods, and faults of physical access (e.g., when users can't get to their computers).

### What Is Necessary for Fault Tolerance?

For a client/server system to be considered fault tolerant, it must continue running properly and without noticeable interruption, even in the presence of one or more significant system faults. The more faults and the more types of faults that the system can survive, that is, tolerate without undue ill effect, the more fault tolerant the system is.

Fault tolerance, then, is not a binary quantity. Any system that can tolerate any sort of fault can, in an academic sense, be said to be fault tolerant. Any client/server application is to some degree fault tolerant, because commonly used networking technologies all incorporate a degree of fault tolerance to deal with inevitable transmission errors, but no system is ever 100.0% fault tolerant: Some level of equipment or environmental failure will bring even the most robust system to its knees.

For practical purposes, the question, "Is this system fault tolerant?" boils down to asking whether it is *sufficiently* fault tolerant. What type and number of faults can it tolerate? How does that compare to the type and number of faults that it can be expected to experience? When is fault tolerance required, and when is fault resilience satisfactory?

Because a fault-tolerant system must continue running properly and without noticeable interruption, it must be self-healing; that is, the system must itself apply any corrective measures that are required to assure continued operation. In a classic model of the healing process, the system must detect, isolate, and correct the fault condition. We'll briefly look at each of these fundamental steps.

- *Detection* consists of becoming aware that a fault has occurred. A system must constantly monitor the performance of any components for which it claims fault tolerance. This monitoring may take any form, but it must always be accomplished by some other component than the one being monitored. For instance, the performance of a database management system can be monitored by client software or by a transaction processing monitor; the performance of a primary power source can be monitored by a component in an uninterruptible power supply.

- *Isolation* is the act of removing the faulty component from the system configuration, so that additional faults will not occur or so the existing fault will not have further consequences.

- *Correction* means providing the system with an acceptable permanent or temporary alternative to dependence on the faulty component. Perhaps the alternative component is already part of the system and activities that the failed component would have performed need merely be reallocated, or the alternative component may have been a standby, whose sole purpose for existing is to step in when the main component fails, as for example in some mirrored server configurations. If so, then steps will be required to substitute the standby seamlessly for the failed, and isolated, component, for example by "hot-swapping" a failed disk drive in a RAID array.

## Client/Server Fault Tolerance (Redundancy)

Note that the correction step, if it is to be executed automatically, requires the existence of an alternative component that can substitute for the one that has failed. Fault tolerance requires some level of redundancy—that is, the provision of multiple components that can substitute for one another. This intentional redundancy can take a wide variety of forms, depending on the portion of the system under discussion.

### Client Redundancy

**Hardware**  The most common form of redundancy in client hardware is simply the provision of more client workstations (PCs) than are actually required. That way, if one of the client PCs crashes or otherwise becomes unusable, the operator can simply move to another machine or swap machines. This arrangement does not meet our ideal definition of fault tolerance (to continue running without noticeable interruption), but it is typically acceptable in today's work environment. People recognize that PCs occasionally die and will generally move willingly from a deceased machine to a live one—so long as it doesn't happen too often.

In the simplest cases of redundant client hardware, the only requirement is that the second PC have access to the same application software that the first PC was executing. In more complex applications, the second PC may need to be identically equipped (hardware) and configured (software) in order to be an acceptable replacement. However, if fault tolerance is the "be all and end all" of your system (as it is with some military command and communication systems), the preferred design is for the second workstation explicitly *not* to be equipped or configured like the first, so that an integration problem affecting the first workstation would not be expected to affect the second.

An additional consideration in terms of client hardware is the location of the redundant PCs. Several companies have experienced business problems when their client workstations became inaccessible because of natural disaster or terrorism. (Think of companies with offices in the World Trade Center, whose employees could not get to those offices for several days after the buildings were bombed.) Prudence often dictates that, although one or two redundant PCs per hundred users may be necessary within the primary work location, some proportionally greater number of redundant PCs be provided (or at least provided for) somewhere off-site. Certain companies have solved this problem by providing modems to employees with PCs at home and testing to make certain that dial-up connectivity works well enough to be acceptable, at least in an emergency.

In a case of client hardware failure, detection and isolation are performed manually. Detection occurs when the user notices that something isn't right. Isolation of the fault takes place when the offending PC is switched off, or at the very least when it is no longer used as part of the client/server application. In some cases, client hardware failure may be quickly traceable to a single component. Here, fault tolerance becomes a measure of how quickly that component can be replaced, which is a function of the company's support organization responsiveness as well as of the technology itself (for example, hot-swappable PCI cards require almost no downtime).

**Software**   Client software faults may take many forms, influenced in part by the extent of system functionality that is implemented on the client. Simply for reasons of opportunity, more client software faults occur in fat-client systems than in thin-client or three-tiered systems. Where there is more going on, there is more that can go wrong.

As with client hardware faults, detection and isolation are typically performed manually. Again, it is up to the human operator to notice that something has gone wrong, and again, fault isolation takes the form of ceasing to use the affected PC, but redundancy, as it applies to client software, takes an entirely different form. When your client hardware is at fault, you move to different client hardware, but when your client software is at fault, you typically just import a new copy. This is true regardless of the category, or general character, of the fault.

To begin with, we must realize that the most common client software operating environment, Microsoft Windows Version 3.x, is inherently unstable. There are many technical reasons for this, but the easiest one to understand is the well-known "memory leak." As programs are run under Windows, for whatever application or combination of applications is being used, main programs and subprograms are constantly being loaded and unloaded from memory, and memory is constantly being allocated and deallocated. Unfortunately, Windows 3.x's deallocation process is not 100.0% effective—not all memory always gets freed up to be reused. Thus, over the course of a lengthy Windows session, Windows will eventually run out of memory, particularly a specific pool of shared memory known as *system resources*. Sometimes, the user gets increasingly urgent messages to close applications and shut down Windows voluntarily. Other times, the voluntary aspect disappears as Windows simply crashes.

Regardless of the form of the client software fault, then, if you're using Microsoft Windows 3.x the resolution may be to simply restart Windows and try whatever you were doing again. (Experienced Windows 3.x users generally do this out of habit.) The basic pattern still applies in that we tolerate faults through redundancy, but here the redundant component is the second copy of software created in your PC's random access memory when you simply try again.

The more permanent solution is to replace Windows 3.x with something more robust. American industry is slowly migrating from version 3.x to a combination of Windows 95 and Windows NT 3.51/4.0, both of which are much less subject to memory leaks. Eventually, Windows 3.x will become an historical curiosity. For the remainder of our discussion, then, we will assume that the cause of the fault is more than just running out of Windows 3.x resources.

For client software *crashes*, the operating assumption is that one or more software components on the client platform have been corrupted. The typical solution, then, is to replace all suspect components (which may be to say, all components) on the client workstation with fresh copies from some master (redundant) library, typically on a server. This process of "refreshing" all client software can be time-consuming if the client programs are large, but it will fix a large number of problems. (Unfortunately, and for obvious reasons, the fat-client approach to client/server computing, which has the highest incidence of client software faults, also has the largest client software modules and thus the longest refresh times.)

A similar solution is applied to client software *omission* faults. The symptom of such a fault is some form of message that states "Program xxxxx not found," or sometimes "not installed properly." Here, the operating assumption is that the PC's file system has simply lost track of the program file. The obvious solution is to obtain a fresh copy of the program in question, again from a library of programs residing on a server. Because the problem appears limited to a single program, it is not necessary to refresh all the programs in your system. A fresh copy of the missing module will generally suffice, although with client operating systems that rely upon a centralized database of configuration data, such as the Registry in Windows 95, a complete application reinstallation using the application's setup utility may be necessary

A bulletproofed client/server application, then, contains one or more servers with verified clean and up-to-date copies of all client-side software (operating system, GUI environment, application programs, and configuration database) available for downloading in case client software corruption is suspected. This downloading may be large-scale (in case of a crash) or selective (in case of an omission fault), but the form of the resolution is the same, regardless.

*Timing* and *Byzantine* faults on the client side are typically handled like hardware faults. That is, the user moves to a different machine and the offending PC is examined and corrected as soon as practical.

**Data**   In most client/server applications, the major store of data is located on a server, rather than on a client. However, there can be many smaller data stores which reside on each client platform. Such things as validation tables, sets of transactions, subsets of the data, "what if" scenarios, and personal preference parameters are often more efficiently stored on a person's client machine than centrally on the server.

Data cannot "crash," but data can be missing or corrupted in such a manner as to cause a Byzantine fault. When data is missing or data corruption is suspected, the safe course of action is to restore the data to its pristine condition, using a backup copy. If the data has been corrupted by one or more unintended operations, that is, a "user fault," the client-side application may be able to correct the fault through the use of an "undo" command. Bulletproofers may wish to evaluate the "undo" capabilities of client applications: Do they permit multiple "undos" or just one? Is the setting adjustable? To have an effectively fault-tolerant system, it may be necessary to back up not only your central database (probably on a server) but also any critical system files religiously, regardless of where they reside.

Backup copies of files that should be identical on all clients are best taken and provided centrally—if your reference table of regional offices becomes corrupted, you simply get a fresh copy of the official reference table from your server. However, backup copies of files that exist only on a single client machine, or that will have different contents on different client machines, must be taken individually, and are often best maintained at the individual client PC. Truly bulletproof fault tolerance requires backing up any system files that have changed on a regular and periodic basis (at least daily). The recommended arrangement is to back up each such file twice—once to some other file on the hard disk of the client computer (for ease of restoration), and once to some offline storage medium (such as diskettes or magnetic tape) for safety and for ease of transportation to another client PC, if necessary.

Expecting PC users to take responsibility for backing up files that reside on their own hard drives has proved through the years to be a risky proposition. As a result, bulletproof client/server systems often use server-based backup utilities that can communicate with a client-based TSR or "agent" to back up designated files, directories, or even disks across the LAN cable to high-capacity network backup devices. Performing such backups at night is usually necessary to avoid overloading the infrastructure during work hours. Newer LAN technologies, such as 100-Mbps Fast Ethernet and high-capacity, high-speed backup devices have made server-based backups of workstation data more practical.

We should also mention client-side add-in utilities, such as those from Octopus Technologies, that perform real-time mirroring of disk operations. That mirroring can occur to the same disk device, a secondary disk, or a network drive. The space and performance impacts of such a scheme can both be reduced if the add-in utility mirrors *deltas*, that is, changes to data files, rather than the entire data files themselves.

### Communications Redundancy

In any client/server system, if the network goes down or stops functioning reliably, the entire system is affected. Therefore, bulletproofing your client/server fault tolerance always means bulletproofing your network. Again, the primary technique is to provide redundancy, in this case redundant connectivity. However, the form of the redundancy will vary, depending on whether the network (or network segment) concerned is local area or wide area in scope.

The key concern in providing a fault-tolerant network for client/server computing is to enumerate all the network components that come between your clients and your servers and to have a tested alternative, or backup plan, for each component. Please note that "tested" means not just component-level testing, but rather integration testing of each mathematical permutation—testing of each possible combination of components, of each possible network configuration.

For instance, if your client/server system uses a PC client workstation, which uses an attached modem to dial into one of the nationwide value-added commercial carriers, which is connected to a communications server at your company's home office, which is tied into a LAN, on which resides your database server, then there are four communications components: the local phone company, the value-added carrier, the communications server, and the LAN. Your system will only be as fault tolerant as its most brittle component.

**Local**  Making a single local area network fault tolerant typically means making the network server redundant. Major network operating systems offer add-on features to achieve this, and competing third-party products are available for the most commonly used NOSs, as well.

Add-on programs provide the ability to mirror (that is, maintain a full redundant copy in real-time mode) the network server, including all data files and all network administrative information. Should the primary (regular) network server crash, the mirror-image server will immediately take its place. These programs also alert the network administrator that a failure has occurred so that a permanent resolution can be implemented and mirroring reinstated.

Because typical client workstations (that is, PCs) can only address one network adapter card, and because such LAN components as cabling and hubs very rarely fail, mirroring the LAN server is generally considered sufficient. However, in the most critical LAN environments, where absolute bulletproofing is considered essential, a second set of cabling can be installed, complete with hubs, routers, and so on. The purpose of the second physical LAN is to preclude all workstations being knocked out by interruption of the cabling at any point. To this end, the two LANs are cabled never to pass through the same wall or the same area of ceiling; the possibility of a single physical mishap interrupting both sets of cable is kept to a minimum. Redundant cabling that passes through the same physical space isn't truly redundant, as the Browns Ferry nuclear plant accident and at least one DC-10 airline crash have proven.

Typically, client workstations will be split, with half tied into one set of cabling and half the other. However, to get everyone back online as soon as possible, all workstations can be supplied with connections to both LANs—if one LAN goes out, the users can merely disconnect from the failed LAN and connect to the remaining LAN. It's somewhat inconvenient, and a bit crude, but this arrangement can give another level of fault tolerance to client/server systems. A higher level of convenience, and cost, is offered by technologies such as FDDI's (Fiber Distributed Data Interface) counterrotating ring design.

**Wide Area**  If the network to be made fault tolerant is wide area in scope, a number of redundancy options exist. To begin with, recognize that any commercial wide area communications carrier provides a high level of redundancy and fault tolerance as part of its normal offerings. That's not to say that commercial networks never go down—even AT&T loses a midtown switching center occasionally—but it is to say that they don't go down very often. (Let's face it, if they did, losing a switching center wouldn't be nationwide news.)

If your primary wide area communications are provided by a commercial carrier, you may still need to arrange for additional redundancy, but most of the job is taken care of. The common means of providing additional redundancy is to make arrangements with another commercial carrier (which could even be an Internet Service Provider—see "Virtual Networks"). Perhaps you split your everyday network traffic between the two, and perhaps you use one regularly and keep the other on standby, for emergencies only. The key point is that it's unlikely that both networks will fail at the same time.

## VIRTUAL NETWORKS

A new phrase is making its way into the client/server technical lexicon: *virtual networking*, or *virtual private networking*, which usually means using the Internet in place of (or in addition to) traditional wide-area network carriers to link geographically remote business sites. Internet-based WANs represent an almost complete inversion of the Internet's original intentions, in that the Internet was supposed to be a completely public network for the noncommercial transfer and dissemination of data, and virtual networks use the Internet to create private network links purely for business purposes. However, there was never supposed to be advertising on the Internet either, and we all know how that situation has changed! The modern view of the Internet, for better or for worse, is as a business resource to be taken advantage of in any way possible, and virtual networking takes this view one step further than simply hosting a commercial site on the Web.

In a virtual network, remote sites each use a high-speed link (such as a short-distance leased line) to an Internet Service Provider (ISP) to create a wide-area network configuration. This approach can have several benefits to the customer:

- It may not be necessary to buy, configure, and manage as many routers at each site, simplifying system design and reducing support costs.

- The overall cost may be lower. The leased lines between remote sites and nearby ISPs will be much shorter than leased lines between the remote sites themselves, especially for geographically distant sites. Further, ISPs often charge much less for T1 Internet access than traditional commercial carriers charge for leased T1 lines in private networks. Finally, your organization may already be paying for high-speed Internet access, reducing the incremental cost of implementing an Internet WAN.

- The availability of multiple communications pathways between ISPs provides good to excellent redundancy for fault tolerance.

- There are disadvantages to virtual networking, however:
- It does not provide the guaranteed data transfer rate or response time of private digital leased lines, at least not yet, so it might not be suitable for WANs carrying audio or video data streams or other types of timing-sensitive data.
- There is still a single point of failure in the connection from the office to the ISP, suggesting that an alternate network link of some sort is still required for very high availability.
- The security level of a virtual network is inherently lower than that of a private network, because data is traversing the Internet, meaning that your organization will need to implement encryption and authentication technologies to achieve acceptable security (see Chapter 6).

Perhaps, then, the best use of a virtual network would be as a less-expensive backup system for an existing private WAN, especially one that connects sites separated by long physical distances. As the Internet matures, virtual networking may become an even more economically attractive option than it is today, while coincidentally providing a high level of fault tolerance from the multiplicity of pathways between ISPs. It's not unreasonable to forecast that in a few years, there may be more private network traffic on the Internet than public traffic—standing the Internet concept on its head.

---

If "unlikely" is still too much risk (after all, both commercial networks could be purchasing capacity on the same cable, and that cable could go out), then redundancy should be provided using an alternative technology. If your primary carrier uses cable, then your redundant carrier should be based on satellites, for example. (This is a common scheme—all the world's undersea communications cables are backed up, on a contingency basis, by satellite carriers.) If your primary communications are via virtual private satellite network (VPSN), on the other hand, your backup communications should be via land line.

Using a backup communications network may or may not be transparent to the user. If each client workstation accesses the network individually (each is equipped with its own modem), then the user will have to select a different telephone number within the communications software to access the alternate network. However, if users access your wide area network through a communications server on your LAN, then the communications server can be programmed to use the alternate network whenever the primary one is unavailable. If your primary wide area communications network is privately owned or constituted of leased lines (the usage of which your company manages), commercial networks can still provide reliable backup service.

### Server Redundancy

**Hardware**  Probably the most widely discussed issue in client/server fault tolerance is the one of server—mostly database server—redundancy. Because fat-client systems are the most common form and the server is seen as the critical (yet complex and therefore vulnerable) component of fat-client systems, this is where most discussions begin. Unfortunately, it is also where many of them end.

The form of redundancy best suited to providing fault tolerance in server hardware depends, in large part, on whether the server provides database, or only business application processing, services. Ignoring for the moment the issue of distributed databases, let us make two broad generalizations:

- For servers providing database services, whether or not they are also the platform for business application processing, redundancy takes the form of a server that will not crash or of a mirrored "hot standby" server ready to step in instantly if the primary server does crash.

- For servers that provide only business application processing support, redundancy takes the form of multiple servers, so that any particular transaction can be processed on more than one machine and, should one server crash, alternatives are inherently available.

- Lesser degrees of hardware fault tolerance for both database servers and application servers include error-correcting memory, external disk enclosures, and redundant disk subsystems such as RAID arrays. The latter typically support hot-swapping so that disk failures require no downtime. Although these steps certainly help, server motherboard and CPU failure may remain single points of failure.

We deal first with the more common instance—the database server. Let us begin by emphasizing a difference in terminology between this discussion and earlier chapters in the book. For most purposes, a computer is a "database server" if it provides database management services exclusively—if it provides business application processing *and* database management services, as in a thin-client arrangement, then it is referred to as an "application server." However, for purposes of redundancy analysis, a server is a "database server" if it provides database management services, *regardless* of whether it provides other services as well. In redundancy planning, the driving factor is the need to maintain a single, controlled, master copy of critical production data; everything else is secondary. For database servers, then, the industry has evolved a number of solutions to single-server redundancy requirements:

- Traditional *nonstop* computers provide two coordinated processors within a single cabinet. The processors are coordinated in such a way that, should one of them fail, the second will continue uninterrupted. Services will normally be provided by only a single processor, so if that processor fails, performance will not be degraded. In addition to redundant processors, these machines can provide separate memory banks, mirrored disk drives, and even redundant power supplies so as to be able to guarantee uninterrupted operation in spite of any form of hardware crash.

- *Clustered* servers are separate machines, usually of the same make and model line, which can be addressed across the network as if they were a single computer. Clusters are better, under normal operations, than a nonstop server, because they can allocate work to all processors all the time. However, they exhibit degraded performance in the case of a processor crash, as now the same amount of work must be spread across a smaller number of processors. For use as a database server, a particular cluster must offer the capability to share disk drives without a requirement for file locking, so that a single copy of the database can be accessed, simultaneously, by all machines in the cluster. (See Figure 7.2.)

- *Symmetrical multiprocessing* (SMP) servers are single computers with multiple processor boards inside the cabinet. SMP technology offers good scalability and is cost-effective, but SMP in and of itself is only fault tolerant within limits. A typical SMP server will have multiple processor ships, all sharing the same pool of memory and the same disk drives, but SMP servers do not have the ability for processors transparently to take over tasks in case of a hardware crash. If any processor

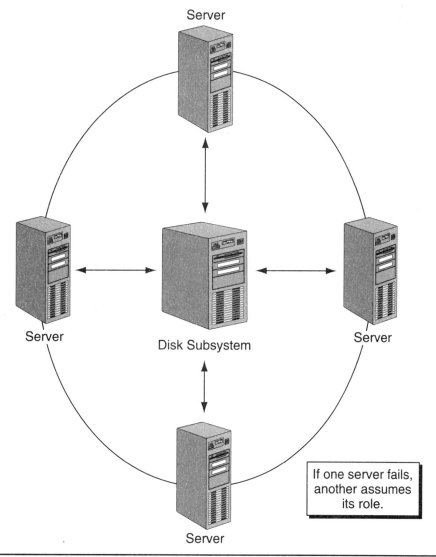

**Figure 7.2:**    A Fault-Resilient Server Cluster

fails, an SMP server must typically shut down, check its disks for corruption, and then restart. This process can take as little as a minute or two, but interruption *does* occur.

- *Hot standby* database servers are supported by many of the major relational database management systems. In a hot standby arrangement, one of a pair of computers is the primary database server and performs all database processing neces-

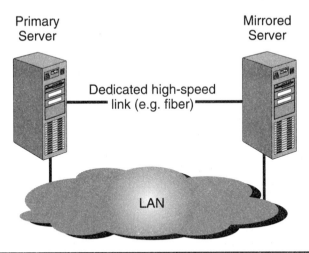

| If the primary server fails, the mirrored server takes over. |

**Figure 7.3:**   A Fault-Tolerant Hot Standby Server Configuration

sary to support all client workstations. The secondary computer, typically a clone of the first, spends all of its resources mirroring the actions of the primary server. If the primary server ever crashes, the secondary server takes over in a transparent, seamless transition (see Figure 7.3).

- *Warm standby* database servers are configurable for any DBMS (or any version of any DBMS) that does not support hot standby. In a "warm" arrangement, two computers are still required, and all visible work is still performed by only a single machine. The difference is that if the primary server fails, some human action is necessary before the secondary server can take over from the primary one. Perhaps the last few database updates have to be applied. Perhaps some network addresses have to be changed. Whatever the specifics, the need for operator intervention means that the switchover can never be transparent to the user.

Redundant application servers (which contain no database) are less complex to implement. Because they contain no database themselves, presumably the business logic executing on the application server uses a database on another machine. Because that database server manages competing user requests, a three-tiered system can have as many application (business logic) servers as might be desired. The machines need not be of the same make, model, or configuration. The only requirement is that they all be addressable by (some portion of) the client workstation population and that they all address the same database server (or server cluster).

Redundant application servers typically split the processing load based on a static allocation of users or network addresses. One bank of users always uses the first server, another bank the second server, and so on. In the event of application server failure, most network operating systems will handle an alternate address (alternate server). One of the advantages of using a transaction process monitor (see Chapter 4) is its ability to dynamically balance transaction loads across a number of fully or partially redundant application servers.

**Software**   Server software consists of a finite number of programs, be they application programs or the components of a database management system. Redundancy in this situation consists of having two or more copies of each program that might need to be executed.

The first copy is always online. It is the copy, the executable file, that is intended to be loaded into memory and executed whenever anyone needs to run that program.

The second copy, and any subsequent copies, may or may not be online. These copies are intended to be moved on top of a failed primary copy, if necessary. The purpose of having a second copy online is to make the process of moving it as quick and as painless as possible. The purpose of having a copy offline (on tape, or removable disk, or some other medium) is to store it securely, away from the computer, so that no single event will wipe out all copies of any program.

At present, no operating system we know of offers the functionality to detect a bad copy of a program and automatically "fail over" to a second copy stored online. In the absence of that functionality, the only way to have a seamless transition from one copy of a program to another is for a TP monitor to move the transaction from one server to another.

**Data**   Modern industrial-strength database management systems provide a great deal of fault tolerance as part of their basic functionality. Backward error recovery (recovering the database to some previous state) and forward error recovery (reapplying all database update transactions up to, but not including, the one that caused a problem) are widely available. For example, a DBMS might save a record just before it is deleted or modified; if the transaction completes successfully, the extra saved copy of the record is discarded, but if the transaction does not complete successfully, the extra saved copy is used later for transaction rollback. Bulletproofing your server data fault tolerance, then, is limited to complementing the basic DBMS functionality and safeguarding any files not contained in a database.

As regard complementing DBMS functionality, the main form of redundancy required is offline storage of a copy of the database, to assure the ability to do backward recovery. Many organizations take full backups of all production databases on one cycle, plus incremental backups at shorter intervals (e.g., a full backup weekly and incremental backups daily). In theory, these organizations can restore the database to any previous condition by overlaying the data files with the appropriate full backup copy, then updating that copy with each incremental backup (in succession), and finally by reapplying any appropriate database updates from a database update log file.

Determining an appropriate backup scheme and schedule is not necessarily a simple or obvious task. Daily full backups permit more rapid file restoration, by not requiring multiple successive restores, but they require more time, more media, larger capacity backup devices, and perhaps even faster LAN infrastructure (e.g., dedicated high-speed server channels) to perform the necessary file transfers in the time available. System designers must also consider media wear when devising a backup strategy, and choose from different media rotation schemes, such as Grandfather-Father-Son and Tower of Hanoi. Fortunately, newer standalone network backup devices can simplify the bulletproofer's life by performing automatic media set rotation with autochanger hardware.

All this is not to imply that your only choices are online and offline storage. A third option, often termed "near-line" storage, forms a compromise between the very slow retrieval times associated with offline storage and the expensive storage space requirements of online storage. Near-line storage systems typically use optical media or automated tape "jukeboxes." Balancing the costs and benefits of online, near-line, and offline storage is the purview of Hierarchical Storage Management (HSM) systems, but whatever the system, true fault tolerance means the ability not only to retrieve data files from a redundant and/or physically secure location, but also to restore those files quickly enough so that costly downtime is kept to a minimum.

Providing redundancy for nondatabase files is a less sophisticated process. Depending on the volatility of the data in question, daily, weekly, or monthly backups are usually taken and retained for purposes of backward error recovery only. Lacking the update logging that goes on in a database environment, these files rarely offer forward error recovery. As a result, any updates made since a backup will, following backward error recovery, often have to be made manually.

### Environmental Redundancy

A final aspect of fault tolerance for client/server systems is the quality and reliability of environmental services—that is, of services that are not technically part of the computing architecture, but that certainly affect the performance of that computing architecture.

**Power**  How reliable is your electric power? Unless you can answer that question "absolutely!" you have an opportunity to increase your system's fault tolerance. Managing your power supply to increase system fault tolerance has a number of aspects.

Although it's not technically a matter of fault tolerance—more one of fault avoidance—the quality of the electrical flow being used by your computers will affect system reliability. All commercial electric power is subject to voltage fluctuations all the time. Normal electrical and electromechanical equipment—lights, heating elements, motors—is minimally affected by these fluctuations, but electronic equipment (especially computers) can be significantly affected. Too high a voltage spike can fry your processor chip or your memory. Too low a voltage valley at just the wrong time can prevent your data from being written properly to your hard disk. As a result, any client/server system that is important enough to require fault tolerance should be running on electrical power that has been "conditioned." That is, the highest spikes and the deepest valleys should have been smoothed off to decrease the incidence of system faults.

Redundancy of electrical supply, to achieve true fault tolerance, can be achieved in a number of ways. In the "olden days," companies would sometimes locate their (mainframe) computer centers at the service area boundary of two electrical utility companies, bringing electrical feeds from both companies into the building. This way, if one company had an outage, the other probably wouldn't.

For a less geographically restrictive solution, many companies installed gasoline- or diesel-driven motor/generator combinations, combined with banks of batteries. These "uninterruptible power supplies" (UPSs) might provide power just to the computer center or to the whole building (as in a hospital). Several companies installed two or more of these UPSs, each capable of powering the critical aspects of their operations, so that if one backup system failed they had a backup for the backup! If your objective is to supply continuous electrical power for an extended period of time, or to a whole building or other large operation, motor/generator units are probably still the way to go. They can be cost-effective (although never cheap) and they will run more or less forever, given sufficient fuel.

However, if your objective is to supply power to a smaller operation (such as a network of a half-dozen PCs) or for a shorter period of time (perhaps half an hour, to allow files to be saved and the system to shut down gracefully), then smaller, independent battery units are generally the answer. These units, sold as UPSs and costing in the low-to-mid hundreds of dollars, both condition the power flowing to your computer equipment and provide a period of continued electricity following an interruption of external power. At the very least, every critical component of a fault-tolerant client/server system—and this includes hubs, gateways, routers, bridges, and modem racks as well as servers—should be able to count on 10 or 15 minutes notice before losing power. It's also worth investigating UPSs that automatically alert servers of a power cut, usually via a serial link, so that the servers can initiate an orderly shutdown.

One last tip on battery backups: Audit them periodically for both performance and correct size. Batteries typically last only 3 to 4 years before requiring replacement. Furthermore, it's quite common for network managers to add disk drives, memory, and other devices to LAN servers without beefing up the battery backup capability. If its circuit breaker trips because a UPS is no longer capable of handling the current draw, you get exactly zero seconds of protection!

**Communications**  Data communications, and the redundancy necessary to make them fault tolerant, is a subject that we have already discussed, but what about voice communications? Would your client/server system be truly useful in the absence of normal voice telecommunications? Or would it be "up" yet inactive?

Especially in an emergency situation, telecommunications capability is often an early casualty. As a result, customers and suppliers can't contact your staff, your management can't direct your staff, and too often staff can't really coordinate their efforts at the very time when coordination is most important.

Some sort of redundant voice communication system, using two-way radios, cellular phones, or VSDN (voice synchronous data networking), can make all the difference if normal phone service goes out. VSDN sends voice across the same network wires as are used to transmit data. As a result, so long as there is any system to talk about, the communications capability will exist!

**Fire, Flood, and Other Protection**  Again, falling perhaps as much into the category of fault avoidance as fault tolerance, the redundancy characteristics of any special equipment that helps control the environment in which your computers operate should be examined.

- Cooling (typically, air-conditioning) equipment will affect the lifetime of your computers. Electronic equipment hates heat, and computers generate a lot of it. Particularly if some of your computers are in enclosed areas for security purposes, heat can build up rapidly in the absence of air conditioning. How do you make your cooling system fault tolerant? Install two or more independent systems, typically sized smaller than a single system would be, so that if any one of them goes out you still have some or most of your cooling capacity available. Also, make certain that all of these systems cool (or can be made to cool) your specially enclosed computer areas.

- Positive air pressure, which decreases the amount of dust in an area or building, can be achieved with one large air blower or with several smaller ones. The multiple-blower arrangement is more fault tolerant.

- Fire detection equipment can give early warning of fires caused by electrical or other problems before serious damage occurs. Multiple independent sensors are best.

- Special areas or rooms in which servers reside may be equipped with fire-suppression equipment. To protect the computers, this equipment should use a gaseous fire suppressant, not water! Again, multiple independent systems provide a higher level of protection than a single large system can.

- Air filtration equipment can prevent smoke and other particulates from getting into your computers. Smoke damage resulting from a fire elsewhere in the building can destroy a computer.

- Water detection equipment can alert you to flooding on the lower levels of a building. This is particularly important to companies that run network and power cables through a basement, or beneath raised flooring.

**Access**    Finally, reconsider the question of what happens in a disaster situation where, perhaps, your servers are fine, your client workstations are all working, your network is operating entirely up to specification, there is power to your building and your phones are ringing off the hook...and your staff can't get to any of it!

Again, the bombing of the World Trade Center in New York is the best-known case, but by no means the only one. Downtown Chicago was closed for days when the Chicago River broke through into some hundred-year-old coal delivery tunnels. There have been, and will continue to be, other such cases. If, in a country with an aging infrastructure and an increasing exposure to terrorism, your organization depends for its survival upon its computers, you must answer the question, "How will we use them if we can't get to them?" The answer can take many forms:

- Multiple business locations, with similar operating capabilities and proper data access, can back each other up. For example, a database server in the Dallas regional office can perform a nightly backup to a database server in the Chicago regional office, and vice versa.

- Modems and "remote control" software can let your employees operate their office computers (with some performance penalty) from computers located in their homes. (Of course, certain office computers and modems must be left powered on, if this is to work.) "Remote node" software can let employees use home computers as long as a network modem is running in the main office.

- Commercial disaster recovery services are beginning to offer support for client/server computing, although these offerings will probably never be as comprehensive as they were in the mainframe environment.

- You may even decide to create a second business location to allow your organization to provide its own off-site recovery services. If so, the second location should probably be cabled for electric power and more data and voice communications than would otherwise be necessary.

Note: Please don't run into your boss's office, saying "See? Martin and Weadock say we've got to invest in all sorts of special equipment!" We're not saying that at all. What we are saying is that any of these risks that you don't protect against has the ability to bring your system down. Each risk has some chance of occurring and some associated cost.

Of course, the likelihood of any particular risk will vary from company to company, and from location to location. If you get your electric power from a small local cooperative with a limited maintenance staff, you may have a higher-than-average risk of power loss. If your offices are on the third floor of a building halfway up a mountain, you may have a lower-than-average risk of your premises flooding. What risks you protect against is a management decision, and properly so.

What we *are* saying is this: Consider these types of risk. Consider the consequences of each to your business. Don't think that simply bulletproofing your hardware, software, and network can bulletproof your entire system. For any environmental risks that you decide to protect against, look for ways to get some redundancy into the solution. Why use two when one will do? Because, in an outage situation, starting with two still leaves you with 50% of your original capacity. Starting with one will leave you up the creek!

## Issues Regarding C/S Fault Tolerance

### Complexity

Any single chapter on the subject of fault tolerance can only skim the surface. Indeed, entire books are dedicated to the use of a single technology (one of a number of possible choices) to address a single type of risk (among all the possible risks). Worse, your choice of a fault-tolerance approach will be affected by your other architectural choices, and your options in one area of fault tolerance will be limited by other fault-tolerance decisions, already made.

The whole subject just gets very complex, very fast.

As a result, it's generally not productive to attempt total (or even near-total) fault tolerance at system implementation. Instead, a phased approach is generally better, starting from the most critical components and then moving the perimeter of fault tolerance gradually outward. A typical order of progression might be as follows:

1. Local Area Network
2. Database Server(s)
3. Client Workstations
4. Wide Area Network
5. Application Servers
6. Environmental Services

### Security

One of the complexities of fault-tolerance planning is that it often conflicts with security planning. There is a natural contradiction, not so much between the two sets of objectives, as between the approaches by which they can be achieved. Here are some examples:

- Fault-tolerant data means data that is stored in several copies, ideally in multiple locations. Each copy, and each location, must be secured or your data may fall into the wrong hands.
- Fault-tolerant systems should be able to recover from any software failure, yet a failure that destroys an encryption key cannot be recovered. Once a key is lost, your organization will be in precisely the same situation as some cracker trying to break in. Your security measures will work against you.
- Fault tolerance means that authorized users may be accessing the system from equipment other than their normal computer, from somewhere other than their normal work location, at some time other than normal business hours. Yet these very conditions should trigger a security alarm, as they could be the symptoms of a cracker attacking your system with a stolen user ID/password combination.

Some reasonable compromise between security and fault tolerance can generally be worked out, but the inherent conflict

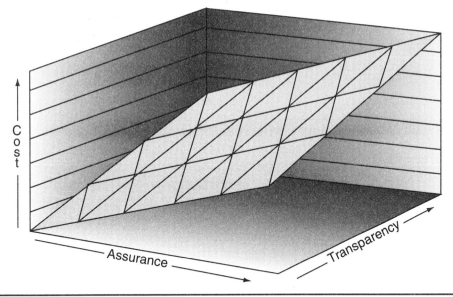

**Figure 7.4:**  Assurance, Transparency, and Cost

between the two approaches must be recognized, so that trade-offs and relative risks can be analyzed rationally.

There is, in fact, a common three-way trade-off in client/server fault tolerance. It relates to the levels of assurance that are required for any system, the transparency with which the fault-tolerant technologies must operate, and the amount of money all of this is going to cost (see Figure 7.4).

## Assurance Levels

Assurance levels are merely a semiquantified expression of the amount of risk that the system is going to crash. No system is ever 100.0% assured, but we can get pretty close. To estimate the assurance levels of your system, list the risks that you have not specifically addressed via security or fault-tolerance measures. Then estimate the likelihood that each of them will occur and the severity of consequence (catastrophic, serious, moderate, minimal) for each. An expression of your assurance levels might end up looking like this:

| | |
|---|---|
| Assurance that nothing catastrophic will occur: | 99.85% |
| Assurance that nothing serious will occur: | 99.25% |
| Assurance that nothing moderate will occur: | 96.50% |
| Assurance that nothing minimal will occur: | 68.00% |

Note that, as severity decreases, assurance level drops. That's not to say that you can't guard against every little thing—you probably could—but the benefit isn't there, and the cost goes through the roof.

### Transparency

Similarly, transparency to the user is the objective of all fault-tolerant technology. Ideally, we would like the user to not know, and not care, whether the primary or backup component or configuration is in place. We want the user to have to take no action and to notice no difference in system appearance or performance.

There are legitimate reasons for these objectives; they're not just pipe dreams or "nice-to-haves." The dynamics of humans and computers are seriously affected by how confident the people are that they know what the computer is doing and what it's going to do next. If the system exhibits inconsistent performance, or if users constantly have to tinker with it to get it to work right, user confidence drops off markedly. Intimidated users are not empowered users.

Nonetheless, the practical reality is that some of the most common, reliable, and affordable fault-tolerance techniques we have do not promote complete transparency. Some of them (switching your PC's connection from one network outlet to another, for instance) don't even approach what we sardonically refer to as "translucency."

Again, the three-way trade-off appears. How transparent does your system's fault tolerance need to be? Do you really need to protect against a low-level risk if the result of that protection is a longer, more complex user manual or training class and decreased user confidence? If a transparent solution is available, but it costs ten times as much to implement as the opaque one, which should you choose? What if it costs twenty times as much? Fifty times as much?

### Cost

At the end of the day, cost always becomes a constraint. System users always say they want 100% availability, 100% security, and 100% fault tolerance, yet no one's information technology budget is truly unlimited. Decisions about how much fault tolerance is required, which risks to protect against, and which ones to monitor and accept, are always constrained by how much is in the budget.

One of the main reasons to estimate risk and consequences, both for security and for fault tolerance, is to be able to justify technical decisions based on sound business logic. If you can show that a particular form of risk is likely to cost you X dollars over the next two years, then it makes sense to spend some fraction of X dollars now, to preclude that risk.

"Bulletproof" is a concept we believe in, and one that we promote widely, but there is wisdom in determining what type of fire your system is likely to take, and in spending limited system development dollars on the levels and forms of protection, both security and fault tolerance, that will give your system the best achievable chance of survival.

# 8

# Bulletproofing
# Client/Server Support

Consider the following true stories:

- A Colorado insurance company buys a very expensive support contract with the vendor of one of its client/server database systems. Surveying the company's technical staff reveals that the vendor is only able to answer one question out of four accurately, and vendor representatives often know less about the product than the insurance company's own support analysts.

- A Canadian accounting and consulting firm employs several hundred computer users who work with its client/server systems. The Help Desk that handles employee trouble calls is spotless—the unit's manager proudly points out that nary a manual or piece of paper is to be seen. A model of efficiency? The support analysts have to leave the Help Desk and go to a different room on the same floor to look anything up in a book, meaning that 90% of all incoming trouble calls must be handled on a call-back basis.

- At a New York bank, a top technical trainer quit to join an independent consulting firm because the bank wouldn't let her take time off from giving courses to learn about the products she was teaching to users and she wasn't able to answer questions about new versions and upgrades. Her frustration escalated to an intolerable level, and she also worried that her knowledge was growing outdated.

- A California defense contractor cuts computer support staff and dollars to a third of the prior year's levels while adopting a zero-defect management philosophy. It is unfashionable, even heretical, for managers to admit that anything the company creates, from defense weaponry to client/server applications, might not be perfect and trouble-free. The mere presence of a computer Help Desk flies in the face of zero defects, with the result that no midlevel or senior managers champion its effectiveness or even existence, making it a convenient target for cost-cutters. Users with computer problems no longer call the Help Desk unless there's absolutely no alternative, and when they do, they face an average wait time of 3 days.

- A Midwest real estate development company does not allow users to take computer classes on company time. The company president's dictum: Read the manuals—but do it at home. We're too busy for classes.

These stories suggest that many organizations are better at building client/server systems, difficult though that job can be, than they are at supporting them once they're in place. The result is a disconnect at the point of end use—where the computing rubber meets the road. We'll begin approaching this critical issue by defining what we mean by "support."

## Defining "Support"

*Support* means two things in the context of client/server computer systems:

- Educating everyone involved to avoid problems and work efficiently with the systems
- Providing effective mechanisms for resolving problems or questions

Bulletproofing design, performance, security, and fault tolerance—all examined in the previous chapters—will certainly make computer systems more reliable, but no computer system in existence is completely trouble-free. As we saw in one of the opening vignettes, getting some organizations to recognize this fact is no trivial matter.

Even when they do begin to understand the need for support, those organizations may define the concept too narrowly. Many companies think of support, when they do think about it, solely in terms of end users. However, the technicians and analysts who support end users also require their own support resources and system training. Bulletproofing support, therefore, means not only taking care of system users, but also taking care of those who take care of system users. It also means making allowances for the special case of executive education, as we'll see.

Bulletproofing education and problem management makes both computers and people more reliable—and this fact is the main reason this book's title contains the word "systems," because people comprise a key link in any client/server system. The best-designed client/server system won't pay off if employees only use it grudgingly, but uneducated and poorly supported computer users will not be motivated to make the system work. Rather, they'll find excuses for avoiding it, or worse, torpedoing it. We'll take a look at technical education, and then at problem management, to see what some of the common pitfalls are and how companies can bulletproof against them.

## Education Challenges

For users, perhaps the primary hurdle any technical education plan must face is that today's client/server systems and applications still aren't easy to use.

*Technojargon* gets in the way by forcing users to learn technical industry terms for which convenient English replacements often exist. It's a problem for technicians, too, who must master an ever-expanding vocabulary of acronyms and obscure alphanumeric product names.

*Command-oriented applications* get in the way, too. The *Wall Street Journal*'s Walter Mossberg has written about the many "secret handshakes," or nonmnemonic key combinations, that users must master to use today's systems. (Windows locks up on your PC? Press Ctrl-Alt-Del. Want to move to a previous data field? Press Shift-Tab.)

*User-ignorant systems* don't provide enough feedback or guidance. This is partly the result of the common practice of having the developers who work on the internal structure of computer programs also be the ones who design user interfaces. Don Norman, author of *The Design of Everyday Things*, believes that most programmers don't have the necessary skill sets for designing user interfaces. Indeed, because programmers conceptualize what a computer or system is doing differently than typical users do, Bruce Tognazzini (the former "User Interface Evangelist" of Apple Computer Co., now with Sun Microsystems) has stated that programmers are never the best people to design user interfaces.

If systems aren't easy to use, documentation is even less so. System manuals often assume knowledge that users do not have and fail to provide glossaries or indexes to help them understand foreign terms. They're often written by programmers who don't understand writing or by writers who don't understand the programs. Manuals often don't differentiate between key features and less-used advanced features: All are listed in alphabetical order, for example. Manuals are often bound so that they don't even allow the user to lay them out flat on the desk while working with the computer.

Another factor reducing ease of use as averaged over time is the *pace of change* of client/server software. The software industry is ramping up the frequency with which it issues product upgrades and enhancements in an attempt to regain the profits lost by fierce competition and large market penetration. With every new version, new training becomes necessary, and some prior training must be unlearned.

A final fact mitigating against ease of use is that the *complexity* of today's software applications is growing dramatically as software becomes bloated in size ("fatware"). We could debate whether software complexity produces less reliable systems, but it undeniably makes educating both users and technicians more time-consuming and difficult.

We'd be remiss if we didn't admit that graphical user interfaces have advanced ease of use in most cases. Our point is that if you take one step forward and three back, you're still going backward.

## Bulletproofing Education

### Demonstrating and Reinforcing the Need

Senior managers who don't understand client/server systems tend to minimize their complexity. Naive business managers who believe industry claims about ease of use are not only less likely to allocate funds for user education, they're more likely to

believe that they can hire technicians who already know everything about the technology and won't require education, either.

A large part of bulletproofing technical education, therefore, is
educating decision makers about the realities of client/server
products' ease of use, as discussed in the preceding section; that
is, demonstrating the need. Once that's achieved, it's important
to reinforce management support for an aggressive education
program by demonstrating the return on that investment wherever possible.

- A division of one Atlanta soft-drink company does this by asking employees to write up a list of specific benefits following
  every computer class or seminar they attend. (This is not a bad
  technique for winnowing out the less valuable training sessions, also.)
- Motorola performed a study concluding that each dollar spent
  on computer education returned 30 dollars in productivity
  gains over 3 years.

Bulletproofers will amass support for their position that technical education makes sense, and they will present that support to
key decision makers and system "champions" on a periodic basis.

### Allocating the People

Many companies don't offer much in the way of computer education because the in-house computer staff are too busy fighting fires,
designing new networks, and implementing new technologies. The
typical response is to outsource computer education, and U.S. companies spend about $4 billion annually doing just that, according to
market researcher Dataquest. External training sources include
product vendors, public seminars, independent training companies, and diversified accounting and consulting firms.

There are risks in outsourcing technical training, however.
Vendor trainers may not understand how their product is being
used in a particular organization and therefore won't tailor their
classes around features that organization uses most heavily.
Single-vendor classes also don't typically address issues of inter-
operability with other vendors' products, an issue of real-world
concern to many users. For political reasons, vendor trainers
aren't likely to dwell on products bugs and limitations, which
are of primary concern to technicians and analysts who must
support the products.

The outsourcing decision seems to hinge on the uniqueness of the organization's client/server systems. The more highly customized the system, the less likely it is that outsourced education will prove satisfactory, in which case bulletproofers will ensure that project budgets include staff provisions for ongoing (*not* one-time) technical education for both users and technicians. If technical education isn't in the system budget, it can be very difficult to gain authorization for later.

### Teaching the Right Material

There is a common assumption about training users to operate a business computer system—that the developers of the system know the best way to operate it. However, as we said earlier, the users are the real experts in business problems and system use. What system developers can teach is the way the system was *intended* to be used, but that's not always the *best* way to operate it.

In fact, for custom client/server applications, we've found that the best ideas for new and creative ways to use the system come from the user community. System training can still provide value, not by instructing new users in how the system *should* be used, but by helping the majority of users learn techniques originated by the most creative among them. Often, the scenario will go something like this:

- Initial training will be designed and delivered by the systems analysts who worked on the system requirements (functional, performance, operational, and process). This training will be given to acceptance testers and pilot users of the new software, but will be phrased *as suggestions, not as the only way to use the system.*

- During acceptance testing and pilot use of the software, certain users will prove more efficient and effective at using the system. These users can be identified visually, or by automated productivity statistics. The systems analysts/trainers determine what techniques make these individuals productive, and redesign system training to feature those techniques before training the bulk of system users.

- Three to six months after system implementation, the most productive users are identified, their techniques studied, and a second round of training ("technology updates" if politically necessary) is conducted.

- Six to twelve months after implementation, the process is repeated.

It's difficult to perform a double-blind study to measure the benefits of this training approach, but real-world experience has convinced us that its benefits far exceed its costs. It does require that the Information Technology department practice a certain humility and recognize the contribution of the user community, so it's not easy to implement in all organizations.

### Defining Subject Matter

Organizations making plans for technical education typically take a product focus, laying out a curriculum to cover each of the various modules and applications within the new system. We have seen many cases where problems occur because end users are product literate but not computer literate; that is, they understand what specific commands do within a specific application, but they do not understand how RAM memory (primary storage) differs from disk memory (secondary storage).

One bulletproofing suggestion, therefore, is to ensure that end users have access to a core curriculum in computer and network basics so that they can see forests and not just trees. Data entry clerks don't necessarily have to understand the details of middleware, but they are likely to ask fewer simple questions and make fewer obvious mistakes if they understand computer fundamentals. For example, a core computer curriculum might address some of the following points:

- Why leaving for lunch with your PC logged into the network might create a security problem
- What computer viruses are, and how they can enter a network
- How to tell when a workstation is malfunctioning
- Where to get help for computer problems, either within or outside the organization
- How to use corporate e-mail systems
- How to back up local data files that aren't stored on the network
- How to type

## Documentation that Works

Great documentation remains a rarity in the world of information systems. However, it's a key element of any successful education plan, because great documentation not only permits user education, it facilitates it. What are some ways organizations can create useful end user documentation?

- One way is to limit its *quantity*. Too much documentation may be even worse than too little. Providing excessive detail in user manuals contributes to the user perception that these manuals are overwhelming and intimidating. It can also encourage software and hardware "tinkering" by users who aren't trained in those areas, creating unnecessary configuration problems that can be time-consuming to troubleshoot.

- Another way is to improve its *physical format*. Manuals that don't lend themselves to easy updating provide an excellent example: A perfect-bound or spiral-bound book must be completely replaced when an updated version comes out, meaning that any marginal notes or dog-eared pages in the older version hit the trash can. Loose-leaf binders are much to be preferred in this regard.

- Bulletproofers might want to consider providing convenient "guides to the guides," such as two- or three-page summaries of key product features at the front of the book, with appropriate references to the more detailed chapters or sections that follow.

- Documentation can be greatly improved by the simple step of having it prepared or even just edited by *experienced writers*. The same expertise and familiarity with technical terminology that helps programmers and developers create useful applications can work against them when they try to explain the use of those applications to nonexperts.

- Another idea for improving printed documentation is to break out sections for beginners and for advanced users separately. Many software companies have begun using this model, and users seem to prefer it.

- Finally, putting documentation online in the form of electronic hypertext "help" files has the appeal of making user manuals continually available and easily searchable. There can be significant expense associated with digitizing printed manuals, but one long-term benefit that may outweigh the initial cost is

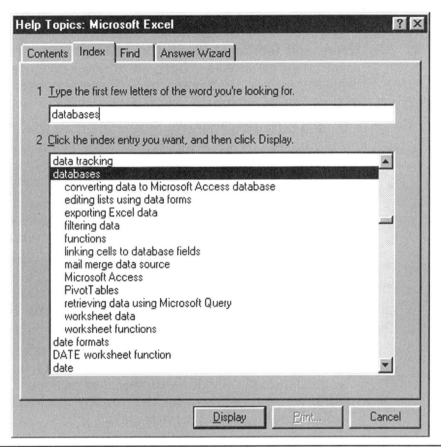

**Figure 8.1:** A Flexible Online Help System

that such documents can be updated and distributed much less expensively. It's important to recognize with online documentation that special design skills are required: the "page size" is less than half that of a printed page, for example, and there are practical limits on the complexity of an on-screen document.

- Figure 8.1 shows a flexible online help system engine used in Windows 95. Users can navigate the system using a book-and-chapter metaphor, a searchable index (shown), a full-text search engine ("Find"), or a procedure-oriented "Answer Wizard." Several third-party tools exist for companies wanting to create their own customized help systems with this engine.

### Maximizing Training Benefit

Users and technical staff alike may attend numerous technical seminars and classes, both in-house and outsourced, but not reap the maximum benefit from those expensive sessions. Some of the reasons include the following:

- Inadequate prescreening of technical courses results in users and analysts alike attending courses at an inappropriate level of expertise—either too fundamental to provide useful new information or too advanced to be understandable.
- Technical staff and employees alike often carry cell phones or pagers that permit their technical training sessions to be interrupted to the point that learning becomes difficult or even impossible.
- After the course, employees return to work to face a backlog of e-mail and phone messages which they scurry to clear, not leaving time to practice and reinforce the concepts they've learned.
- Course attendees don't document the sessions adequately. If they don't take notes for transcription and distribution to colleagues, and if they don't tape-record or even videotape the sessions where permissible, the course's value is transient and limited to the individual attendee.

To bulletproof against the inefficiencies of typical technical seminar attendance, then, an organization could take the following specific steps:

- Ensure that a technically knowledgeable individual screen proposed seminars with an eye to the appropriate level of expertise required.
- Arrange for education to be delivered in an environment free of interruptions, by designating others to take attendee calls and pages.
- Allocate time for employees to reinforce what they learn at seminars and classes after they conclude.
- Urge employees to document training sessions by taking notes and recording sessions so that the knowledge can be shared with their colleagues later, at least to some extent.

Some of these suggestions are illustrated in the time-line diagram of Figure 8.2.

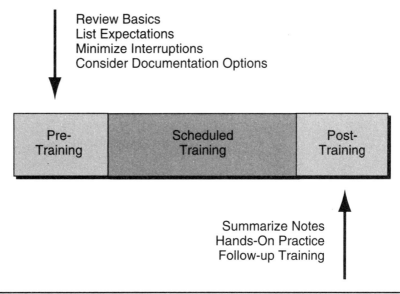

**Figure 8.2:**   Maximizing Training Benefit

## Creative Instruction Delivery Methods

"Instruction delivery methods" is usually a fancy way of saying user manuals. Printed documentation is necessary, but it's usually not sufficient. Providing several avenues for both system users and system technicians to learn is key to accommodating individual differences in learning style. Some people learn well from printed materials: Sit them down with a good manual and a workstation, and they can advance quickly, especially if they have previous experience with computers. Others learn well in a structured classroom-type environment. Still others can learn on their own, but need guided Computer-Based Training (CBT) programs to provide a greater degree of structure than user manuals provide.

Let's take a look at four different avenues for delivering technical education: personalized hands-on, straight lecture, CBT, and "just-in-time" (see Figure 8.3).

**Personalized Hands-On**   Training users on specific applications is probably best accomplished in a learning-lab environment, where a professional instructor leads a small group of similarly expert users through a series of exercises that the users can perform on workstations at their desks. Technology is available for setting up such a learning lab so that the instructor can "take

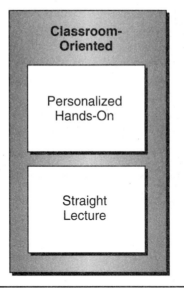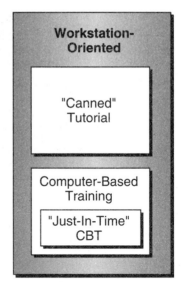

**Figure 8.3:** Instruction Delivery Methods

over" each PC to demonstrate a procedure, then relinquish control to them while they run through it themselves in a "learn by doing" paradigm. The users' active involvement means two things: The amount of material that can be covered in a given period of time is limited, but retention is significantly better than in a nonparticipatory setting such as a straight lecture environment.

**Straight Lecture**  The straight lecture format has the advantages of covering a greater volume of material per hour to a larger number of students. Its disadvantages include lower retention and more difficulty in determining how well individuals are assimilating the material.

Making lecture sessions as informal as possible, setting aside time for question-and-answer sessions, including quiz questions after every subtopic, and incorporating numerous demonstrations (e.g., with notebook PCs and LCD projectors) are all ways to help bulletproof against the disadvantages of this training format.

**Computer-Based Training**  Computer-based training (CBT) is gaining in popularity because of its low cost compared to the preceding two methods and because of the increasing ability of the average desktop PC to handle graphics and multimedia elements (such as interactive screen demos, animation, and even digitized video). The approach is hands-on, self-paced, highly interactive, available and repeatable on demand, and individualized, but the CBT software itself can be distributed to every desktop at low cost by direct downloading, CD-ROM, or even running the software from designated LAN servers where modern high-speed and switching network hubs permit sufficient bandwidth. CBT is well suited for delivery via the corporate *intranets* that are gaining popularity.

The better CBT applications modify lesson plans on the fly to accommodate the particular expertise levels and needs of individual students. Many "authoring" applications now exist to permit trainers and analysts to prepare their own CBT courseware without having to learn the intricacies of 4GL or procedural languages.

**"Just-In-Time" Training**   A relatively new trend in technical education takes a page out of the manufacturing technique known as kanban, or "just-in-time," where component parts arrive at the plant when and where they're needed. Although this method poses risks for manufacturers during an extended supplier strike, as the 1996 GM brake-components supplier strike made very clear, it makes a lot of sense as a supplement to the other three training delivery methods discussed here.

The idea is that online or CD-ROM programs, or tech-note fax-on-demand ("fax-back") systems, offer highly targeted education on applications and procedures that users can consult just before they need to learn those procedures. Kanban CBT requires a high degree of material organization by topic and subtopic, and a high degree of lesson modularization, but it may better reflect how people actually use their computer systems than the more traditional methods of intensive classes supplemented by reference documentation in printed form. It also shares the CBT benefit of being impossible to "lose."

## Technician Education Notes

Poor or inadequate technician education is a common reason client/server computing projects fail. Client/server expert Raymond Martin (no relation) has said that "moving the cavalry from horses to helicopters with nothing more than a set of manuals is a quick way to ensure the troops' ignominious death."

Expecting technicians to learn a whole new computing paradigm by reading books and trade journals is wildly unrealistic.

Whereas end users may acquire basic expertise through online tutorials and CBT, technicians and support analysts require a certain amount of technical education in an interactive format, where they can pose specific questions to technology experts.

It's also relevant to note that technical support analysts who must deal with a wide variety of end users must possess not only technical skills, but sophisticated communications skills as well. Not every computer expert is an expert at interacting with novice users or busy executives. However, the marketplace offers a wealth of seminar opportunities for technical analysts to refine their communications skills, so that they can listen better, minimize misunderstandings, speak to users in terms they understand, avoid wasting time on the phone, and provide solutions in a way that does not demean, confuse, or intimidate the user—guaranteeing that the user will not hesitate to call again next week when another problem rears its ugly head.

### The Special Case of Executive Education

We conclude our look at the education side of computer support by mentioning a unique audience that many organizations overlook: the reluctant executive. These individuals are using client/server systems more and more for decision support, yet in many cases their special needs aren't considered by technical education programs. What are those needs?

- Senior managers may not do well in a mixed-classroom environment because they don't want to appear computer illiterate in front of peers or subordinates
- Executives prefer minimalist education that focuses on the practical aspects of accomplishing a small number of frequently performed tasks, such as generating summary reports with a database query module
- These individuals may have very limited computer background in terms of the basics of using the keyboard and mouse
- These individuals are often unable to set aside large contiguous blocks of time for intensive, seminar-type classes

Some successful responses to the particular needs of this group have included the following:

- Classes focusing on using systems for communications, e.g., e-mail and groupware

- Technology briefings that provide high-level, nondetailed overviews of key computing trends, with a minimum of techno-jargon
- Computer "boot camps" for executives only, perhaps held off-site, such as those offered by CEO Institutes and Computer Associates
- One-on-one sessions rather than group classes

## Problem Management Challenges

OK—we plan to educate both our end users and our support technicians to bulletproof against breakdowns on the human side of the keyboard. Everyone with any experience in the field knows that despite the most thorough and aggressive program of employee training, users and technicians alike are still going to run into problems. Many modern trends increase the likelihood of this happening; we've looked at some of these already in particular contexts:

- Few organizations can afford, or can justify, total fault tolerance for computer hardware.
- Today's systems mix and match hardware and software from many different vendors, creating an unmanageably large universe of possible problematic interactions.
- Industry standards may lag product development by several years, so products are not designed with a uniform set of specifications or rules.
- In distributed computing, the physical environment is no longer a controllable variable, and users and technicians alike can make hardware and software modifications in the field much more easily than in the days of "glass houses."
- Software vendors who have traditionally offered application support are easing out of the business. Vendor-supplied system and application software support is increasingly expensive and decreasingly competent.
- Software vendors who now charge high fees for support have less motivation to design reliable products, as support contracts now represent significant revenue. Stratford Sherman has commented in *Fortune* that "One of the remarkable aspects

of the [computer] business is the way it first causes you horrific problems, and then takes your money to solve them."

- Computer user populations are typically growing faster than support staff populations.
- Many managers don't realize any of these trends and don't appreciate how problematic their systems can be, largely because they don't interact with the systems on a daily basis themselves.
- Those same managers may believe vendor support to be much more efficient than it is, for the same reasons.
- Managers tend to project their mainframe and minicomputer budgeting models to client/server systems, failing to recognize that distributed systems support typically costs as least three times as much, as estimated by Forrester Research Inc.

## Consequences of Inadequate Technical Support

What happens when users and technicians can't get fast, accurate responses to questions and problems? The usual effect is that costs are shifted from the IS organization to the user community, where they become impossible to track, correct, budget for, or manage. Specific problems include the following:

- Employees avoid using the systems companies have created
- Employees will use the systems, but avoid advanced features
- Users try to fix problems themselves, wasting time and often making things worse
- Users and technicians alike become frustrated and "burn out"
- Serious system problems never get fixed
- Expensive system designers have to spend time on support issues

It should be obvious that these consequences can be extremely expensive, and can even negate many of the productivity gains client/server computing promised in the first place.

## Bulletproofing Problem Management

### Building a Case

The shifting paradigm of client/server computing means that more users have access to more data than ever before. Those users will therefore be doing more with their computing tools. Increasing functionality means increasing use, and an increasing need for help when things go awry.

Just as we saw with technical education, so it is with technical support: Project managers and client/server implementers must build a case for it to garner sufficient management support. We have seen time and again that organizations in a cost-cutting mode tend to reduce expenditures on activities that are widely perceived by senior management as being ancillary, or nonessential to core business activities. The attitude often evidenced is that of the company president in the opening vignette who believes that if computer users run into a problem, they can consult the manual and figure it out.

Managers know that hiring (or keeping) people, especially technical support people with both good communications skills and strong technical background, is expensive. What benefits does a human support analyst bring that the online resources discussed above don't? Flexibility, for one: A human technician can advise a user on a temporary workaround while working to achieve a permanent fix. Interactivity, for another: A support analyst can quickly explain the answer to a technical question, taking the user's knowledge level into account. People are still better than computers at recognizing patterns, recalling past experience, and applying analytical logic to guide them when troubleshooting problems. We should also mention understanding: The ability to empathize with a frustrated user's concerns and fears and feelings of inadequacy when that user can't seem to get the system to do what he or she needs it to do.

Convincing management of the desirability of providing strong technical support for end users, whether provided internally or outsourced, hinges not on demonstrating how many minutes per day the support function can save, or whether it can decrease time to resolution for user problems, or whether it contributes to computer literacy. It hinges, instead, on demonstrating that the support function contributes in some significant way to the organization's business goals. Can good tech support help win new customers, keep existing ones, improve time to market, reduce the cost of goods sold, free up technical experts to design new networks to enhance interdepartmental communication, or improve service quality? Focus on building a case for such assertions and you're much more likely to garner management support for your Help Desk than by talking about reducing hold times on the tech support hot line as an end in itself.

## The Help Desk

The first step in bulletproofing problem management for users is to institute a Help Desk: a formal unit whose primary responsibility is the timely resolution of users' technical questions and problems, with the goal of maximizing their productivity and minimizing downtime. The Help Desk might be one person in a smaller organization, it might be two hundred in a larger company. It might consist of seasoned technical experts, or it might be a "technical switchboard" where first-level analysts direct trouble calls to the appropriate technical group. It's a key bulletproofing step because it offers the convenience of a single phone number for users to call: a one-stop shop.

Many organizations have "islands" of support: an application help center, a network help center, a hardware maintenance group, and so on. Bulletproof against user frustration, problem resolution delays, and finger-pointing syndrome by consolidating support groups into a central clearinghouse for all information technology questions.

Some of the advantages of a centralized computer support unit include the following:

- Faster responses
- Faster solutions
- Documentation and tracking of all requests
- Offloading of specialists and experts from routine support responsibilities
- Promotion of company technology standards through problem prioritization
- Convenience of one-stop shopping in an increasingly complex computer environment
- Localization of responsibility for the support function
- Documentation to provide trend identification and, ultimately, improvements in systems, documentation, and training

## Defining the Support Role

Help Centers are often pulled in many different directions, which limits their ability to meet any single objective successfully. Bulletproofers know that it's worth spending time defining the Help Desk mission statement to minimize wasted effort. Commonly assumed support goals may often be at odds with each other; for example, if the support staff is charged both with resolving problems as quickly as possible, and with educating users so that they won't make the same mistakes over and over again, analysts don't know whether to fix a problem themselves with a minimum of communication or take the time to explain what they're doing so the user can understand it and do it himself next time.

A good way to bulletproof against this problem is to make the support group's overarching objective to increase user productivity. That is, get the user up and running as soon as possible, either by performing some remote administration, swapping hardware components, or rerouting output to a different printer, then later spend a few moments with the user if appropriate to correct procedural problems or mistakes of comprehension.

Some of the possible Help Desk objectives to consider are

- Reduce problem frequency in the future
- Reduce user question frequency
- Improve system flexibility
- Increase workstation and network uptime
- Improve system performance (speed) when possible
- Improve user understanding
- Identify trends: problem products, growth patterns, training issues, design issues
- Improve user documentation
- Improve ability to isolate problems quickly
- Solve problems with a minimum number of people involved

Another key question to resolve in the design of any computer support unit is whether to focus on *technology* assistance or *procedural* assistance. The technology support unit will answer technical questions and stop there. The procedural support unit will consider the user's situation in light of company policies and procedures and provide advice oriented toward getting the user's job done, using the available technology as a tool in a broader context. Traditionally, computer support units have focused on providing technology support ("Do I transmit a departmental requisition form using the corporate e-mail system as an ASCII or binary file?"), but procedural support might be more useful ("What steps do I take to requisition computer hardware for my project team?").

Finally, bulletproof against support organizations that don't meet user needs by periodically asking the users what they feel they need. Is fast response their top priority? Organize the unit so that a person handles the calls initially, takes down essential information, and arranges for a suitably expert technician to call the user back—don't make users wait on hold for 20 minutes because each call is being fully and painstakingly resolved in a serial fashion. When Stac Electronics, a disk-compression software firm, implemented such a call-back scheme, 90% of their customers got the information they needed with a smaller total time investment. Is convenient reporting for lower-priority calls a hot button? Set up a fax line or e-mail account so that users can document their nonurgent questions or problems and submit them via fax or e-mail, again avoiding long wait times on the phone. Surveying client/server system users a couple of times a year can yield great insights about what users want and need from a support organization.

The end result of efforts to define the support role should be a Help Center mission statement (short, static) and charter (more detailed, periodically revised). These documents, far from being mere writing exercises, can provide the following concrete benefits:

- A written vehicle for discussing the support function with managers and users, to ensure relevance
- A convenient means for educating users as to available support services
- A starting point for creating support analyst job descriptions
- A philosophical basis for prioritizing support requests
- A means of preventing the support group from becoming a "catch-all" unit that is assigned tasks that don't advance its mission
- A better image of the support group within the organization
- A baseline document for comparing against during periodic performance evaluations

## Staffing Up

One of the first mistakes organizations make when planning a support staff is to use industry rules of thumb for estimating how many analysts and technicians will be required to adequately support X number of end users. It's necessary to start with an estimate, of course, but that number should never be cast in stone from the outset. Many variables can affect the user-to-technician ratio that's appropriate for a given company:

- *Support Staff Responsibilities*. If the staff is also responsible for workstation installation and setup, hardware preventive maintenance, training, etc., then the ratio must be less than if the staff's time is dedicated entirely to phone support.

- *User Sophistication*. A computer-literate population may or may not require a lower support staff ratio than a naive population. When the more sophisticated users do ask questions, they're typically more difficult ones, requiring more time and effort per call.

- *Analyst Expertise Levels*. Less-expert technicians will spend more time in training and less on direct support, necessitating a higher analyst-to-user ratio.

- *Service Level Commitments*. Help Desks committed to solving 90% of all problems within ten minutes will generally need more analysts than support units committed to solving 10% of all problems within one hour.

The second common mistake in assembling the personnel plan is to underestimate the salary levels required to attract individuals with strong technical and communications skills. These kinds of people are among the most desirable and marketable available, and the salary structure should reflect that reality. It's also necessary to build in a growth path, or job ladder, so that ambitious and high-performing support analysts don't need to move outside the support organization to advance within the company—necessary, that is, if keeping their expertise and talent is a priority! Analyst turnover in support centers is high (the average stay is 18 months), and poor opportunity for advancement is a primary reason.

### Avoiding Burnout

Any service organization, especially those chartered to deal with problems or complaints, must concern itself with burnout, or job fatigue. Over 70% of technical support staff report moderate to severe burnout after only a year and a half on the job. Typical burnout symptoms include

- Exhaustion (whether through excessive hours or excessive, unrelenting pressure)
- Detachment—that is, an excessive separation between one's self and one's work
- Boredom (usually the result of doing the same things all the time)
- Cynicism—that is, questioning the validity or helpfulness of one's organizational role
- Impatience (usually with end users)
- Irritability
- Feeling unappreciated (usually a result of low Help Desk visibility)
- Feeling indispensable ("If I take all of my vacation time, the place will fall apart.")
- Rigidity—that is, going by published policies and procedures to avoid thinking of creative solutions to user problems
- Negativity

Among the best ways to bulletproof against technician burnout are these:

- Career path clarification ("What is this job preparing me for later on?")
- Task diversification (changing responsibilities periodically)
- Adequate training (time to read manuals, in-house training, outside seminars, etc.)
- Positive feedback (from users and from peers)
- Sustainable workload pacing (achieved through prioritization and proper staffing levels)
- Physical comfort (equipment and furniture ergonomics, lighting, noise, etc.)
- Respect from within the organization (prerequisite: publication of Help Desk performance statistics)

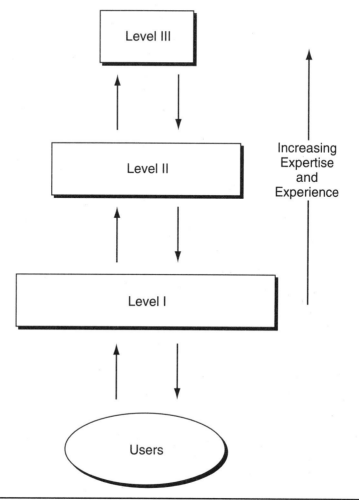

**Figure 8.4:** A Typical Three-Tiered User Support Organization

- Rewards for performance (based on well-understood performance criteria)

### Helping the Helpers

Help Center analysts may support system users, but who supports them? Larger organizations often set up a tiered support structure (IBM's terminology is Level I, Level II, and Level III) providing an escalation path to more experienced and expert technicians when lower-level technicians can't solve a problem in a given period of time or after a predefined sequence of steps (see Figure 8.4). Today, it's possible to provide Level I analysts with some sophisticated tools that can reduce the frequency of such escalations. This is highly desirable, because problem escalations are extremely expensive in terms of resolution time for users and technical staff time for the troubleshooters.

What are some of the weapons that we can provide Level I Help Center analysts to reduce escalation frequency and increase the percentage of calls that get resolved with a single phone call?

- A complete technical reference library is one. It should include complete user documentation as well as supplemental technical documentation. It may also include industry periodicals, but the utility of a magazine reference shelf can be enhanced greatly by CD-ROM databases, such as Information Access Company's Computer Select product, that permit keyword searching of tens of thousands of magazine articles at one time.

- Online documentation from product vendors is another arrow in the tech support person's quiver. Microsoft's TechNet CD-ROM, for example, contains the same set of technical notes on products such as SQL Server as Microsoft support representatives consult when called by customers. Novell's CD-ROM Support Encyclopedia is another example of electronically searchable technical documentation. Digital Equipment Corporation makes nearly all of its product documentation available on CD-ROM. The ability to search vast amounts of technical material by key words and product names in a matter of seconds is a tremendous benefit for support personnel.

- Vendor bulletin boards and Internet sites can be an excellent source of bug notes, tech bulletins, and product patches.

These weapons can be highly effective, but by far the most powerful tool in the support analyst's possession is the Help Center's database of problems and solutions (see "Features of Good Help Desk Software"). Every client/server system has its own set of unique characteristics: design choices, combinations of products, usage procedures, and so on. The problem management database is the only online reference that accurately reflects the specific client/server systems in use at that organization.

## FEATURES OF GOOD HELP DESK SOFTWARE

Probably four or five dozen reasonably good Help Desk automation tools are now available. How can you distinguish between them? We've put together a short but suggestive list of features to consider.

- Shareability. There are degrees to which Help Desk software is truly "multiuser." Clearly, several support technicians may need to use the system simultaneously, but also consider the circumstances in which one technician may be locked out of a record in use by another. Also, ask whether "Level II" or "Level III" technicians, to whom the Help Desk may need to refer knotty technical problems or questions, can easily access the Help Desk tracking system (e.g., for recording solution information). Finally, what would be involved in extending the problem reporting system to end users, so they could submit their own incident reports on line? (The latter generally only works with relatively sophisticated users who understand the need to provide adequate detail.)

- Multitasking and multiwindowing. It's important for Help Desk analysts to be able to actually run a user application in one window while running the problem management system in another (usually omnipresent) window. It's not uncommon for support analysts to have several windows open on-screen at any given time, linked to several different systems, applications, or servers. What is the problem management system's performance impact in a multitasking environment? How much memory does it require to run briskly?

- Speed of data entry. A key to convincing technical support staff to even use a problem tracking system at all is streamlining it for input speed. No analyst will want to document a one-minute call if the documentation process takes three minutes. Keys to speed of data entry are the ability to program default values for most fields, the ability to "look up" user and configuration data based on index fields, such as a property tag number or user phone number, and, for analysts new to the Help Desk, the use of field-level pop-up windows to correlate alphanumeric codes with verbose descriptions.

- Flexibility of data entry. Does the system permit the support analyst to record information supplied by the end user in any sequence, e.g., by pointing and clicking, or does it impose a rigid order for keying in data fields? Can Help Desk managers and analysts design different screen forms for different situations, or does the software impose a monolithic, "one-size-fits-all" data entry form?

- Programmable callback reminders. Can the system prompt the technician that, for example, "it's time to call Wendy Jones back at extension 339 to verify that her report ran correctly this month"?

- Compatibility with common database formats. Better problem tracking systems permit easy importing of data from existing databases to load the inventory and user data tables. For example, client system hardware configuration data might be already available in a purchasing system database; user profile data (phone, address, department, etc.) might already be available in a human resources database.

- Speed of historical searches. How well does the software perform when performing keyword searches through thousands of records?

- Flexibility of historical searches. Does the search engine permit boolean logic, or is it limited to a list of key words? Can analysts search on any data field, or just the statements of problem and solution? Can a default date range (e.g., the past six months) be programmed into the system, or must it be specified with each search? Does the search engine provide a "synonym dictionary" for matching records with equivalent, but not identical, key words? Can the software perform proximity searches; that is, can it find words specified to be within X number of words of each other?

- Canned reports. How many predefined reports come standard with the product? How many of those match your needs? You don't want to have to spend a great deal of time with a report generator.

- Report generator. However, you do need one for those few special reports you need to generate that the software creators didn't anticipate. How easy is it to use? Can it easily cumulate data over time periods you specify? Can it generate reports in the form of disk files that you can use to feed spreadsheet templates? Does it "do" graphs?

- Availability and cost of customizations and/or source code. Some problem management system vendors provide their software "as is" and do not offer customizations; others can customize the product to fit your special needs, but the cost of doing so varies widely. If the tracking system is built on a standard database platform, you may be able to perform your own modifications in-house, in which case the availability and cost of source code becomes significant.

- Availability of a knowledge base module. Whether this is a sophisticated, pattern-matching advisory module or an elaborate programmable decision tree, some form of knowledge base can save technicians a great deal of time. The better ones learn on their own and don't require periodic manual redefining of logical decision trees.

Experienced staff with programming talent can certainly create their own custom support database systems; however, doing so is probably not the best use of their time, and the questions of who will document the system and upgrade and maintain it over time deserve serious review. The range of commercially available software, in terms of both cost and features, is wide enough today that no organization with one or more full-time technical support analysts has to go without a commercially available problem tracking tool. Whether it costs $100 or $100,000, such a tool helps analysts avoid researching what has already been researched and recording what has already been recorded, and is one of the best ways to bulletproof client/server system support. It will also enable IS managers to identify trends and target areas for future improvement—and this, in fact, is where its greatest value lies.

## The Problem Management Database

Figure 8.5 shows the typical organization of a problem management database system. Ask any Help Center manager to estimate the percentage of trouble calls that are unique and have never been reported before by any other computer user, and it will always be less than 50%. Most problems are repeat problems. However, support organizations commonly waste a tremendous amount of time reinventing the wheel, troubleshooting anew problems that were resolved (often by a different technician) only weeks or months before.

Of course, the utility of any problem management database hinges on the dedication of technicians in properly documenting the problems and solutions they encounter and provide. That's not always something that technicians are highly motivated to do, especially with twenty pending trouble calls in the hold queue. It's the responsibility of support managers to make online documentation a top priority. It slows response time in the short run, but speeds it up in the long run as the database grows and becomes a more useful tool. Bulletproof further against the problem of inadequate problem documentation by customizing the design of the trouble ticket entry screen to use system defaults and field lookups wherever possible, to minimize the amount of redundant and unnecessary data entry the support analyst must perform.

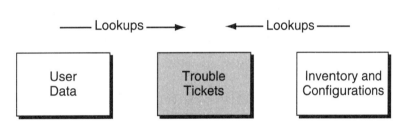

**Figure 8.5:** Problem Management Database Design

Combining a problem management database with an inventory database can be a powerful way to save support analyst and end user time. Often, the first step in resolving a problem is to determine what specific software and hardware a user is running. Few users, however, are prepared to provide that information to any useful level of detail. A common response to the problem is to build a software and hardware inventory database so that Help Desk analysts can quickly punch up a list on the screen. (In the most sophisticated systems, the database is indexed by the user's phone extension, which an internal caller ID system detects automatically, displaying configuration details on the analyst's screen almost immediately after the call comes in—much like the "911" systems most major U.S. cities use to identify caller addresses.)

Creating a comprehensive database, however, and keeping it up to date, can be a massive task. Andrew Grove, Intel's CEO, commented in the *Wall Street Journal* that "Nobody has a clue where all that stuff is." Many organizations change workstation and server configurations so frequently that maintaining an accurate, current inventory isn't a practical idea. In that case, the support staff should explore software that can remotely query PCs on an ad hoc basis to determine configuration details. Network Management Systems (NMSs) often include such capability, and workstation operating systems (such as Windows 95) that support remote querying can facilitate it. It might be limited, and not completely accurate, but it might be better than nothing.

### Automated Troubleshooting Assistance

It's not too fashionable nowadays to speak about "expert systems"—the term, if not the technology, has been so widely applied as to be almost meaningless—but many Help Center problem management systems do offer automated troubleshooting assistance in one form or another. These systems learn from experience, and advise the analyst about probable problem causes based on past history (see Figure 8.6).

Whether the underlying technology uses decision trees, neural-network pattern matching, or simple keyword searching, it can often help analysts solve more common problems faster than they could do otherwise and is worth exploring when shopping for problem management software.

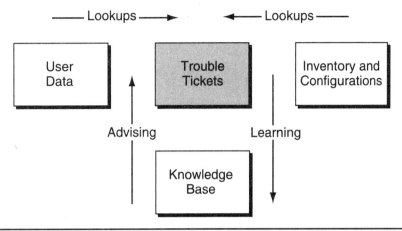

**Figure 8.6:**  Adding Intelligence to Problem Management Systems

## Marketing Support Services

Most technical support centers are so busy, they don't devote any time to promoting their operation to users and managers. The benefits of marketing support services include the following:

- Greater end user awareness
- Greater service utilization
- Higher user satisfaction levels
- Increased user productivity
- Easier justification for training, staff, and equipment
- Lower technician job fatigue
- Greater technician visibility and motivation
- Greater likelihood of continued management support

What are some elements of a "marketing plan" for the support center? For one, performance reporting. The Help Desk should distribute periodic (e.g., semiannual) memos summarizing improvements in service levels. For another, awareness promotion. The Help Desk won't be successful by any yardstick unless users know of its existence: a support newsletter, a listing in the computer user manual, flyers detailing access methods and hours of operation, periodic e-mail bulletins, and the like can help raise user awareness. For support units that must support geographically remote sites, a once-yearly junket in which a support manager or articulate technician visits major branch locations to speak to (and listen to) users can be a valuable and informative goodwill gesture. Follow-up calls and occasional user surveys, with published results, can also enhance user perceptions and increase the likelihood that they'll use in-house support services.

### Closing Feedback Loops

We often surprise those who attend our technical seminars by asserting that the most important long-term function of a Help Center is not the everyday resolution of user problems and answering of technical questions. Rather, the key organizational benefit of a properly implemented support center is the gathering of intelligence about what's going wrong out there in the field and how changes in training, documentation, and even system design can correct those problems.

For those changes to occur, the organization must ensure that problem management data does not reach a dead end at the Help Center, but rather flows back to system designers, trainers, and documentation specialists so that those persons can evaluate what's working and what's not in these three areas and take steps to improve matters. Which hardware products seem to have a higher failure rate than others? Which data entry or query screens seem to be the most unintuitive for users to understand? What sorts of features are users requesting, that might make sense to include in the next upgrade of the client-side software? Are the users able to make heads or tails out of the manuals or online help systems, and if so, which ones seem more useful than others? Which concepts are getting across in company computer classes, and which aren't, based on the kinds of questions and problems users are reporting?

Mining the tech-support database for the answers to these sorts of questions will increase the reliability, usability, and productivity of client/server systems over time. Failing to do so ensures that the same old problems will keep recurring and needed improvements will take longer to achieve—if they ever occur at all.

There are other steps that companies can take to close feedback loops and take advantage of the support staff's experience and knowledge. For example, the support group can become involved in the design and/or selection of new computer products. Support analysts, by virtue of their frequent interaction

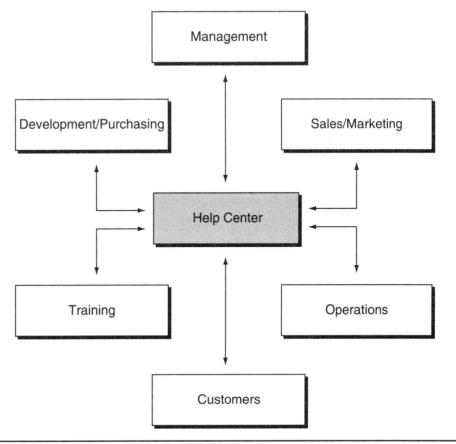

**Figure 8.7:**   Help Center Organizational Links

with end users, become experts in usability and supportability. Taking advantage of that expertise is a more productive approach than simply saying to support analysts, "Here's what's out there, now support it." Figure 8.7 shows how a productive support center will establish bidirectional communication channels to maximize its effectiveness.

We've seen in this chapter that great technology won't make client/server systems successful without attending to user and technician needs for adequate education on that technology, and for efficient support when the technology doesn't work smoothly. Organizations that include an aggressive education and support plan for their client/server systems from day one of implementation take a giant step toward success—and toward productively applying today's most exciting organizational computing model.

# 9

# Intranets and Extranets

Intranets and extranets form a uniquely appealing subset of client/server technology—indeed, a subset that may ultimately prove more successful than many more "traditional" types of client/server system—so we close this book with a concise look at these new types of systems and a few ideas for how we might go about bulletproofing them.

## Defining Intranets and Extranets

We defined intranets in Chapter 3 as networks using technologies that were developed for the Internet, such as Web servers and Internet e-mail, on an internal network for internal customers. Extending the concept somewhat, extranets are intranets that a company makes available to those with whom it does business, primarily customers and suppliers. In their simplest form, intranets and extranets merely put a Web front end onto data that's already available.

Intranets and extranets are becoming very well accepted in the corporate world—so much so, that International Data Corporation forecasts that intranet server licenses will outpace Internet server licenses ten to one by the year 2000.

Intranets are already very popular for publishing certain types of information that most employees have a need to see, and Human Resource departments have been among the earliest adopters of intranet systems, which are now moving into the realm of line-of-business enterprise applications formerly served by mainframes and "traditional" client/server systems. This trend is motivating IS departments to become involved in a technology that initially concerned individual departments with highly specialized, local applications.

Intranets and extranets are not usually considered "client/server" systems in the trade press; in fact, some commentators describe intranets as the apparent successor to client/server systems. In truth, though, intranets and extranets meet the criteria we set forth in Chapter 2 to define client/server systems. A worker is performing a job using information retrieved with a personal computer but stored or processed on a networked server computer, and at least two computers (e.g., a workstation and a Web server) are performing cooperative processing.

The following examples describe current intranet projects, but could as easily be used to illustrate the client/server concepts we've been discussing throughout this book:

- Federal Express employees who used to access customer data through a mainframe will soon be doing so via an internal Web server.

- Rail transportation company CSX Corp. permits employees and customers to use an intranet/extranet application called TWSNet (Transportation Work Station Net) in which users can click on a map of the United States to "drill down" and see individual rail hubs and even individual trains and rail cars, with schedule and contents data available at a click of the mouse.

- Computer maker Silicon Graphics uses an intranet called Silicon Junction to streamline internal purchasing procedures (cutting process time by over 80%), provide marketing data to salespersons, and link employees with back-end databases for checking order status. Silicon Junction consists of hundreds of Web servers throughout the organization.

- Shipping container company Trans Ocean Ltd. provides a server system that its customers can connect to directly in order to obtain product information and place orders. The server happens to be an Internet-style Web server.

- Xerox now provides product data and customer history on an intranet that field sales representatives can access directly with their desktop and notebook PCs, saving the step of having to call up support staff, who would then look up the requested information and respond hours or even days later.

- Billion-dollar electronics component distributor Marshall Industries Inc. makes information available online to key suppliers, who can obtain data about sales volume and sales opportunities. Marshall also publishes information on the system for its customers to check credit information, pricing, inventory, and shipping status. A third constituency of users, company employees, access the server for human resources information: retirement plans and company insurance policies.

Call the above examples intranets, call them extranets, they're still fundamentally client/server systems—with the clients running Web browsers and speaking HTTP (HyperText Transfer Protocol) and HTML (HyperText Markup Language) instead of SQL, and the servers running Web publishing services. In fact, intranets and extranets can also be a form of middleware, in that they can act as an intermediary between client workstations and back-end databases. Typical intranets are also being used in the same manner as Executive Information Systems and Decision Support Systems, that is, to present operating data to managers who can then use that data to fine-tune decision making. For example, rail transportation company CSX Corp. uses an intranet to report 35 critical performance statistics to managers.

Our point is that almost everything we've discussed so far in this book is as applicable to intranets and extranets as it is to "traditional" client/server systems that are not based on Internet technologies.

## Advantages and Risks

The main advantages and risks of intranets and extranets are summarized as follows:

- Familiar and reasonably standardized user interface
- Built-in hypertext capability for user-controlled navigation
- Preexisting infrastructure for less expensive, quicker deployment on heterogeneous systems
- Relative ease of application development (two-edged sword)
- Relative ease of scalability
- Facilitation of information sharing
- Ability to publish many types of data, including audio and video
- Reduction of paper publishing costs

- Ability to update information more promptly than is feasible with paper documentation
- Reduction of support costs
- Possible duplication of effort
- Potential for user interface inconsistency (Web page design)
- Ability of departments and workgroups to implement without necessary expertise
- Poor support for WYSIWYG printing

Let's examine these pros and cons in a little more detail.

One of the most obvious benefits of intranets and extranets is that their user interface is reasonably standardized and, by now, reasonably familiar. Although the "look" of a Web page can of course vary radically between sites, the basic navigational tools of the Web browser provide an anchor—a constant and unchanging aspect of the user interface, or UI—that makes the user feel "at home." Users who have Web-surfing experience are already comfortable with the hyperlink concept. Compared against the inconsistent and diverse user interfaces that have bedeviled many organizations' moves to client/server systems, the constancy of using the same UI all the time has great appeal and comfort for business users.

The intranet/extranet UI supports hypertext links that permit users to navigate the Web site easily and, more important, without following a deterministic path. That is, users can go where they want to go by clicking the links, and they don't have waste time going where they don't need to go. This advantage is especially important in an age when information overload is becoming more of a problem than information availability.

Another key advantage is that because of the explosion of interest in recent years in the Internet, much of the technology infrastructure that intranetting requires is already in place.

- At the client side, the Web browser is becoming as commonplace on the typical PC desktop as the mouse. Indeed, Microsoft is working hard to achieve total integration of the desktop OS and the Web browser, so that PC users will employ the same tool to navigate their own PCs as they use to navigate the Internet. At that point, the browser will become the only system-level user interface on the machine. Of course, browsers run on Macintoshes and Unix systems as well as PCs, so even if an organization has a mix of heterogeneous client microcomputer architectures, intranets can still run on all of them without new technology.

- On the server side, most companies by now have acquired and implemented the technology to publish a corporate presence on the World Wide Web and to make data files available through FTP servers. E-mail servers already have the capability to handle Internet mail. Creating an intranet server uses tools with which companies have already developed experience.

- A number of commercial products, many of them developed for use on the Internet, can provide functionality that was previously difficult, prohibitively expensive, or even impossible to attain. Such tools as search engines, workflow managers, and document imaging systems can readily be implemented in an intranet environment because most of the development work has already been done.

- Finally, on the network side, TCP/IP is fast becoming the most widely used LAN and WAN network protocol. Its major competitor in years past, IPX/SPX, is not only considered passé by its detractors, it has been essentially disavowed by its major champion, Novell. Shops running IPX/SPX can usually run TCP/IP as well on clients such as Windows 95 or Windows NT Workstation, which support multiple simultaneous network protocols.

Another advantage of intranetting is speed of application development. It is becoming commonplace to see complete intranet applications developed in a month or two. The relative ease of developing intranet applications can be a two-edged sword, of course: Although one can create an intranet in a month, it may take longer to create an intranet with acceptable performance, security, and fault tolerance.

Intranet technologies are fairly scalable; that is, one can add capacity as usage increases and as organizations add new functions and features. This fact is especially conducive to setting up small-scale pilot projects because such projects need not be discarded or even substantially reworked if the organization wants to expand them.

Internet technologies are inherently oriented toward information sharing. Computers linked to an intranet or extranet can (with upload permissions) share data easily with any other computers on the same net. A training department that wants to publish a PowerPoint presentation to everyone on an intranet need only place it onto a Web server for downloading. Alternatively, the training department can save the presentation in a special Web-compatible format so that even users who do not have PowerPoint can still run the slide show from their browser. More and more office application documents can be published in this Web-friendly way, facilitating information sharing even further.

The type of information that intranets and extranets can share includes multimedia information, such as audio and video (and even videoconferencing). Client/server database vendors have been struggling for the past few years to integrate these "new" data types into their relational database models, for example by working on "object-relational" database technology. Informix is making such integration a high priority, and Oracle is working hard on it also. That work will continue, as organizing multimedia objects and integrating them into the relational DBMS structure has great value for expanding the utility of today's databases. Meanwhile, intranetting is a convenient technology for publishing multimedia data, even if it is not yet mature in terms of organizing and managing that data.

Intranetting may be the best single set of technologies for reducing paper documentation. The "paperless office" has been mentioned more in the context of cynical humor than serious planning for many years now, and information systems have proven more of a godsend to the paper industry than a threat. Intranets, however, are already reducing paper consumption dramatically at companies such as Sun Microsystems, Silicon Graphics, and Hewlett-Packard. The direct cost reduction is welcome, especially when one considers not just paper but also document printing, warehousing, and distribution, but so is the reduced environmental impact of business operations, which is becoming a larger priority for many corporations.

When organizations publish documents on an intranet or extranet, it becomes possible (and even easy) to update those documents on an irregular, ad hoc, timely basis—something that was impractical for paper documents, which organizations typically update on a fixed periodic schedule. Further, the cycle time of creating and publishing a new employee document can be much shorter on an intranet compared to paper. Intranetting can therefore improve the quality of published information, if (and this can be a big "if") the organization dedicates sufficient personnel time to keeping those online documents up-to-date.

Intranets can help reduce support costs. We'll examine this issue in more detail later in the chapter, but suffice it to say for now that it's probably easier for an organization to update an application executing on a single intranet server than it is to update an application executing on hundreds or thousands of client PCs.

One risk of intranets is duplication of effort. Whenever a "grass-roots" computing phenomenon arises, one of the IS department's first concerns is that users and departments will be reinventing wheels. Even though intranet applications may be a great idea, if six different project teams are developing substantially the same application, the intranet activity is not a very efficient one for the organization.

A related risk is that with the diverse and uncoordinated development of workgroup and departmental intranets, the user interface, taken as a whole, could conceivably become even less consistent than it is with today's client/server systems. That is, although the navigational tool is a constant, the ability to design a Web page any way you want could create wildly varying intranet home pages that may be more difficult for users to switch between than the programs they use now.

Another risk is that companies will run into a situation similar to that encountered several years ago when organizations began deploying LANs on a large scale: Although the tools for setting up an intranet site are widely available and relatively inexpensive, departments and project teams may not have the expertise to design those systems for performance, security, ease of use, and ease of administration.

An inherent drawback of intranets is that there isn't usually a built-in method for interrupting one task, going somewhere else (e.g., a help screen), and then returning precisely where you left off. It's not impossible to provide such functionality, but intranet applications are usually designed to run from start to finish as a single activity, at which point the user can execute another intranet application. Implementing interruptability can be a more challenging design task with intranet and extranet applications than with more traditional software programs.

Finally, we should mention that although HTML is a convenient tool for getting information to a user's screen, it is not yet a completely capable tool for getting information to a user's printer. Intranet proponents have stated that this limitation misses the point, which is to obtain data without requiring a printout, but the reality is that many intranet and extranet users will want a hardcopy of the data they've retrieved. Here are a few of the printing-related problems that HTML-based intranets and extranets face:

- Inability to print portions of a Web page
- Text and graphics appropriate for low-resolution monitors, not for high-resolution printers
- Very limited font support
- Limited number of text heading sizes

Although particular browsers employ proprietary means to overcome such problems, generalized cross-platform solutions—such as the OpenType specification sponsored by Adobe, Apple, Sun, and Microsoft for using TrueType and PostScript fonts in HTML files—are sorely needed.

## Integrating Intranets with Existing Client/Server Systems

Does the advent of intranets mean that all that development work your company has done with client/server databases is doomed to extinction? Despite the hasty actions of some firms that have thrown out existing projects in their zeal to embrace intranetting, clearly the answer is "no." There are various ways to tie Web intranet or extranet servers into existing, traditional client/server systems, even though such connections have been relatively slow in emerging amid the frenzy of other intranet and extranet technology developments.

### Intranet as Data Collection Device

Many of the most widely used "intranet" transaction processing applications are, in fact, traditional client/server or even mainframe systems under the skin. An intranet can easily be used to provide a user interface, collecting transactions and other input from system users spread across the organization. For applications in which users do not require instantaneous confirmation or results from their activity (for instance, in an office-supply ordering intranet), transactions that are entered via a Web browser cay simply be collected in a file on a Web server and periodically passed off to some nonintranet processing system for fulfillment.

An advantage to such an approach is that it provides a modern, distributed user interface to certain types of applications, with little or no custom programming required. The data can be collected using simple HTML forms and can be stored in a file on the server using such products as FrontPage (from Microsoft) or PolyForms (from O'Reilly and Associates).

### Common Gateway Interface (CGI)

Although HTML is useful for creating forms in which users can enter data, some additional mechanism may be needed to take that form-based data and hand it off to another program on the Web server (or, for that matter, any other accessible server) for immediate processing and response. One way to achieve this handoff is by using CGI, or Common Gateway Interface, developed several years ago by CERN, the European nuclear research center. One of CGI's primary advantages is that most Web servers "speak" CGI and most Web browsers can submit CGI scripts.

CGI is not a programming language per se, but rather an interface between a browser and a Web server that defines how data is shuttled between an HTML form and an external program. When you hear intranet designers speak of "CGI programs," they are really speaking of programs designed to be triggered by data delivered through the CGI interface. Typically, a browser sends user data to a Web server via a CGI string embedded in the URL, which the browser creates based on user entries in an HTML form that may have radio buttons and check boxes as well as text-based fields. The Web server passes the data along to an external program (which can be anything from a compiled C++ program to an interpreted Visual BASIC program or a PERL script), receives the results, and returns them to the user's browser as a separate HTML Web page.

CGI is powerful, and it works with most browsers, servers, and databases, but it can be a rather difficult technology to master. It can also be tough on a Web server's CPU, imposing significant processing overhead. Additionally, CGI programs operate on an "open-and-close" model rather than maintaining a continuous connection to a DBMS. A single user can easily create many connect-disconnect operations in the space of a few minutes, impos-ing much more processing overhead than a system permitting establishment of a continuous database connection.

### Proprietary Web Server APIs

Web server vendors provide proprietary APIs that may offer var-ious advantages over CGI in terms of simplicity, security, error checking, ability to maintain database connections over time, and functionality. For example, Microsoft's Internet Information Server permits the use of ISAPI (Internet Server API) as an alternative to CGI, and although ISAPI may not be as widely portable as CGI, it's likely to impose less server CPU overhead. Additionally, O'Reilly and Associates offers WSAPI (Web Site API); Netscape offers NSAPI (Netscape Server API). Companies developing interactive intranets or extranets that will trigger external programs must weigh CGI's portability advantage against the advantages offered by proprietary APIs.

### The Java Approach

Yet another way to link Web browsers to existing databases is provided by Sun's JavaSoft operating unit in the form of the JDBC (Java Data Base Connectivity) API. Java applets can use JDBC, which can communicate with ODBC or other SQL APIs to directly access client/server databases from the client end with-out using the Web server as an intermediary.

This approach is quite different from the server-oriented approach used by CGI and many proprietary Web server APIs, in that the Java applet executes on the client and can access back-end databases without going through a Web server. This shifting of responsibility from server to client has the appeal of burning client CPU cycles rather than server CPU cycles, follow-ing the performance guideline of minimizing the use of less-available resources that we discussed in Chapter 5. Depending on the specific implementation, however, the strain on database servers might be greater than with the other Web server–based approaches discussed previously. Also, Java applets, which run in interpreted mode rather than a true compiled mode, have shown a tendency to run slowly, although this situation is likely to change over time.

Java has been eliciting a great deal of attention because of its platform-independent design, support for multithreading and multitasking, and object orientation. Nearly all the major client/server DBMS vendors are conforming their products to support the JDBC API. Companies developing applications in Java should become familiar with JDBC if they want their intranets to provide access to back-end databases without straining intranet Web server resources.

## Bulletproofing Intranets and Extranets

Now that we have a better idea of what intranets and extranets are, what are some ways we can bulletproof them? The technologies are new enough that we are still learning about the common failure modes and pitfalls, but it's possible to identify some bulletproofing opportunities even at this early stage.

### Design

Bulletproofing tips for intranet and extranet design include the following:

- Choose pilot projects having a defined business purpose, measurable cost/benefit, and a good technology fit.
- Start with simple applications and design interactive and real-time systems later.
- Develop expertise with intranets before deploying extranets.
- Don't try to overcentralize intranet development.
- Do publish technological and organizational guidelines for implementers.
- Plan extra design time to allow for unsophisticated or difficult Web programming tools.
- Track development of early projects to build a knowledge base for budgeting and scheduling future projects.

The first point about designing intranets and extranets sounds trivial, but it is ignored surprisingly often: Build these systems where they serve a demonstrable business purpose, not because it's "the thing to do." As with all client/server systems, the most successful ones are those that advance the business goals set by top management. Politically, implementing early intranets and extranets that deliver clear benefits, after performing at least an informal needs analysis, is a good way to win upper management support for the intranet/extranet concept. Selecting a project that permits fairly straightforward cost/benefit analysis will help build a consensus as to intranetting's advantages.

A corollary to this first point is to build intranet applications that fit well with the technology's capabilities. At this point in their evolution, intranets and extranets are not particularly appropriate vehicles for delivering large applications or for performing high-speed online transaction processing; they're more appropriate for delivering relatively small data sets to a large number of users who make occasional connections.

The second main design point is to start with the easy projects. For example, an intranet Web site is much easier to design, support, and manage if it contains information that doesn't change each minute or each hour. It's therefore logical to cut your intranet teeth on relatively static information-publishing projects, such as employee directories, insurance policies, retirement plans, human resource policies, product specifications, competitive product analyses, internal training schedules, quarterly financial reports, and so on. Once you've successfully implemented simpler intranet pilot projects such as these, you can move on to the more complex issues of bidirectional communications (employees filling out expense reports or modifying W4 withholdings online, team members collaborating on projects, appointment scheduling, technical support for system users), frequently updated documents (company news bulletins, project management schedules), and links to real-time back-end databases (employees checking customer order status).

Extending the guideline a step further, recognize that intranets can benefit from a remarkable range of commercially developed tools and applications. Not all of these will be the sort of standard business application (accounting, operations, inventory, etc.) that your organization might tend to think of, but many of them can (if applied with a little creativity) provide tremendous business value. Search engines, for example, have proven particularly beneficial to organizations with large volumes of machine-readable text already stored on their LANs, and because there's no significant development work, they qualify as "easy projects."

Third, develop a pretty good level of experience and competence in intranets before creating your first extranet. The face your company presents to the customer must be friendly, professional, and efficient, whether it's on a human salesperson or an electronic Web server. Ultimately, of course, you want your intranets to be just as polished and bug-free as your extranets, but problems are slightly less embarrassing when your employees see them than when your paying customers see them.

The fourth point is to avoid the tempting but ultimately counterproductive approach of overcentralizing intranet design and development. One of the key advantages of intranets is that they can be small in scale and developed by departments or even project groups. Encourage intranet application development; for example, Xerox holds an annual Internet Trade Fair where employees can demonstrate their "homemade" intranet applications.

Having said that, the fifth point is to publish technology and organizational guidelines for those departments and teams that are designing, or will soon design, their own intranets and intranet applications. For example, letting departments and project teams know about corporate standards for database connectivity can help avoid the emergence of a hodgepodge collection of intranets using several different DBMS access methods. For another example, corporate guidelines for Web page design might help avert the UI problem of highly inconsistent intranet "faces." An example of an organizational guideline might be to recommend that each department designate "Webmasters" for particular intranet or extranet sites, or even for specific Web pages, to help ensure that content is kept current.

Sixth, we should mention that intranet/extranet application developers may not find the level of sophistication in code generators and debuggers than they are used to with more mature technologies. Budget some time for building in lots of checkpoints and timing loops manually in order to compensate for the lack of debugging assistance provided by the new development tools.

Finally, intranet/extranet development is in many ways inherently less predictive than traditional client/server systems development. That is, the flexibility of intranets can make it more difficult to nail down a system specification and therefore to perform the budgeting of time and dollars necessary for larger projects. Probably the only ways to effectively bulletproof against runaway intranet projects are to build in considerable leeway for initial projects, track the progress of systems as they are developed, and create an experience knowledge base to apply against new projects.

## Performance

Tomes have been written in the professional press about optimizing Web sites for Internet use, and most of the techniques espoused in these magazine articles and computer books apply equally to Web sites for intranet or extranet use.

- A big advantage of intranets is their ability to present data in graphical form. There is a difference between utilitarian graphics and window dressing, however. For performance management, avoid large decorative graphics (such as complex, multicolored bitmapped backgrounds) that take a long time to download; instead, use smaller images that can pop up quickly on the user's browser. Color-reducing Web page graphics down to 8-bit color can produce much snappier performance than using 15-, 16-, or 24-bit images.

- If there are objects that will take longer than a few seconds to download, such as Adobe Acrobat PDF files containing extensive documentation on specific topics, provide users with options to download what they want and provide file size information (or, even better, download time estimates) to help them decide if they want to download a file immediately or at a later time.

- Use compression technologies for audio and video as well as for static graphics; often, sacrificing a small degree of accuracy can result in files an order of magnitude smaller but having acceptable quality levels.

- Match multimedia files to the power of the clients that will play them back. It's usually better, for example, to create a digitized video clip with a less ambitious frame rate so that it does not drop frames when viewed at the client PC.

- Dedicate servers to intranet and extranet services, even though it may be possible to layer those services on PCs already performing other server functions.

- Use high-speed LAN interfaces for intranet servers to avoid throughput bottlenecks.

- Equip intranet and extranet customers using dial-up access with the fastest available modems and with client-side software that supports data compression.

- Educate users about the network performance impact of their work habits. Leaving a browser connected to a real-time, continuously updated Web page can impose significant network traffic overhead.

Other performance issues may arise for intranets and extranets that link to existing client/server systems. As we saw in our discussion of database connectivity approaches, the choice of server-based versus client-based processing of database access can have a large performance impact. In addition, it may be desirable to separate out intranet query traffic from other operational traffic to avoid slowing down line-of-business systems; for example, CSX Corp. moved to a data warehouse approach for its "Integrated Measures" business performance reporting intranet.

Organizations may need to perform the same type of performance analyses for intranets and extranets as they do for traditional client/server systems in terms of the amount of data to be transferred, processing loads on servers, processing loads on clients, and burden on LAN and WAN infrastructure.

The easier a company makes information access, the more its employees (and suppliers and customers) will use the information systems. Organizations are likely to find that users already familiar with Internet technologies will spend more time accessing intranets than they spend accessing systems with unique user interfaces having a steeper learning curve. Therefore, intranets and extranets may accelerate the need for more modern LAN infrastructure technologies such as fast and switched Ethernet.

However, realize that intranetting, at least for now, is not so much about processing high-volume transactions (where performance is often a key issue) as it is about providing easy and more flexible access to data. With the user interface tools that exist for intranets today, many performance-sensitive applications are simply not good fits for intranetting.

## Security

Just as ease of use can create performance problems by increasing network usage, it can also reduce security by making data easier to find (and, in some cases, easier to upload as well).

Review the user/workgroup/domain access restriction capabilities of Web server systems before choosing one for your intranet or extranet. The ability to restrict access by specific IP address is probably much less useful in terms of creating a manageable intranet than the ability to designate privileges by group or supergroup, especially in networks where IP addresses are assigned dynamically from a pool of addresses. If a Web server can leverage an existing LAN security database, such as an NT Server's Registry or NetWare's NDS, intranet security implementation will prove much easier both to set up and to manage over time. If you must have a custom security database, bulletproof it by choosing a Web server that allows you to create such a database with a common and familiar tool.

Internet firewall technology is reasonably mature at this point (we discussed it in Chapter 6) and should be applied to intranets and especially to extranets. Firewalls can have several functions, including protecting Internet-connected intranets from outside crackers and restricting the access levels available to legitimate extranet users. Whether simple router filtering or more sophisticated proxy server firewalls are required will depend on the sensitivity of the data that the intranet or extranet is publishing and/or receiving. If your organization implements proxy servers, check to ensure that they support FTP and gopher as well as HTTP requests (most do).

Of course, nothing in the definition of intranetting requires a connection to the Internet. Most intranets do, over time, connect to their massive common parent, but for complete security from hackers and crackers, many intranets simply stay isolated.

Intranets or extranets that do link to the Internet will require encryption to protect data from unauthorized access as it traverses the public Internet cloud. Transaction encryption can be implemented with Secure Hypertext Transport Protocol (SHTTP, an extension to HTTP) and Secure Sockets Layer (SSL, pioneered by Netscape but now supported and extended by several vendors). For dial-up connections, Point-to-Point Tunneling Protocol (PPTP) is an extension of the popular PPP dial-up communication protocol that adds encryption capabilities; PPTP made its first widely publicized commercial appearance on Microsoft Windows NT 4.0 servers. It supports IPX, NetBIOS, and NetBEUI as well as IP. Although PPTP is not yet a formal standard, it has been submitted to the Internet Engineering Task Force and is likely to become a de facto if not a de jure standard.

If you use CGI as a means for linking your intranet/extranet Web pages with other programs or databases, you'll need to take some steps to ensure that unauthorized individuals can't add their own CGI scripts or programs to the server. One typical step is to localize CGI scripts and programs to a server directory (e.g., CGI-BIN) with restricted access. Another issue is to make sure users have no direct access to lower-level tools, such as DOS or PERL command interpreters, that might reside on a Web server.

Secure intranet/extranets may need authentication technology as well as encryption technology to verify that users are who they say they are. The types of products are similar (and in many cases identical) to those discussed in Chapter 6.

Finally, organizations should consider security issues from the user's standpoint as well as the organization's. If you are going to ask employees to use an intranet to look up information on the company's drug use policy, for example, you may need to be able to demonstrate that the intranet server is not recording such accesses in a site log. Alternatively, you may wish to set up a nonprivileged account that users can log into anonymously when they want to safeguard their privacy.

### Fault Tolerance

Fault tolerance is an area where intranet and extranet design is still immature. For example, although LAN operating systems provide built-in mechanisms to replicate key data across multiple servers, there are no standards yet in the Web server world for such redundancy. Chapter 7's suggestions regarding client, communications, server, and environmental redundancy all apply to intranets and extranets, and they may be even more important because of the technology's relative immaturity in this area.

### Support

Intranets and extranets present new support challenges as well as opportunities.

**New Support Challenges** Technical support must be available for intranet and extranet users, just as it must be available for traditional client/server system users. Intranets and extranets may be inherently easier to use than other systems because of the constancy of the Web browser interface, but a number of support issues will come up, including

- Configuring a Web browser for TCP/IP access, including how to specify domain name servers, how to get IP addresses, etc.

- Configuring dial-up links for users in the field: phone numbers, communications protocols (e.g., PPP, SLIP), whether to use data compression, modem configuration, handshaking, etc.
- Troubleshooting slow intranet/extranet performance

Support staff education will have to focus more intensively on such subjects to handle the deployment of intranets and extranets. That is, although support requirements in total may not change, or may even decline, the subject matter will certainly change. Help Desks will have to become as expert in supporting Internet technologies as they have become in traditional client/server technologies and applications.

In addition to end-user support, intranet server site management and support presents new challenges. Perhaps the largest of these is keeping intranet-published information current. As is the case with desktop PCs, the largest cost of an intranet is probably not getting it established, but keeping it up to date. Organizations implementing intranets and extranets must be careful to budget serious personnel time and to document management systems for this purpose. Users are likely to have higher expectations for intranets and extranets in terms of assuming current content, as a result of their browser experience on the Internet. The quickest way to turn users off is to leave "stale" data on Web and FTP servers. Doing so also negates much of the value these systems can add, because users will have to pursue other avenues to get the current information they need.

Finally, whereas remote LAN server management tools have had several years to evolve, the technology for remote management of Web servers is still immature by comparison. Companies moving to intranet/extranet systems should carefully review the remote site management tools compatible with their Web server software to ensure that support staff and system administrators can perform some level of remote performance monitoring, troubleshooting, and content updating.

**New Support Opportunities**  A key support benefit of intranetting is the ability to deliver "help" files online. Although designing customized help files in traditional client/server systems can be a forbidding task, the built-in availability of hyperlinks in the intranet environment can ease the task greatly. Therefore, another new subject area for Help Desk analysts and managers is the design of user-friendly Web-based help systems to answer

FAQs (Frequently Asked Questions) and FEPs (Frequently Encountered Problems). As we saw in the previous chapter, there should be a feedback mechanism so that common problems and questions can periodically find their way into online FAQ and FEP areas.

Another support benefit is the ease of disseminating software patches, fixes, and updates via Web servers. Many software vendors have been using their Internet sites for such purposes for years, and corporations deploying intranets can do the same.

**The "Net PC"**   We should comment in this section on the "network PC" or "net PC" for short. Several major software and hardware companies, including Apple, IBM, Netscape, Oracle, and Sun, have posed the hypothesis that a stripped-down client PC, with no local disk storage, could create a client/server environment that is inherently easier to support and administer, because the PC would essentially download all applications from the network as well as data. (Rather than a "thin client" architecture, we could call the net PC a "skeletal client.") A net PC would load its BIOS and operating system software from a ROM chip and/or a special network directory, much as diskless workstations do today. All programs, as well as all data, would have to be loaded across the network for execution.

The net PC is in stark contrast to the traditional, or "powerful," PC. Doing away with the diskette drive is a step that most organizations will applaud for security reasons, and one that most users frankly won't mind very much (the days of backing up hard disks to diskette are over). The same is true of the CD-ROM drive, which is more of a necessity in the home PC than in the office PC. Doing away with the hard drive, however, is a much more complex proposition.

There is little reason to consider the net PC approach for cost reasons alone, given the extraordinarily low cost-per-megabyte of today's disk devices. (A much greater potential for workstation cost reduction lies in the monitor, which now constitutes almost half of the cost of a typical PC.) In fact, the hardware cost savings of the net PC may be illusory: The improvements to LAN infrastructure that net PCs require may easily cost more than one saves by removing $100 hard drives. Rather, the net PC's reason for being would be that administrators could enjoy complete control over applications and workstation configuration for the first time since the PC arrived on the computing scene.

Several serious questions arise when considering the net PC as a standard client. First, will users accept it? One of the main reasons PC-based networks became so popular in the first place is that users no longer had to rely on central IS departments to write programs for them; for example, users could run spreadsheets to do their own data analysis and reporting. Widespread implementation of net PCs in an organization might mean that users could no longer run software of their own choosing, but would rely completely on whatever server-based "applets" network administrators provide.

Although total user independence in choosing what software to install and run is probably not a good thing, the net PC model may very well feel like too far of a pendulum swing back to the central-administration model of the mainframe era, a paradigm that most users and even managers are not anxious to revisit. The degree to which users will resist net PCs on the grounds of losing control, choice, and flexibility will be largely determined by the number and range of server-based applets that net PCs will have access to on any given system. As we'll see, most of today's general-purpose business software wasn't written to execute over a network and may bring network performance to a crawl if forced to do so.

The second concern is, do IS departments have the resources to handle the extra workload? Can they manage the demand for data processing that will shift to them? Or, stating this question more precisely, will the time savings on the technical support side make up for the time requirements on the application development side? Although the ability of departments and users to deploy their own tools for data manipulation, processing, and analysis has undoubtedly increased the burden on support professionals, it has shifted much of the responsibility of application development to users, workgroups, and departments (remember our discussion of ad hoc, single-user, workgroup, and departmental software projects in Chapter 4).

Third, can today's networks handle the large increase in LAN and WAN traffic that net PCs portend? For years, applications have been growing in size ("fatware") as the cost of PC memory and disk space has plummeted and software vendors have learned that the demand for compact programs is minuscule compared to the demand for more and more features. It's not uncommon for Windows applications to require 40 MB or more of local disk space, and attempting to rewrite such applications as "bite-size" Java applets may be unrealistic. Merely moving such applications to the network, without a rededication on the part of application developers to tight, efficient code (which could take a decade or more), is likely to increase network traffic at least tenfold and perhaps much more. This is not an increase that many networks have the bandwidth to manage without major redesign. One can mitigate the fatware traffic problem by equipping net PCs with lots of primary memory for caching, reducing the need for repeated access to application modules, but this approach is only useful where users run a small number of fatware applications—and it does increase the net PC's hardware cost.

Fourth, the net PC may make the client/server environment less fault tolerant. If a network server is unavailable, the user may not even be able to load the PC's system software: The net PC is useless. In networks of powerful PCs, users can typically still perform certain tasks during periods of server unavailability.

Net PCs may be able to reduce support costs over time for some classes of users. However, organizations must understand the sizable hidden costs of net PCs, and the net PC is in no way required for organizations to reap the key benefits of intranets and extranets.

## Summary

Intranets and extranets present a great opportunity for organizations to leverage existing technology investments and overcome the problems of inconsistent and unique user interfaces that have plagued many client/server systems in the past. They can help companies reduce costs, improve communications, and create more intimate supplier and customer relationships. It may be that by developing intranets and extranets, many organizations will reap greater rewards than they currently enjoy by using the Internet itself for marketing and commerce.

Rather than viewing intranets as a "new" phenomenon, there are many reasons to view them as an extension or application of the fundamental client/server model. Most of the same concerns that apply to any client/server system also apply to intranets and extranets. Companies that extend the bulletproofing philosophy to their Web-based information services will enjoy the same benefits that they will enjoy applying that philosophy to traditional client/server projects: better design, performance, security, fault tolerance, and support. That is to say, information systems that really work.

# References and Resources

## Printed and Electronic Resources

This section contains information on books, magazines, CD-ROMs and online information services that might be of interest to readers of this book.

### Books

We recommend getting on the mailing list of the major computer book publishers and looking over their catalogs periodically. Some of the phone numbers for that purpose are listed here.

| | |
|---|---|
| Addison-Wesley | 800-447-2226, 617-944-3700 |
| Bantam Books | 800-347-7828 |
| Howard W. Sams & Company | 800-428-7267, 317-298-5566 |
| IDG Books | 800-762-2974, 317-596-5200 |
| John Wiley & Sons | 800-225-5945, 212-850-6000 |
| McGraw-Hill | 800-822-8158 |
| Microsoft Press | 800-MSP-RESS |
| New Riders Publishing | 800-858-7674, 317-581-3500 |
| O'Reilly and Associates | 707-829-0515 |
| Osborne/McGraw-Hill | 800-227-0900, 510-548-2805 |
| Peachpit Press | 800-283-9444, 510-548-4393 |
| Sybex | 800-227-2346, 510-523-8233 |

Here are some of the books we've found useful over the years and feel are worth a look, as well as a couple of other titles in the "bulletproofing" series that take a more detailed view of narrower subjects than this book does.

*Bulletproof Your PC Network*   by Glenn Weadock, McGraw-Hill, 1996. The chapters on NetWare and security are covered more thoroughly in *Bulletproofing NetWare,* but the earlier book contains more material on DOS, Windows 3.x, and memory management.

*Bulletproofing NetWare*   by Mark Wilkins and Glenn Weadock, McGraw-Hill, 1996. Covers versions 3.11, 3.12, 4.0 and 4.1, providing 175 bulletproofing tips in 7 areas.

*Bulletproofing Windows 95*   by Glenn Weadock, McGraw-Hill, 1996. Applies the bulletproofing philosophy to Windows 95 workstations in-depth, with 160 tips in 8 areas.

*Client/Server Strategies*   by William Marion, McGraw-Hill, 1994. A textbook-style work that is targeted largely for readers well versed in the IBM computing paradigm.

*Client/Server Technology for Managers*   by Karen Watterson, Addison-Wesley, 1995. A short, lucid overview mainly for non-technical managers making decisions about client/server.

*DataPro Directories & Market Research Articles*   Expensive but well worth it. Call 800/DAT-APRO or 609/764-0100. Lots of industry directories and topical market studies.

*The Essential Client/Server Survival Guide*   by Robert Orfali, Dan Harkey, and Jeri Edwards, Wiley, 1994. Contains much product-specific information and details on client/server standards.

*Help! The Art of Computer Technical Support*   by Ralph Wilson, Peachpit Press, 1991. A quick read with some good tips for tech support professionals.

*Implementing Client/Server Computing*   by Bernard Boar, McGraw-Hill, 1993. Builds an excellent case for client/server computing.

*LAN Disaster Prevention and Recovery*   by Patrick H. Corrigan, PTR Prentice-Hall, 1994. Very interesting and entertaining book on disaster prevention.

*Technical Foundations for Client/Server Computing*   by Carl Hall, Wiley, 1994.

*The Mythical Man-Month*   by Frederick P. Brooks, Jr., Addison-Wesley, 1982. A timeless and essential book for anyone involved in large software development projects.

## Magazines

Here are a few periodicals worth considering for a "core" library. Even if you subscribe to a CD-ROM service that includes the text of some or all of these magazines, you'll still want the hard-copy for figures and graphs.

**Byte: The Magazine of Technology Integration**
One Phoenix Mill Lane, Peterborough, NH 03458
603-924-9281

**Client/Server Computing**
One Research Drive, Suite 400B, Westborough, MA 10581-3907
508-366-2031

**Computerworld**
500 Old Connecticut Path, Framingham, MA 01701
508-879-0700

**DBMS**
411 Borel Avenue, Suite 100, San Mateo, CA 94402
415-655-4243
http://www.dbmsmag.com

**InformationWeek**
600 Community Drive, Manhasset, NY 11030
516-562-5051

**Infoworld**
P. O. Box 1172, Skokie, IL 60076
800-457-7866

**LAN Magazine**
600 Harrison Street, San Francisco, CA 94107
800-234-9573

**LAN Times**
1900 O'Farrell Street, Suite 200, San Mateo, CA 94403
800-525-5003

**Network Computing**
CMP Publications, 600 Community Drive, Manhasset, NY 11030
516-562-5882

**Network World**
151 Worcester Road, Framingham, MA 01701-9524
800-643-4668, 508-875-6400

**PC Magazine: The Independent Guide to Personal Computing**
One Park Avenue, New York, NY 10016-5802
212-503-5255

*PC Week*
10 Presidents' Landing, Medford, MA 02155
617-393-3700

*Software Magazine*
One Research Drive, Suite 400B, Westborough, MA 01581
508-366-8104

*Telecom & Network Security Review* (monthly newsletter)
Pasha Publications, 1616 N. Fort Myer Drive, Suite 1000,
Arlington, VA 22209
800-424-2908, 703-816-8639

*Windows Magazine*
One Jericho Plaza, Jericho, NY 11753
516-733-8300

## CD-ROMs

CD-ROM databases permit keyword searching and save great amounts of time. If dollars permit, it's great to have several of these references available simultaneously on a dedicated CD-ROM server.

The art of searching takes some practice; if you want to find all references to RPC, for example, you'll need to search on "RPC" and "remote procedure call" because both are widely used. Some time spent mastering Boolean phrasing and search techniques is well invested.

### Computer Select
Information Access Company
800-419-0313, 212-503-4400, 212-503-4487 (Fax), cdorders@iac-net.com (Internet)
$1250 (standalone), $8995 (six concurrent users)

Computer Select provides a running 1-year database of over 80 full-text periodicals and over 20 abstracted periodicals in digital format (updated monthly), which can be searched electronically (and therefore quickly).

It also provides industry information, including 10,000 computer company profiles; data on 70,000 hardware and software products; and 19,000 computer terms defined in an online glossary.

**Microsoft TechNet**
Microsoft Corporation
One Microsoft Way, Redmond, WA 98052-6399
800-344-2121
$295/year for a 12-month subscription
This monthly CD-ROM with Microsoft's complete Knowledge Base and other reference documents, drivers, and updates should prove a good investment for any shop supporting Windows and other Microsoft client/server products.

**Network Support Encyclopedia ("NSE")**
Novell Inc.
P.O. Box 5205, Denver, CO 80217
800-377-4136, 303-297-2725
$1395 for a 12-month subscription
The NetWare Support Encyclopedia contains software updates, product manuals, patches and fixes, technical information documents, Novell Labs hardware and software test bulletins, Novell application notes and the NetWare Buyer's Guide.

## Online Information Services

Information services can provide

- Product-specific utilities
- Driver updates
- Direct tech support via e-mail
- Participatory forums or Special Interest Groups (SIGs)
- Press releases on new products
- Online tech publications
- Online troubleshooting databases

Here are some of the more popular online resources. You may wish to check with your software and hardware vendors and distributors periodically to see if they offer specific services via BBS systems.

**America Online ("AOL")**
8619 Westwood Center Drive, Vienna, VA 22182
800-227-6364

Freeware and shareware are available here, via a convenient Windows interface. AOL now offers good Internet access, including the World Wide Web, as long as one runs version 2.5 or higher of the Windows client.

### BIX (Byte Information eXchange)
Owned by Delphi Internet Services Corporation
1030 Massachusetts Avenue, Cambridge, MA 02138
800-695-4775, 617-354-4137, 617-491-6642 (Fax)

BIX is a useful service for moderate to advanced PC users and support professionals. It offers over 600 access numbers throughout the United States; you can also connect to BIX through the Internet (the address is info@bix.com).

BIX offers a Windows program, BIXNav, to make it easier to get around BIX. It's run by *Byte* magazine, one of the longstanding standards and home to many influential columnists and reviewers. BIX also includes a searchable full-text database of *Byte* articles.

### CompuServe
Owned by H&R Block
5000 Arlington Centre Boulevard, Columbus, OH 43220
800-524-3388; 800-848-8199; 614-529-1349

Virtually every PC (and Macintosh, for that matter) hardware and software vendor is now providing one or more levels of support via CompuServe. It's also a popular vehicle for distributing software updates and new drivers.

In addition to MCI Mail, you can access the *Internet* through CompuServe. Spry's Mosaic Web browser and ImageView viewer are bundled in a downloadable package CompuServe calls "NetLauncher."

CompuServe's WINNEWS forum is a useful way to get Windows 95 information sent to you automatically every 2 weeks. GO WINNEWS and follow subscription instructions. WINNEWS is also available via Prodigy (JUMP WINNEWS) and America Online (key word WINNEWS).

### Dialog Information Services (Knight-Ridder)
2440 El Camino Real, Mountain View, CA 94040
800-334-2564
Encyclopedic, if expensive, databases on every subject.

### Microsoft Network
Microsoft Corporation
One Microsoft Way, Redmond, WA 98052-6399
800-386-5550

Although Microsoft seems to be backing off from making MSN a strong information service in its own right, it's useful particularly for downloading fixes and updates from Microsoft.

### NetWire
(see CompuServe)

NetWire is Novell's electronic information service, which it provides via CompuServe with the command "GO NETWIRE." Over 125,000 NetWare users participate in NetWire, which Novell updates on a daily basis.

NetWire provides 24-hour tech support via Novell sysop, queries to "message board" for 24-hour response, product enhancements, patches, and fixes, shell drivers, utilities, technical bulletins, press releases, and an events calendar.

### ZiffNet
Owned by Ziff-Davis Publishing
One Park Avenue, 5th Floor, New York, NY 10016
800-848-8990
Utilities and online computer magazine text.

## Client/Server Companies

Here's a partial listing of companies and organizations that have established a prominent position in the client/server marketplace.

### Borland International, Inc.
100 Borland Way, Scotts Valley, CA 95066-3249
800-233-2444, 408-431-1000
http://www.borland.com

### Centura Corp. (formerly Gupta)
1060 Marsh Road, Menlo Park, CA 94025
800-876-3267, 415-321-9500

### Cognos Corp.
67 South Bedford Street, Burlington, MA 01803-5164
800-4-COGNOS, 617-229-6600
http://www.cognos.com

### Computer Associates International, Inc.
One Computer Associates Plaza, Islandia, NY 11788-7000
800-225-5224, 516-342-5224
http://www.cai.com

### Digital Equipment Corp.
146 Main Street, Maynard, MA 01754-2571
800-344-4825, 508-493-5111
http://www.dec.com, http://www.digital.com

### Easel Corp.
See V-Mark

### Forte Software Inc.
1800 Harrison Street, 24th Floor, Oakland, CA 94612
510-869-3400
http://www.forte.com

### Gupta Corp.
See **Centura Corp.**

### Hewlett-Packard Company
3000 Hanover Street, Palo Alto, CA 94304
800-752-0900, 415-857-1501
http://www.hp.com

### IBM Corporation
Old Orchard Road, Armonk, NY 10504
800-426-3333, 914-765-1900
http://www.ibm.com

### Information Builders, Inc.
1250 Broadway, New York, NY 10001-3782
800-969-INFO, 212-736-4433
http://www.ibi.com

### Informix Software Inc.
4100 Bohannon Drive, Menlo Park, CA 94025
800-331-1763, 415-926-6300
http://www.informix.com

### JYACC Inc.
116 John Street, 20th Floor, New York, NY 10038
800-458-3313, 212-267-7722
http://www.jyacc.com

### Micro Focus, Inc.
2465 East Bayshore Road, Suite 200, Palo Alto, CA 94303
800-872-6265, 415-856-4161
http://www.microfocus.com

**Microsoft Corporation**
One Microsoft Way, Redmond, WA 98052
800-426-9400, 206-882-8080
http://www.microsoft.com

**NCR Corp.** (formerly AT&T GIS)
1700 South Patterson Boulevard, Dayton, OH 45479-0001
800-447-1124, 513-445-5000
http://www.ncr.com

**Novell, Inc.**
1555 North Technology Way, Orem, UT 84757
800-453-1267, 801-222-6000
http://www.novell.com

**Open Software Foundation, Inc.**
11 Cambridge Center, Cambridge, MA 02142
617-621-8700

**Oracle Corp.**
500 Oracle Parkway, Redwood Shores, CA 94065
800-633-0596, 415-506-7000
http://www.oracle.com

**Platinum Technology, Inc.**
1815 South Meyers Road, Oakbrook Terrace, IL 60181-5241
800-378-7528, 630-620-5000
http://www.platinum.com

**Powersoft Corp.**
561 Virginia Road, Concord, MA 01742-2732
800-395-3525, 508-287-1500
http://www.powersoft.com

**Progress Software Corp.**
14 Oak Park, Bedford, MA 01730-9960
800-477-6473, 617-280-4000
http://www.progress.com

**SunSoft, Inc.**
2550 Garcia Avenue, Mountain View, CA 94043-1100
800-SUN-SOFT, 512-345-2412
http://www.sun.com/sunsoft

**Sybase Inc.**
6475 Christie Avenue, Emeryville, CA 94608
800-879-2273, 510-922-3500
http://www.sybase.com

**Unify Corp.**
3927 Lennane Drive, Sacramento, CA 95834-1922
800-455-2405, 916-928-6400
http://www.unify.com

**Vinca Corp.**
1815 South State Street, Suite 2000, Orem, UT 84058
800-934-9530, 801-223-3100
http://www.vinca.com

**V-Mark Software, Inc.** (formerly Easel Corp.)
50 Washington Street, Westborough, MA 01581-1021
800-966-9875, 508-366-3888
http://www.vmark.com

# Glossary

**4GL.** A fourth-generation programming language is one that requires fewer commands (typically by an order of magnitude) than a traditional programming language such as COBOL or C.

**8-mm Tape.** Exabyte Corporation is the sole supplier of this Sony-licensed technology for helical-scan recording that offers high tape capacity on small cartridges (3.75" x 2.5" x 0.5") using 8-mm tape. Typical cartridge capacity is 1.5 GB and 5.0 GB uncompressed, though recent models can store 14 GB compressed and can transfer data at 60 MB/minute. These tape systems typically perform immediate read-after-write verification.

**10Base-2.** The standard for "thin" shielded coaxial Ethernet cable; usually RG-58 cable with BNC-type connectors. The "10" means 10 MBps speed, and the "Base" means baseband network.

**10Base-5.** The standard for "thick" shielded coaxial Ethernet cable.

**10Base-T.** The standard for twisted-pair Ethernet cable, either shielded or unshielded.

**10Base-F.** The standard for fiber optic Ethernet cable.

**100Base-VG.** A network protocol developed by Hewlett-Packard and AT&T, running Fast Ethernet over all four twisted pairs in Category 3 cable.

**100Base-T.** See **Fast Ethernet.**

**Ad Hoc Application.** An application that is created, used once, and discarded, e.g., to solve a nonrecurring business problem.

**ANSI.** American National Standards Institute, one of the primary U.S. computer standards organizations.

**AMP.** Asynchronous (also Asymmetric) MultiProcessing is an option, built into certain network operating systems, that splits processor duties between two mirrored servers, one handling input/output and the other handling network services. See also **SMP**.

**API.**   Application Program Interface; a defined set of commands or "calls" that application programs use to communicate with underlying services, software, or devices. MAPI, for example, allows applications to interact with Microsoft Mail.

**Application Layer.**   Highest of the seven OSI-model layers of network software; where file transfer and e-mail functions occur, for example. The interface between the network and application programs.

**Application Program Interface.**   See **API**.

**Application Servers.**   LAN servers that provide specialized functions such as communications, database, or backup. Lotus Notes and WordPerfect Office are typical applications that run on application servers. These typically run network "runtime" code, which excludes file and print services, and have their own dedicated PC.

**Archives.**   Permanent copies of data files for long-term storage, e.g., for one or several years.

**ARCNet.**   Attached Resource Computing Network, a Datapoint-developed network known for low cost and easy installation. It can handle 255 nodes and runs at 2.5 Mbps or 20 Mbps (ARC-Net-Plus) with a token-passing protocol.

**Asymmetric Encryption.**   See **Public-Key Encryption**.

**Asymmetric Multiprocessing.**   See **AMP**.

**Asynchronous Transfer Mode.**   See **ATM**.

**ATM.**   Asynchronous Transfer Mode, a newer network protocol designed to guarantee a certain high throughput rate for the duration of a session; useful for digital video and other demanding needs. ATM requires compatible network cards and hubs.

**Attachment.**   In many e-mail packages, a data file or program to be sent along with a mail message. Attachments may be in any form, text or binary.

**Attenuation.**   The weakening of a signal (e.g., in a cable) over distance or time.

**Average Access Time.**   (1) How long it takes a hard drive read/write head to find a specific track and sector location on the disk; in milliseconds. (2) How long it takes to transfer a byte to or from memory.

**Back End.**  Usually synonymous with "server."

**Backbone.**  The part of a large network, typically a trunk connecting servers, that manages the lion's share of traffic and links LANs together.

**Backup Agent.**  A program that runs on a target computer, either server or workstation, and communicates over the network with the computer running the backup program. PC backup agents are implemented as TSRs or as Windows 95 network services. Server backup agents are usually implemented by add-on modules that extend the NOS.

**Bandwidth.**  The capacity of a data channel, typically in kilobits per second (kbps).

**Baseband.**  Single-signal, unmodulated transmission of digital information. Baseband LANs are typically Ethernet or token-ring and are geographically limited.

**Basic Rate Interface.**  See **BRI.**

**Baud Rate.**  Technically not the same as the bit-per-second (bps) rate, the baud rate represents signal modulations over a serial link—how often frequencies change. Advanced modems can send more than one bit for each modulation, so the bps rate exceeds the baud rate.

**Beaconing.**  In token-ring networks, an alert broadcast by a NIC that has detected a problem, such as an off-line upstream PC that is not passing the token.

**Binding.**  The process of logically connecting a network driver to an NIC driver; usually done at PC startup.

**BIOS.**  Short for Basic Input-Output System. ROM-based software that loads prior to the operating system and handles low-level data transfer between disk drives, printers, keyboards, monitors, and memory; also includes Power-On Self-Test code. Devices such as video adapters and disk controllers typically have their own BIOS in addition to the main PC BIOS.

**BLOB.**  Binary Large OBject, a database field that may consist of a large graphic image, digital video clip, sound file, or other large nontextual element.

**Boot-Sector Virus.**  A type of virus that infects a PC disk's Master Boot Record (MBR); an example is the famous Michelangelo virus.

**BRI.** Basic Rate Interface, the most common type of ISDN connection, consisting of two digital 64-Kbps voice-and-data channels and one digital 16-Kbps signaling channel. The BRI is designed for an individual line connection over standard copper telephone lines.

**Bridge.** A device connecting one network to another and able to pass data between the two; usually, a computer with two network boards in it (but not necessarily the same cable type). Bridges operate on Layer 1 (physical) and the MAC sublayer of Layer 2 (data link) of the OSI model; they don't provide route optimization.

**Broadband.** Multiple-signal transmission of digital and analog (e.g., voice, video) data on different frequency channels. Broadband transmission can span longer distances than baseband.

**Broadcast.** To send information to all networked clients. For example, servers typically broadcast their availability periodically to let workstations know they're on line.

**Brouter.** A device that can perform both bridge and router functions.

**Buffer.** An interim storage location for data in transit; usually used to smooth out data transfer between devices capable of operating at different speeds.

**Bus Mastering.** Said of high-performance adapter cards that can temporarily take control of the bus and perform tasks without CPU intervention. Bus mastering is generally used by disk controllers, network adapters, and video cards.

**Bus Topology.** A network layout in which a single cable, terminated at each end, connects all PCs. Inexpensive for very small networks, but failure of the cable renders the whole segment inoperable.

**Byzantine Fault.** A computer system fault in which one component of the system (hardware or software) alters a condition that another component assumes to be true. For example, one program may change the contents of a particular memory location, accidentally overlaying a variable that was stored in that same location (and will soon be relied upon) by a second program.

**Cache.** An intermediary memory storage location, usually to help smooth over speed differences between devices. A *disk cache* is a memory region that stores disk data recently read or considered likely to be read again soon. A *CPU cache* is usually high-speed SRAM that caches main memory in the same way.

**CAD.**   Computer-Aided Design or Computer-Aided Drafting, software (e.g., AutoCAD) and hardware (e.g., powerful graphics workstations and graphics tablets) that accommodate traditional product design and drafting functions on the computer.

**Callback Modem.**   A security modem that returns a call initiated remotely by calling back to a predetermined number, based on a password entered on the first call.

**CAS.**   Communications Application Specification, Intel's fax-modem standard that puts more intelligence in the modem and permits binary file transfer between two CAS modems. It often requires a TSR and works with a very limited variety of modems, including Intel's SatisFAXtion line.

**CASE.**   Computer-Aided Software Engineering, a broad term for any software that facilitates the design, coding, or revising of other software.

**Category 1 Cable.**   Twisted-pair cabling suitable for analog voice transmission, but not for digital data, according to the Electronic Industry of America's performance standards.

**Category 2 Cable.**   Inexpensive twisted-pair cabling that can move data at up to 4 Mbps.

**Category 3 Cable.**   Twisted-pair cabling that can handle data rates of up to 10 Mbps, or higher with four-pair configurations.

**Category 4 Cable.**   Twisted-pair cabling that can handle data rates of up to 20 Mbps; often used for token-ring networks.

**Category 5 Cable.**   Presently the most expensive and flexible grade of twisted-pair cabling, Category 5 can manage data rates of up to 100 Mbps and higher, making it suitable for Fast Ethernet, ISDN, and ATM connections.

**CBT.**   Computer-Based Training, any application that facilitates self-paced user education, but especially those that do so interactively by providing information in either text or graphical form and then providing a mechanism for the user to validate the training, for example, with a self-test.

**CCITT.**   Consultative Committee on International Telephone and Telegraph, an international unsponsored standards-setting body for data communications, based in Geneva. Now called ITU-TSS.

**CD-R.** Recordable CD-ROM technology has supplanted Write-Once, Read-Many (WORM) optical formats and is rapidly dropping in price. CD-R provides about 650 MB of data storage per optical disk.

**CGI.** Common Gateway Interface, a standard interface between a browser and a Web server that defines how data is shuttled between an HTML form and an external program. CGI, developed at Europe's CERN nuclear research center, provides one mechanism for executing external applications (e.g., to access back-end databases) via Web servers.

**CHAP.** Challenge-Handshake Authentication Protocol, a password encryption technique that makes it virtually impossible for an eavesdropper to pick the password off the data stream. Windows 95's Dial-Up Networking supports CHAP if the encrypted passwords option is enabled.

**CheaperNet.** Synonymous with ThinNet (see **ThinNet**).

**Circuit.** Transmission medium connecting two or more communications devices.

**Class 1.** A Group III fax standard extension allowing the control of fax-modem functions using Hayes-style "AT" commands.

**Class 2.** A Group III fax standard extension similar to Class 1, but that allows the fax-modem to offload the CPU somewhat in managing connection chores; not completely defined, it may present annoying incompatibilities.

**Client.** (1) A workstation that is connected to a shared resource on another workstation (in a peer-to-peer network) or on a server (in a client/server network). NetWare clients, for example, can be running DOS, Windows 3.x, Windows 95, OS/2, Unix, or MacOS. (2) An application running on a client workstation. (3) The combination of client hardware and software.

**Client/Server Network.** A network (e.g., NetWare, NT Server) in which a dedicated PC running a Network Operating System handles all resource-sharing responsibilities (such as file and print sharing).

**Client/Server Computing.** Client/server computing is the subset of cooperative processing that is based on a simple, stable, hierarchical control relationship between any two cooperating programs, which may be running on two separate computers.

**Client/Server System.** A cooperative processing environment in which, typically, a front-end process executes on the client and one or more back-end processes execute on one or more servers, sometimes with intermediate software and hardware handling communication chores. A client/server system is broader in concept than a client/server network: It often makes use of server computers entirely separate from the common network server or servers, and typically requires services such as messaging and security authorization, among others.

**Cluster.**  (1) A collection of computers, generally of the same make and model, that share processing chores. (2) The smallest unit of storage that an operating system can allocate (expressed in sectors) given the limitations of its file system.

**CMIP.**  Common Management Information Protocol, the ISO's network management standards. CMOL (CMIP Over LLC) is the subset relevant for Ethernet and token-ring networks.

**CMOS.**  Short for Complementary Metal-Oxide Semiconductor, a memory type PCs use for storing system configuration information. Since CMOS RAM uses little power, it's a good choice for this battery-backed-up usage.

**Coaxial Cable.**  Network cabling with a central insulated copper conductor, a braided, jacketed shield and a plastic or plastic/Teflon cover; typically used for its superior resistance to electromagnetic interference and its ability to handle 100-Mbps data rates, but more costly than twisted-pair cable.

**Cold Site.**  A network set up at an alternate site for use in disasters, with hardware ready to go but without preloaded applications and data.

**Collision.**  What happens when two network clients try to send information packets across the LAN cable simultaneously, which causes lost data and slows the network by invoking a retransmission.

**Communication Buffers.**  Server memory devoted to caching network card read and write activity.

**Communications Server.**  A LAN server that shares modems or fax-modems for inbound access, outbound access, or both. Communications servers manage queues and assign devices much like print servers do; they may be dedicated or nondedicated.

**Comparison Pass.**  A backup operation that compares files on target media with files on source media; also called a verify pass.

**Compound Document.** A document containing data created by more than one application; the result of a link or embedding operation. See also **OLE.**

**Computer-Aided Design.** See **CAD.**

**Computer-Aided Software Engineering.** See **CASE.**

**Computer-Based Training.** See **CBT.**

**Concentrator.** Typically, a network device linking workstations in a physical star topology; often used synonymously with "hub."

**Conditioning.** (1) Improving AC line power quality by correcting variations in voltage waveform and frequency. (2) Improving telephone line quality by reducing noise.

**Container.** In Windows OLE terminology, an object that can contain another object.

**Contention.** When two programs vie for the same resource, e.g., a serial port or an Ethernet cable.

**Continuity.** The quality of an unbroken electrical pathway, e.g., in a LAN cable; one of the simplest functions of a cable tester is to test continuity.

**Control.** A programmed action button, multiple choice ("radio") button, or on-off button ("checkbox") that a software user can select to perform a predefined procedure.

**Conventional Memory.** Also known as DOS, low, application, and base memory; the area where DOS programs execute. From 0 to 640 K.

**Cooperative Multitasking.** A type of multitasking in which programs must periodically relinquish control to other programs and be "good citizens" to avoid hangups; used in Windows 3.x, and with Windows 3.x programs running under Windows 95.

**Cooperative Processing.** The closely coordinated use of more than one computer to solve any given business problem, and a distinguishing characteristic of client/server systems. Modern cooperative processing systems typically involve multiple brands and models of computers, and often unpredictable combinations of computer types. They address business problems and tasks that are not necessarily fixed, predictable, or well understood such as monthly production reporting. They may even address multiple business problems simultaneously.

**Cracker.** An individual who attempts to gain unauthorized access to a computer or network.

**Crash.** The event that causes a computer system or application to stop working suddenly, immediately, and irrevocably.

**CRC.** Cyclic Redundancy Check, an error-checking algorithm (e.g., for link level transmission); CRC values derived from the data to be sent are generated by the transmitter and verified by the receiver.

**Crosstalk.** Interference from an adjacent wire or cable; one of the potential problems cable testers can measure.

**CSMA/CD.** Carrier-Sense Multiple Access/Collision Detection; the Ethernet standard for arbitrating cable access by multiple devices and for dealing with collisions. CSMA allows nodes to transmit any time they sense the LAN is available; two nodes transmitting simultaneously each wait a random amount of time and then retry.

**Custom Control.** A specially made control (e.g., a VBX file in Visual BASIC) that extends the functionality of a given programming environment or application. See also **Control.**

**DAT.** Digital Audio Tape, a Sony-licensed technology for helical-scan recording with high capacity on small cartridges (2.9" x 2.1" x 0.4") using 4-mm tape. Typical cartridge capacities are 1.3, 2, and 4 GB. These systems also perform read-after-write verification.

**Data/DAT.** A Hitachi-sponsored DAT standard that has lost momentum compared to the various DDS standards.

**Database Management System.** See **DBMS.**

**Database Messaging Middleware.** A form of middleware that uses one or more client/server databases as message repositories. Instead of sending an e-mail message to another program's in-box, this approach inserts a row (or record) into another program's database. The DBMS then alerts the receiving program, or the receiving program simply looks at the database and notices the message. See also **Middleware.**

**Database Server.** A specialized server that accepts requests from clients and selects only relevant data for sending across the LAN to satisfy those requests.

**Datagram.** Generic term for a message in a predefined format, which includes some sort of transaction identifier and the associated data fields or strings.

**Data Link Layer.**   The second-lowest OSI model network software layer, governing low-level communication (messaging); the area where LAN drivers and bridges operate.

**Data Migration.**   A generic term for moving little-used files off from server hard disks and onto slower media that have a lower cost per megabyte, such as optical disks. See also **HSM.**

**Data Warehouse.**   A database (typically relational) that is intended solely to support data retrieval, analysis, and presentation. Data warehouses are physically separate from the databases and files that operational systems update on a regular basis.

**DB2.**   IBM's mainframe relational database management system.

**DBMS.**   DataBase Management System, an application that typically provides for data entry, validation, updating, querying, reporting, and archiving data related to one or more particular business functions.

**DC2000.**   A quarter-inch tape "minicartridge" standard measuring 3.25" x 2.5" x 0.6" and used with QIC-40 and QIC-80 tape drives.

**DC6000.**   A quarter-inch tape "full-cartridge" standard measuring 4" x 6" x 0.675" and used with higher-capacity QIC tape drives.

**DCE.**   Distributed Computing Environment, a set of standards developed by the Open Software Foundation (OSF) to aid in the development of client/server applications running on different platforms. See also **OSF.**

**DDE.**   Dynamic Data Exchange, a technique Windows programs use when data and/or commands exchange between two simultaneously-executing programs. NetDDE is an extension used in Windows for Workgroups and available in Windows 95.

**DDS.**   DDS-1 (Digital Data Storage-1) is a DAT standard developed by Hewlett-Packard and Sony that specifies a 2 GB uncompressed capacity and an uncompressed transfer rate of about 200 KBps. DDS-2, developed to support SCSI-2 burst mode, supports a 4-GB uncompressed capacity and a 400- to 500-KBps uncompressed transfer rate for 120-meter DAT cartridges. DDS-3 offers 8 GB of uncompressed capacity and can provide read and write compatibility with DDS-2.

**DDS-DC.**   Digital Data Storage—Data Compression, a hardware-based data compression standard for DAT.

**Decryption.** The decoding of an encrypted file or message. See also **encryption.**

**Defragment.** To reassemble a file so that all its sectors are physically contiguous, or adjacent. Improves performance of disks and disk caches.

**Departmental Application.** An application that fully automates or significantly supports the major function of a department

**DES.** Data Encryption Standard, the National Institute of Standards and Technology's algorithm for encrypting files for secure transmission or storage.

**Device Driver.** Software that enables a PC to communicate productively with a particular input or output device (e.g., mice, networks). Device drivers interpret computer data and provide the commands or signals needed by the device. They can be considered as "add-ons" that, when loaded, become an extended part of the operating system.

**DID.** Direct Inward Dialing, a technique for automatically routing incoming fax or voice messages to the intended party. Typically, the phone company will send the last two to four numbers of the dialed number to the customer's routing equipment.

**Differential Backup.** A backup scheduling method calling for periodic backups of all files that have changed since the last full backup. A file restore requires two backup sets, the last full backup and the last differential backup.

**Directory Services.** Network software that makes resource information (such as user names and addresses) available to everyone on the network. NDS (Netware Directory Services) is an example.

**Digital Audio Tape.** See **DAT.**

**Digital Linear Tape.** See **DLT.**

**Diskless Workstation.** A PC without floppy or hard drives; DOS typically boots from a ROM on the network card. Reduces security risks both outbound (confidential data) and inbound (virus-infected files).

**Distributed Computing Environment.** See **DCE.**

**Distributed Processing.** A computing model emphasizing that two (or more) computers are located in multiple physical sites. Distributed computer systems are often designed to make allowance for the fact that human work goes on in multiple locations, and to locate computer processing near the work to which it relates.

**DLL.** Dynamic Link Library; in Windows 3.x, Windows 95, and OS/2, basically a group of program subroutines collected together that perform related functions. Code modules in DLLs can be loaded and unloaded as needed at runtime, instead of at compile time (when the program is created). Software vendors often distribute bug fixes in the form of updated DLLs.

**DLT.** Digital Linear Tape is a fairly expensive, half-inch format developed by Digital Equipment Corporation, supporting capacities from 10 GB on up and transfer rates of about 1.25 MBps.

**DMA.** Direct Memory Access, wherein data transfers between devices do not require the direct involvement of the PCs CPU but rather are managed by a separate processor (e.g., on a disk controller). Hard disk backup programs often use DMA for better performance.

**DMI.** Desktop Management Interface, a network management system offered by the Desktop Management Task Force (DMTF). Similar in concept to SNMP; memory-resident "agents" can report on PC configurations and problems.

**DoD.** The United States Department of Defense.

**Domain.** In networking, a group of servers or "subnetwork" governed by a single security database; intended to ease network management.

**DPP.** Demand Priority Protocol, a non-collision-oriented access method used in the 100VG-AnyLAN network. DPP is a two-tiered protocol: One level of priority is for data and the other is for multimedia. A real-time video request would get priority over a simple data request.

**DRAM.** Dynamic RAM, the type most often used in PC main memory subsystems; it consists typically of one transistor and one capacitor, which must be "refreshed" continually by the power supply.

**Driver.** See **Device Driver.**

**DSS.** Decision Support System; see **EIS.**

**DUN.** Dial-Up Networking, Microsoft's Windows 95 remote node software allowing remote PCs to access NetBEUI, TCP/IP, and IPX networks over phone lines.

**Duplexing.**  A network server reliability technique whereby redundant disk controllers and drives protect against failure of either component. Built into NetWare as part of System Fault Tolerance Level II (SFT II). See also **Mirroring.**

**Dynamic Data Exchange.**  See **DDE.**

**Dynamic Link Library.**  See **DLL.**

**EC-1000.**  A software upgrade for QIC-80 tape drives permitting an uncompressed capacity of 400 MB on 1000-foot tapes.

**ECC.**  Error Correction Coding, a technique often used by backup software that adds redundant information to a backup set to permit rebuilding of records damaged as a result of media failure.

**ECU.**  EISA Configuration Utility, a program used to define operating characteristics for circuit boards installed in EISA slots.

**EDA/SQL.**  Enterprise Data Access/Structured Query Language, a "de facto" open database middleware product developed and sold by Information Builders Inc. EDA/SQL establishes a gateway server to which client applications issue their database calls. The EDA gateway then interprets and resolves those calls by issuing native SQL commands to any of a wide mix of database servers and DBMSs. Widely used for ad hoc and other database retrieval.

**EDC.**  Error Detection and Correction, not used for PC memory systems but often used by network operating systems for hard drive data.

**EDI.**  Electronic Data Interchange, intercompany standards for exchanging information such as orders and inventory.

**EIA.**  Electronic Industries Association, for electronics and communications industries; responsible for standards such as RS-232C.

**EIDE.**  Enhanced IDE, an extension to the Integrated Drive Electronics standard permitting disk drive sizes greater than 528 MB, more devices (usually four) per bus connector, and improved data transfer rates.

**EIS.**  Executive Information System, a "read-only" computer system or application that permits access to corporate data, usually in a summarized (and often graphical) form. Usually synonymous with DSS (Decision Support System), though a DSS may denote wider accessibility.

**EISA.**  Extended Industry Standard Architecture, a 32-bit-capable bus that is backward compatible with ISA boards (unlike MCA). Usually found in high-powered desktops and LAN servers, the EISA standard appeared in 1988. EISA machines have programs to configure adapters in software; they also support bus mastering.

**Electronic Data Interchange.**  See **EDI.**

**Embedding.**  In Windows OLE parlance, embedding is the process of encapsulating one object into another, container object.

**EMI.**  ElectroMagnetic Interference, such as noise from fluorescent lights and dimmer switches, which can corrupt data communications.

**Encapsulation.**  Wrapping one communications packet inside another.

**Enhanced IDE.**  See **EIDE.**

**Encryption.**  The mathematical manipulation of data characters in such a manner as to make them unintelligible to unauthorized viewers.

**Enterprise Application.**  An application whose functionality is necessary to all the employees in the company, not just those in a single department

**Ethernet.**  A 10-MBps networking standard, using either thick coaxial, thin coaxial, or twisted-pair cable, which handles network traffic using a collision-detection technology.

**Ethernet II.**  An Ethernet variant specifying a frame type compatible with TCP/IP, early versions of AppleTalk, and DEC networks.

**Ethernet SNAP.**  An Ethernet variant specifying a frame type with a header extension for compatibility with later versions of AppleTalk.

**Executive Information System.**  See **EIS.**

**Extranet.**  An intranet that provides services to external companies, such as customers and suppliers.

**Fast Ethernet.**  100-Mbps Ethernet that can run on standard twisted-pair cables but requires updated NICs.

**FAT.**  File Allocation Table, a data structure that keeps track of which disk clusters are in use and where the "next" cluster is in a file. DOS uses a 16-bit FAT for hard disks, meaning that larger cluster sizes must be used for larger-capacity disks. Net-Ware's FAT is stored in memory and accessed via the Directory Entry Table (DET).

**Fat Client System.**   A type of client/server system that places the user interface and all the process logic on the client For each user of a fat-client application, the programs that capture, display, and process all the data that the user handles or looks at run on that user's desktop computer. The data storage, typically residing on a database server, will be commonly accessed and shared among all users, no matter how many, but most of the processing for each user is right where the user is, and affects no one else.

**Fault Tolerance.**   Systems that can operate without interruption during a component failure, either in hardware or software, have fault tolerance. Hardware fault tolerance, for example, is achievable through machine design or by coupling redundant systems, e.g., in mirrored servers.

**Fax-Back System.**   A computer-based fax document delivery system whereby users place a phone call, select documents (e.g., technical notes) based on a coded list, and request that those documents be sent to a specified fax number. Also called "fax-on-demand."

**FDDI.**   (pronounced "fiddy") Fiber Distributed Data Interface, an ANSI token-passing network protocol that can manage 100-Mbps data rates and long distances (2 kilometers on fiber cable). FDDI has better immunity to cable failure than token-ring, but it is still expensive.

**Fiber Optic Cable.**   Glass or plastic light conductors; high transmission rates (over 150 Mbps) and best noise immunity of all cable types. Fiber is not subject to crosstalk, capacitance, or attenuation. Because it uses light rather than electrical signals, it's also very secure, though relatively expensive.

**File Allocation Table.**   See **FAT.**

**File Infector.**   A type of virus that attaches itself to executable programs.

**File System Buffers.**   Server memory devoted to caching disk read and write requests.

**Firewall.**   Any system or group of systems that implements and enforces any sort of access control policy between any two networks.

**Firmware.** Software in hardware, that is, nonvolatile memory that keeps its software contents when powered off. It may be updatable, e.g., with UV light. Types include ROM, PROM, EPROM and EEPROM.

**Flash Memory.** Nonvolatile memory such as that used in software-updatable "Flash BIOS" chips.

**Frame.** The envelope of control, addressing and error-correcting information around a packet. Ethernet frame types include ETHERNET_II, ETHERNET_SNAP, ETHERNET_802.2 and ETHERNET_802.3. The frame is specified under the "Link Driver" section of NET.CFG in the IPXODI system, and in the Network control panel's "Configuration" tab in Microsoft's Windows 95 driver for NetWare. An incorrect frame type will result in "Server Not Found" errors.

**Front End.** Usually synonymous with "client."

**Full Duplex.** Permitting simultaneous bidirectional communications.

**Gateway.** (1) A router operating on all seven OSI layers; interconnects completely dissimilar LANs, or LANs and mainframes, by translating protocols. (2) A software tool allowing access to other enterprise mail systems.

**GFS.** Grandfather-Father-Son, a backup media rotation strategy employing three generations of media.

**GPF.** General Protection Fault, a Windows error indicating an attempt to access memory not legitimately available to the application.

**GPPE.** The General Protection Processor Exception, also known as General Processor Protection Error, is a network server error detected by the CPU and usually caused by a program attempting to access a nonexistent physical RAM address.

**Group III.** The most common fax communications standard, specifying 203 x 98 dpi (standard) or 203 x 196 dpi (fine) resolution with data compression and 9600 baud. (Group III bis provides for 14.4-Kbps transmission.)

**GUI.** Graphical User Interface, e.g., Microsoft Windows; as opposed to a text-mode interface, e.g., the DOS command line. See also **OOUI**.

**Header.** In networking, a packet component containing source and target addresses and message type data.

**Helical Scan Recording.** See **8-mm Tape** and **DAT.**

**Help Desk.** A formal organizational unit whose primary responsibility is the timely resolution of users' technical questions and problems, with the goal of maximizing their productivity and minimizing downtime.

**Hierarchical Storage Management.** See **HSM.**

**Hop Count.** How many NICs a network packet traverses during its route from source to destination. After a certain number of hops, typically 16, transmission may not complete.

**Host Adapter.** The controller card on a SCSI device chain. Host adapters are available for ISA, EISA, MCA, VL, and PCI buses.

**Hot Fix.** The ability for an error to be corrected, or a problem repaired, without interrupting operations. Some network operating systems support this for bad sectors, as do many SCSI hard drives. Also called "hot swap," usually for entire components such as RAID hard drives.

**Hot Site.** A network set up at an alternate site for use in disasters, with critical applications and data already loaded.

**Hot Swapping.** The ability to replace a component without powering it or its host computer down; a feature of some RAID disk subsystems and PCMCIA cards.

**HSM.** Hierarchical Storage Management, a mainframe data migration technology finding its way into PC LANs. HSM software typically leaves a zero-length file on the server as a placeholder and reloads the file automatically from optical disk or tape ("near-line" media) when a user performs an operation that requires the file. See also **Data Migration.**

**HTML.** HyperText Markup Language, the most popular coding method for defining documents on the World Wide Web.

**Hub.** Most generally, a device at a central location to which two or more cables connect in a star topology. In a 10Base-T network, the hub is a necessary network component from which unshielded twisted pair cables radiate to individual workstations. Hubs may be separate devices or plug-in circuit boards; they may be powered or unpowered; they may include network management software ("intelligent" hubs) or they may not.

**Hypertext.** A text-based computer document with highlighted links ("hyperlinks") that, when acted upon (e.g., by a mouse click), jump to another document or to another portion of the same document.

**IDE.** Integrated Drive Electronics, currently the most popular hard drive interface standard, in which the controller is integrated with the drive unit and typically plugs into a motherboard connector; maximum throughput is 8 MBps (megabytes/second) in a typical 16-bit implementation. IDE technology obviates many of the drive-geometry and setup problems associated with earlier types, such as MFM and RLL.

**IEEE 802.2.** The Ethernet standard to which NetWare 4.x and 3.12 default. A modification of 802.2 called Ethernet_SNAP adds a header extension for AppleTalk compatibility.

**IEEE 802.3.** The formal name for the "raw frame" Ethernet standard (also StarLAN) and the version of Ethernet to which NetWare 3.11 defaults. See **Ethernet.**

**IEEE 802.5.** The formal name for the token-ring standard. See **token-ring.**

**Incremental Backup.** A backup scheduling method calling for periodic backups of all files that have changed since the previous backup. Less convenient for file restores than differential backups, incremental backups require less space on backup media.

**Instrumentation.** Program code that is not necessary for performing the business function, but that records data about the performance of the application program itself.

**Integrated Drive Electronics.** See **IDE.**

**Integrated Services Digital Network.** See **ISDN.**

**Internetwork.** A network with more than one segment, possibly with different cabling, speeds, Network Operating Systems, etc., typically connected by one or more routers.

**Interrupt.** A signal to the CPU from a device that needs attention, usually to service an input or output demand. When the CPU receives an interrupt, it may pause what it's doing and give control to an *interrupt handler* program that will take it from there.

**Intranet.** A computer system that makes available just about every type of corporate information to all corporate employees, using tools such as electronic mail, Usenet newsgroups, and Web pages. Formatted, structured information, such as is normally stored in a database, is available online for regular or ad hoc retrieval but unformatted, unstructured information—letters, memos, notes, drawings, diagrams, books, manuals, other reference works—is also accessible online.

**Inverter.**  An electrical device to convert DC power, e.g., from a UPS battery, to AC power.

**IP.**  See **TCP/IP.**

**IPX.**  Internet Packet eXchange, a message routing protocol that runs on the Network layer of the OSI model; used by NetWare LANs. IPX by itself does not guarantee message delivery. See also **SPX.**

**IPXODI.**  See **ODI.**

**IRQ.**  Interrupt ReQuest line, basically a hardware "hot line" that devices (such as network boards) use to snag the attention of the CPU. No two devices in an ISA-bus PC may share the same IRQ simultaneously, though MCA and EISA machines permit interrupt sharing under specific circumstances.

**ISA.**  Industry Standard Architecture; the IBM PC-AT bus, capable of handling either 8- or 16-bit-wide boards. Used in most workstation PCs of moderate to low power.

**ISDN.**  Integrated Services Digital Network; allows voice, fax, data, and video on the same network. Telephone companies in major metropolitan areas are starting to offer ISDN connectivity.

**ISO.**  International Standards Organization, headquartered in Geneva, which produces the OSI network model among other standards.

**ISP.**  Internet Service Provider, an organization that offers Internet connectivity, usually for a monthly access fee.

**ITU-TSS.**  International Telecommunications Union Telecommunications Standards Section; an international unsponsored standards-setting body for data communications, with over 100 participating countries. Formerly CCITT.

**Java.**  A full-fledged programming language, developed by Sun Microsystems and modeled loosely on C++, designed for creating applications that may reside on a World Wide Web server and be executed by clients running Web browsers. Java applications require an interpreter that converts the machine-independent "byte code" to machine-specific code at run time.

**JDBC.**  Java Data Base Connectivity, an API developed by JavaSoft (a Sun unit) to permit Java applets to access client/server databases directly.

**Join.**  A relational database operation in which data from one or more tables that have at least one common column is combined to satisfy the requirements of a query or report.

**Kerberos.**  A widely used, software-based authentication technology developed at MIT that allows client and server programs, running on different computers, to prove their identity to each other. Kerberos can also prevent eavesdropping by unauthorized users and can detect interruptions in the stream of data from one computer to another.

**LAN.**  Local Area Network, a network containing servers, workstations, cable, and software all linked together within a relatively small geographical area.

**Landmark Backup.**  A backup performed before a major LAN event, such as an application upgrade or end-of-year accounting close procedure. Also called "milestone" backup.

**Leased Line.**  A telephone line leased from a common carrier and dedicated for exclusive, round-the-clock service between two locations; also called "dedicated circuit." May be conditioned for better data capability.

**Legacy (Device, Application, Data).**  A nice way of saying "old."

**LIP.**  Large Internet Packet, a throughput optimizing technique permitting packets larger than 576 bytes for more efficient internetwork and WAN communications.

**LLC.**  Logical Link Control layer, a sublayer within the Data-Link layer of the OSI network model; sits on top of the MAC layer.

**Local Area Network.**  See **LAN.**

**Local Bus.**  A bus running at higher speeds (often at the CPU's clock rate) and possibly wider data pathways than the PC's standard bus; useful for video, disk, and network adapters. See **VESA** and **PCI.**

**Locking.**  In a DBMS, the act of preventing other users from updating a field or record while one user is already doing so. Locking maintains the data's validity.

**Logical.**  As distinct from "physical," in computer systems, a high-level view independent of underlying detail. For example, a logical connection between two PCs might navigate several physical network devices, or a single physical disk drive might contain several logical drives.

**Logical Map.** A network map showing servers, groups, and users, sometimes including server public and private directories. See also **Physical Map.**

**LSL.** Link Support Layer, part of Unix System V and of Novell's modular ODI client software scheme; resides on top of the LAN driver, between OSI layers 2 and 3, and allows multiple network transport protocols to be used on a single network interface card.

**LZW.** Lempel-Ziv-Welch, a file compression technology that takes advantage of repeating patterns to reduce file size; common in graphics file formats and in file compression utilities.

**MAC.** Media Access Control, a sublayer within the Data-Link layer of the OSI network model, located between the LAN driver and the physical layer.

**Macro.** An embedded program designed to automate a series of operations within a particular application. Microsoft Windows applications, for example, typically use a macro language based on Visual Basic (Visual Basic for Applications).

**Magneto-Optical Storage.** MO is a rewritable, removable optical storage medium with capacities from 650 MB to 2 GB and form factors of both 3.5" and 5.25". The medium is expensive compared to magnetic tape, but very stable and often used for long-term archiving.

**MAN.** Metropolitan Area Network, covering a city or a portion of a city.

**Map.** To associate a network resource (e.g., printer, directory) with a logical name (e.g., local port, drive letter).

**MAPI.** Messaging Application Program Interface, or how programs interact with MS Mail; a way of making workgroup applications independent of the underlying messaging system.

**MAU.** (1) Multistation Access Unit, the hub to which PCs in a token-ring LAN connect. Also called MSAU. (2) Media Access Unit, an Ethernet hub.

**MBR.** The Master Boot Record of a disk.

**MCA.** Micro Channel Architecture, the 32-bit-capable bus used in certain IBM PS/2 machines (and very few others). MCA boards are software configurable and may be 8, 16, or 32 bits wide.

**Media.** Cable between network nodes; twisted-pair, coax, or fiber optic.

**Messaging-Oriented Middleware.**  A form of middleware in which one program (the client) sends a formatted message to another program (the server). By previous agreement, that is, in accordance with the application design, the server knows what action to take upon receipt of each format of message. See also **Middleware.**

**MIB.**  Management Information Base, configuration data files used by the SNMP network management system. See **SNMP.**

**Middleware.**  In a client/server system, software that mediates and standardizes the connections, or interfaces, between different parts of the system's communications pathways.

**MIF.**  Management Information File, configuration data files used by the DMI network management system. See **DMI.**

**Mirroring.**  (1) A network reliability enhancement whereby redundant disk drives are used with the same controller. Protects against drive failure but not controller failure. Built into NetWare as System Fault Tolerance Level II (SFT-II). (2) With servers, two identical machines with a high-speed link and appropriate software to provide fault tolerance.

**Mission-Critical Application.**  An application that may have a smaller user constituency than an enterprise application, but that is essential to the functioning of the business. A common characteristic of mission-critical applications is that the user community extends beyond an organization's employees; if the system goes down, people outside the organization know about it as soon as employees do.

**MLID.**  Multiple Link Interface Driver; an element of Novell's ODI network software scheme that communicates with a specific network interface card below it, and the link support layer above it. The MLID, which is typically supplied by LAN card makers, is independent of protocol stack details and can be updated separately.

**MNP 4.**  A Microcom-developed error correction standard for dial-up modems.

**MNP 5.**  A Microcom-developed data compression standard for dial-up modems. Microcom Networking Protocol 5 has fallen out of favor on many online services because it decreases transmission speed with files that are already compressed, such as .ZIP or .GIF files.

**MO.**  See **Magneto-Optical Storage.**

**MOM.**  See **Messaging-Oriented Middleware.**

**MSAU.**  See **MAU.**

**MTBF.**  Mean Time Before (Between) Failures, a statistical measure of how long one may expect a hardware component to operate reliably before a problem; usually given in Power-On Hours (POH). Good modern hard drives typically have an MTBF of 500,000 hours or more.

**MTTR.**  Mean Time To Repair, how long it takes on average to fix something.

**Multistation Access Unit.**  See **MAU.**

**Multitasking.**  When a computer manages two or more simultaneous tasks, it multitasks. Various techniques (e.g., time slicing) exist for single CPUs to appear to be doing two or three things at once. *Cooperative* multitasking relies on well-behaved applications; *preemptive* multitasking allows the operating system to play traffic cop.

**Name Space.**  A network capability permitting the storage of files on a server that use a file system other than the default.

**NCP.**  NetWare Core Protocol, a set of procedures NetWare uses to deal with all LAN-related client requests. Analogous to SMB on Microsoft networks.

**NDIS**  (pronounced EN-dis). Network Driver Interface Specification, developed by Microsoft and 3Com in 1989; a standard for network drivers, allowing any OSI Level 3 and 4 software to communicate with any NDIS-compliant network card driver at OSI Level 2.

**NDS.**  NetWare Directory Services, a domain naming system for NetWare 4 that may be retrofitted to NetWare 3 servers.

**Near-Line Storage.**  Somewhere between online (server disks) and offline (archived backups), near-line storage is typically optical storage for little-used files that may need to be restored relatively quickly to online server disks.

**NetBEUI**  (pronounced NET-booie). NetBIOS Extended User Interface, a high-speed, nonroutable network transport, residing in OSI levels 3 and 4; controls access to file and print sharing and NetDDE. Originally introduced by IBM in 1985.

**NetBIOS.**  Network Basic Input/Output System, network software residing in OSI Level 5 on DOS or Unix machines, which handles redirection of I/O requests to network resources. Made popular by IBM and Microsoft; supported by NetWare through emulation, though at some performance cost.

**NetDDE.**  Network Dynamic Data Exchange, Windows for Workgroups' technology for linking applications and data files across the network. The ClipBook uses NetDDE, and it is also accessible from many Windows application macro languages.

**NetWare Core Protocol.**  See **NCP.**

**Network Modem.**  A modem (such as those made by Shiva) that connects directly to a network, rather than indirectly through a PC.

**Network.**  Two or more computer systems connected for the purpose of communication or resource sharing: the aggregate of clients, servers, and interconnecting infrastructure. Often informally used as a synonym for LAN.

**Network Interface Card.**  See **NIC.**

**Network Layer.**  Third of the OSI network model layers, where network protocols such as IP and IPX are defined; also where network addresses are defined. Routers operate at the network layer.

**Network Operating System.**  See **NOS.**

**Network PC.**  Also known as "net PC," a networked microcomputer with no local disk storage. Network PCs have been proposed as a way of reducing support and administration costs, as all software—applications as well as data—resides on network servers and is downloaded as necessary.

**NETX.**  The NetWare client redirector software used with 2.x and 3.x servers. NETX.EXE is a TSR that reroutes requests for shared file and print services.

**NIC.**  (pronounced "nick") Network Interface Card, the circuit board that plugs into a PC expansion slot and a network cabling system and manages the physical data transfer between the PC and the network.

**NLM.**  Netware Loadable Module, an extension to the server operating system to provide added functionality, such as interacting with disk and LAN controllers, detecting viruses, providing foreign name space support, or performing backups. NLMs may be loaded and unloaded without DOWNing the server, though in practice the sequence of unloading may be important. Buggy NLMs can cause great problems with NetWare servers as they run at a high privilege level (Intel processor Ring Zero).

**NMI.** NonMaskable Interrupt, such as the interrupt triggered by a memory parity error or bus error, which is too important to allow disabling by software.

**NMS.** Network Management System, such as SNMP.

**Node Number.** A unique identifier for a LAN card. Ethernet and token-ring cards have node numbers burned into firmware at the factory and require no maintenance or administration.

**Nonvolatile.** Said of computer memory that retains its contents without power.

**NOS.** (pronounced "noss") Network Operating System, the core system software running on a network server. Examples include Novell NetWare, Microsoft NT Server, Banyan VINES, etc.

**NT.** Actually Windows NT, for New Technology, the high end of the Windows product line, implemented in 32-bit protected mode in its entirety; targeted for LAN servers and high-end Windows workstations.

**ODBC.** Open DataBase Connectivity, the most widely supported standard for open database middleware, initially developed by Microsoft. All major relational DBMSs support ODBC; DBMS vendors supply their own ODBC drivers. See also **Open Database Middleware.**

**ODI.** Open Datalink Interface, Novell's modular network client software scheme that permits multiple transport protocols to be used on a single network interface card. The IPXODI module moves data between the redirector or requestor and the LSL module. Similar in spirit and functionality to Microsoft's NDIS.

**OLAP.** OnLine Analytical Processing, a "read-only" computer system or application that permits more rapid access to summarized views of large amounts of data than does traditional relational database technology.

**OLTP.** OnLine Transaction Processing, a computer system or application that permits the real-time entry of large amounts of data. For example, airline reservations systems are OLTP systems.

**OLE.** (pronounced "oh-LAY") Object Linking and Embedding, a Windows technology that extends DDE and allows not only the creation of compound documents with data originating in more than one program, but also the editing of pasted data using its originating application without leaving the host application. Now in version 2.

**OOUI.** Short for Object-Oriented User Interface, a GUI in which objects (such as directories, files, printers, etc.) are represented by icons that users can manipulate directly.

**Open Database Connectivity.** See **ODBC.**

**Open Database Middleware.** Middleware designed to allow an application program to access and/or update data in any one of a large number of commercial DBMSs. The application program doesn't need to, and in fact shouldn't, know in which DBMS the data resides. See also **Middleware.**

**Open Datalink Interface.** See **ODI.**

**OSF.** Open Software Foundation, a nonprofit organization based in Cambridge, Massachusetts, that develops, publishes, and licenses standards for open computing. OSF products include Motif and the Distributed Computing Environment (DCE) standards for client/server systems. See also **DCE.**

**OSI.** Open Systems Interconnect, a seven-layer network model established in 1984 by the ISO (International Organization for Standardization) to help enable network software developers to create programs at each level independently.

**Packet.** The unit of data transfer on a LAN; a chunk of data packaged for transmission in a way specific to the network protocol being used.

**PAP.** Password Authentication Protocol, an authentication scheme that permits the client to send a network account password over the remote link in clear text, meaning that an electronic eavesdropper could read it without difficulty.

**Patch.** In networks, a modification to the operating system to correct a problem.

**PCI.** Peripheral Component Interconnect, an Intel-developed high-performance local bus used for video, disk, and network interface cards. The PCI bus runs at 33 Mhz and may support 32-bit or 64-bit cards; it's well suited to Pentium PCs.

**PCMCIA.** (1) Personal Computer Memory Card Industry Association, a set of standards for the 68-pin "credit-card" devices popular in portable computers. Types I, II, and III differ in the thickness dimension only, but share connector specs. (2) Acronym for "People Can't Memorize Computer Industry Acronyms."

**PGP.** Pretty Good Privacy, a public-key computer data encryption scheme developed by Phil Zimmerman and available to individuals (free) and companies (by license).

**Peer-to-Peer Network.** Type of network in which no dedicated PC acts as a server, but in which every PC may share attached printers and local files, with network processing occurring in the background. LANTastic and Windows 95 are peer-to-peer networks. These are suitable for small groups (2 to 20) with few security requirements.

**Physical Layer.** The lowest of the seven OSI network model layers, dealing with the mechanical and electrical connection to a network cable.

**Physical Map.** A network map showing device locations (PCs, printers, servers, routers etc.) and interconnections. See also **logical map.**

**Plenum Cable.** Network cable with fire-resistant coating required by most fire codes for installation through walls and across ceiling plenum spaces.

**Plug-and-Play.** Often abbreviated PnP. A set of standards developed by Microsoft, Intel, Compaq, and Phoenix (among others) to ease the configuration of hardware devices through autodetection of device characteristics, resource allocation, and conflict arbitration. A full implementation requires PnP compatibility at all levels, including BIOS, motherboard, OS (such as Windows 95), adapter, device, and driver.

**PnP.** See **Plug-and-Play.**

**Polymorphic Virus.** A virus that can "change shape" each time it infects a file, making signature-based detection much more difficult.

**POP.** Point of Presence, a telephone number that provides access to a public data network (such as the Internet).

**POST.** The Power-On Self-Test residing in a PC's BIOS that runs on power-up.

**Power Conditioning.** Broad term usually encompassing line voltage surge suppression, waveform regulation, and backup capability.

**PPP.** Short for Point-to-Point Protocol, a standard for communications across relatively slow links (such as dial-up phone lines). The default protocol for Windows 95's Dial-Up Networking facility. PPP is supported by NetWare Connect versions 2 and above.

**PPTP.** Point-to-Point Tunneling Protocol, an extension of the popular PPP dial-up communication protocol that adds encryption capabilities. It supports IPX, NetBIOS, and NetBEUI as well as IP.

**Preemptive Multitasking.** A type of multitasking in which the operating system can manage allocation of CPU and other resources to multiple simultaneous processes. Available in Windows NT, OS/2 and Windows 95.

**Presentation Layer.** Sixth of the OSI model layers; where machine-specific data manipulation (such as internal numeric formats) is translated and encrypted.

**Presentation Logic.** See **User Interface.**

**Pretty Good Privacy.** See **PGP.**

**PRI.** Primary Rate Interface, a commercial ISDN installation consisting of 24 digital channels in the United States and 31 in Europe. In the U.S. version, 23 of the channels carry data and the 24th is used for commands.

**Print-Through.** The corruption of data on physically adjacent tape spool winds by magnetic field effects.

**Process Logic.** The software component of a computer system that implements the business rules that characterize or constitute the business application.

**PROM.** Programmable Read-Only Memory, memory chips that may be "burned in" with program code and that then act as ROMs.

**Protocol.** Rules or standards that control and manage the creation, maintenance, and termination of data transfer on a network or across modems.

**Protocol Analyzer.** Program, or an entire computer system, that listens to a LAN cable and collects data at various levels of the OSI model; used for troubleshooting network links and for performance tuning.

**Proxy Server.** A communications server that typically permits no direct traffic between one network and another, but rather, for security reasons, acts as a store-and-forward device for data or messages meeting predefined criteria. Proxy servers may forward permitted data or messages automatically, or only on request from another computer.

**PSTN.** Public Switched Telephone Network.

**Public-Key Encryption.** Also known as *asymmetric* encryption; a cryptography scheme wherein each individual has a private "secret" key and a published, "public" key. A sender looks up the recipient's public key and uses it to encrypt a message, and the recipient uses the private key to decrypt it. See also **encryption** and **secret-key encryption.**

**QFA.**   Quick File Access, a standard that both the tape drive and the backup utility must support for it to work, specifies a method for repositioning a tape to the start of a file or directory up to 50 times faster than systems without QFA.

**QIC.**   Quarter-Inch Committee, which creates standards for magnetic tape drives. QIC-40 and QIC-80 are popular PC tape drive standards; QIC-40 offers 40 to 60 MB of uncompressed storage depending on tape length, and QIC-80 offers 80 to 120 MB. Defined standards go all the way up to 13 GB, however, and many QIC variants exist. See also **EC-1000, QIC-Wide,** and **Travan.**

**QIC-Wide.**   A Sony-developed extension to the QIC standard that uses 0.315" tape and boosts capacity from 20% to 75%.

**Queue.**   Any kind of waiting or holding location; typically, the list of documents waiting to be printed on a print server.

**Quiet.**   Said of a LAN with no users logged in and a minimal number of executing processes. Backup operations include more files when performed on a quiet LAN, because fewer files are open.

**RAD.**   Rapid Application Development, a relatively new model for developing software applications that typically emphasizes prototyping, modularization, and recursive rather than linear development.

**RAID.**   Redundant Array of Inexpensive Disks, a network reliability enhancement technique usually involving vendor-specific hardware and software that spreads server data across multiple disks. RAID 1 is the same as disk mirroring. RAID 5 is the most popular type and does not require a dedicated parity drive; it's more expensive than duplexing, but has more potential for performance as well as reliability enhancement.

**RAM Disk.**   A portion of RAM made to behave like a very fast, volatile disk drive, usually through a driver such as RAM-DRIVE.SYS.

**RAS.**   Remote Access Server, Microsoft's remote node software allowing remote PCs to access NetBIOS, TCP/IP, and IPX networks over phone lines. RAS is available in Windows for Workgroups, Windows NT, and Windows 95 (where it's called "Dial-Up Client").

**RAW.**   Read-After-Write verification, e.g., of server disk data; faster when implemented in hardware, e.g., in a high-performance controller, but some networks provide RAW functionality in software. Better backup utilities and devices also perform RAW for backed up data.

**Redirector.**   Workstation software that routes read/write requests to network devices as appropriate.

**Relational Database.**   A DBMS in which data is stored in tables with columns and rows. Relational databases support an almost infinite number of relationships among data records, as distinct from other database types that predefine links between records.

**Remote Control.**   A remote PC linked indirectly into a LAN by "taking over" a local, networked PC via modem. This technique depends on the availability of a local PC, but is suitable for lower-speed modem connections because the local host PC processes most of the data. Keyboard, screen, and mouse data traverse the dial-up link.

**Remote Node.**   A remote PC linked directly into a LAN via modem. Remote Node PCs function just as if they were logged in on-site, in that network packets traverse the dial-up link. This technique for remote access requires high-speed modems to handle the traffic.

**Remote Procedure Call.**   See **RPC**.

**Repeater.**   A simple network device that amplifies, or boosts, incoming signals so they can be sent a longer distance. Repeaters do not look at packets or protocols; they just amplify and recondition every bit they receive and retransmit it. They operate on Level 1 of the OSI model.

**Resource.**   Any computer drive, directory, printer, or other peripheral that can be shared among network users.

**RFI.**   Radio Frequency Interference, e.g., noise from radios and televisions.

**RG-58.**   ThinNet Ethernet coaxial cable.

**RG-62.**   ARCnet cable.

**Ring.**   A network topology in which PCs connect via a closed path of typically unidirectional network interface cards. In token-ring networks, the ring topology may reside entirely inside the hub, with the actual cabling in a star topology emanating from the hub.

**RIP.** Router Information Protocol, the protocol routers use to communicate amongst themselves and with workstations. Each router routinely and repeatedly sends its routing tables, with associated network addresses, to all other routers—typically once a minute.

**RISC.** Reduced Instruction Set Computer, a processor design that uses shorter commands compared to CISC (Complex Instruction Set Computer) designs.

**Rollback.** A client/server database feature wherein a partly completed but interrupted transaction is nullified and the data restored to its original state.

**Router.** A network device operating at Layer 3 of OSI; more sophisticated than a bridge, able to perform routing optimization and load balancing by examining packet destination addresses. LANs that are connected by routers form internetworks.

**RPC.** Remote Procedure Call, a technique for computer-to-computer program execution across a network wherein one computer issues a function call that is at least potentially processed by another computer. The calling (main or master) procedure is the client program, and the called (or subordinate) procedure is the server program. For example, Windows 95 uses RPC for services such as the Remote Registry Editor.

**RS-232C.** The EIA's "Recommended Standard" for serial interfaces, incorporating guidelines for modem and printer links. Widely interpreted by different PC and printer manufacturers.

**SAP.** Service Advertising Protocol, a mechanism whereby services broadcast their presence to the network. Routers use SAP broadcasts to maintain LAN configuration databases and to notify the LAN of configuration changes. A high level of SAP activity can slow down a network.

**SCSI.** Small Computer Systems Interface, a separate terminated bus that can support up to seven connected devices; usually used for high-performance, high-capacity server hard drives. The "Fast SCSI-2" variant specifies a maximum sustainable data transfer rate of 10 MBps, with burst transfers that may be significantly higher. "Fast and Wide SCSI" is not yet fully standardized but permits 20 MBps throughput.

**Secret-Key Encryption.**   Also known as *symmetric* encryption; a cryptography scheme wherein each individual has a private "secret" key that is used for both encryption and decryption. See also **encryption** and **public-key encryption.**

**Sector.**   The smallest unit of storage readable or writable to a disk drive.

**Segment.**   A portion of a network electrically connected, e.g., by a cable.

**Segmentation.**   The process of dividing a LAN into multiple segments, or subnets, usually to increase performance. Segmentation or "subnetting" may increase the administration burden for the overall network.

**Server.**   (1) Any computer that provides network services, whether file, print, communication, name space, directory, security, or application services. In peer networks, a server is any PC that is sharing a local resource over the network, and any given PC may be both a server and a client for different resources. (2) A program providing services to a client application, e.g., a database server. (3) The combination of server hardware and programs.

**Session Layer.**   Fifth of the OSI-model network layers; where the network creates, manages, and terminates communications sessions.

**SFT.**   System Fault Tolerance, a NetWare acronym. SFT Level I is the "hot fix" capability and is built into NetWare 2.x and higher. Higher levels of SFT include disk duplexing and mirrored servers (Level III).

**Shadowing.**   Copying ROM code (such as a PCs BIOS) to RAM for faster execution.

**Share-Level Security.**   A network security model whereby an administrator assigns names, passwords, and access privileges on a per-resource basis. See also **user-level security.**

**SHTTP.**   Secure HyperText Transfer Protocol, an extension of HTTP that provides encryption and authentication services for the Internet and intranets.

**Single-User Application.**   An application that does not integrate with other users. Typically, single-user applications read and update data; they may be created by nonprofessional developers.

**SIV.**  System Integrity Violation, a Windows error similar to the GPF but triggered by a DOS application.

**SLIP.**  Serial Line Interface Protocol, a communications standard similar to PPP but less efficient.

**Slot.**  In network parlance, a user license. Certain print servers also use a slot.

**Small Computer Systems Interface.**  See **SCSI.**

**SMB.**  Server Message Block, a network protocol for handling workstation requests on Microsoft networks such as LAN Manager or NT Server. Analogous to NCP on NetWare networks.

**SMP.**  Symmetric MultiProcessing, single computers with multiple processor boards inside the cabinet. For example, Windows NT supports SMP. The effectiveness of SMP is related to the efficiency with which system and application software can divide tasks into separate threads of execution.

**SMS.**  Storage Management Services, a specification that standardizes data storage and retrieval operations to permit different backup utilities to work automatically with different file systems and backup devices. It was designed by Novell and has received support from DEC, IBM, Microsoft, and others.

**SNMP.**  Simple Network Management Protocol, a popular standard that grew out of the Unix world for managing LANs. SNMP specifies a protocol for communication between a management "console" and network devices.

**Socket.**  An IPX or Unix internetwork packet destination. Applications can access a network protocol such as NCP or TCP/IP by addressing the appropriate socket.

**SPOE.**  Single Point Of Entry, an access control system in which a user logs on only once to unlock all the resources to which that user has access privileges.

**Spool.**  Actually an acronym for Simultaneous Peripheral Operations On Line, a spooler is a program that reroutes print output to a disk file before allowing it to go to a printer. Windows' Print Manager is a spooler, as is most network print services management software.

**SPS.**  Standby Power Supply, a backup device that provides power to a server, workstation, or other device from AC power but switches over to battery power in a brownout.

**SPX.**  Sequenced Packet Exchange. Runs over IPX, on the Transport layer, and provides error checking and flow control to make sure packets reach their intended destination and reach it accurately. Used instead of NetBIOS and commonly required by data backup and communications applications. SPX is controlled by software-settable timers on NetWare servers and workstations specifying, among other quantities, how long to wait without receipt acknowledgment before retransmitting.

**SQL.**  Structured Query Language, a set of commands for interrogating databases; very popular among database management system vendors in client/server networks. There are almost as many versions of SQL as there are relational database management products.

**SRAM.**  A high-speed, high-cost memory type, "Static RAM" is most often used for CPU caching in modern PCs and buffers the computer's main DRAM memory; typically used in quantities of 64K, 128K, and 256K.

**SSL.**  Secure Sockets Layer, technology supporting data encryption and authentication between Web clients and servers. Pioneered by Netscape but now supported by several vendors.

**STA Bridge.**  An internal bridge protocol (using a Spanning Tree Algorithm) that determines correct traffic flow across the interconnected topologies in a LAN with multiple bridges, with an eye to preventing message looping.

**Static RAM.**  See **SRAM.**

**Stealth Virus.**  A virus that takes specific steps to conceal its presence.

**Storage Management Services.**  See **SMS.**

**STP.**  Shielded Twisted-Pair cable, with braided metal shielding similar to that used in coaxial cable; used where electromagnetic interference might present problems (see also **twisted-pair cable**).

**Surge Protector.**  A device that is supposed to protect computer equipment from voltage spikes. Most inexpensive surge protectors do not perform this function adequately.

**Swapfile.**  An area of hard drive space used as a low-speed supplement to main memory. In Windows 3.x, a *permanent* swapfile is a contiguous, hidden, position-sensitive file (386SPART.PAR) residing in the root directory. *Temporary* swapfiles are created and deleted on startup and exit and may reside in noncontiguous space on uncompressed, compressed, or network drives. Windows 95 creates a temporary swapfile that it dynamically resizes to adapt to system needs.

**Switching Hub.**  An intelligent device that establishes dedicated, real-time connections between individual computers on a LAN rather than forcing all computers on the LAN to share a single connection.

**Symmetric Encryption.**  See **secret-key encryption.**

**Symmetric Multiprocessing.**  See **SMP.**

**System Fault Tolerance.**  See **SFT.**

**System Resources.**  Local, shareable, fixed-size memory heaps of 64K each used by Windows programs to create menus, palettes, windows etc. This "Achilles' heel" of Windows 3.x limits the number of simultaneous applications and prevents Windows systems from running for long periods without restarting. Windows 95 relocates many system resource structures to 32-bit heaps with practically unlimited size, alleviating the problem almost completely.

**TAPI.**  Windows 95's Telephony API, providing a standard way for programs to use the services of data and voice modems.

**TCP/IP.**  Transport Control Protocol/Internet Protocol is a set of network protocols for file transfer, network management, and messaging. It's popular in the educational, engineering, and governmental areas; it was developed in the early 1970s by DARPA (Defense Advanced Research Projects Agency) for the Arpanet research network. TCP breaks apart and reassembles packets in the correct order, and resends if errors occur; IP handles routing and transmission.

**TDR.**  Time Domain Reflectometer, a sophisticated device for testing LAN cabling.

**Terminator.**  (1) The resistor used at each end of a network cable segment to minimize reflections. A 50-ohm terminator is used in Thin Ethernet systems, a 96-ohm terminator in ARC-Net schemes. (2) In the SCSI bus, a resistor that serves much the same function. SCSI buses require termination at each end of the daisy chain and do not permit terminators elsewhere.

**ThickNet.**  An Ethernet cabling scheme using 0.4$DP diameter coaxial cable.

**Thin Client System.**  A type of client/server system that puts only the user interface component on the client, keeping all the process logic on the server, along with the data storage.

**ThinNet.**  An Ethernet cabling scheme using RG-58A/U type shielded coax cable, which is thinner than the older "ThickNet" cable but still thicker than UTP. ThinNet cable typically uses BNC-type connectors.

**Thread.**  An execution path. In Windows 95, for example, programs can spawn multiple concurrent threads, each of which shares code, data, and window structures with the parent program.

**Three-Tiered System.**  A type of client/server system in which each basic application component (user interface, process logic, and data storage) has its own computer, or its own logical tier of computers. In a three-tiered design, each component can be implemented on hardware specifically selected or designed to perform its specific task.

**Timeout.**  Said to occur when a device or program fails to perform an action within a predetermined maximum time limit.

**Timing Fault.**  A computer system fault in which the appropriate component (be it software, hardware, or communications) is present, is installed correctly, and produces the proper output result for the input in question, but produces that result at such a time that the output is not usable.

**Time Slicing.**  CPU cycle allocation method in which multiple tasks get alternating chunks of CPU time in short intervals, according to a preset prioritization scheme.

**Token.**  A unique sequence of (typically) 24 bits that confers the right to access a token-passing LAN and includes origin and destination data. In a token-ring network, a transmitting station waits for an empty token to circulate to its location, where the station fills the token with destination and message information. All stations monitor circulating tokens to determine if any are targeted to them; if so, the station retrieves the token data and resets the token to an empty state.

**Token Generator.**  A handheld device for user authentication that displays a new and different password in an LCD window at regular intervals. An *automatic* token generator has a unique password algorithm associated with a user's PIN and is time-synchronized with corresponding software or hardware on the server or PC to be accessed. A *challenge-response* token generator has a keypad for the user to enter a code (the "challenge") provided by the server or PC to be accessed, and an LCD window that then displays a coded "response" for the user to enter at the computer.

**Token-Ring.**  A 4- or 16-MBps network standard promulgated by IBM and noted for predictable response and fault tolerance, as well as somewhat higher cost than Ethernet. See also **token**.

**Topology.**  The "shape" or layout of a network cabling and/or signaling scheme; common topologies include bus, ring, and star.

**Tower of Hanoi.**  A backup media rotation strategy, more sophisticated than GFS, that permits administrators to select which days to do backups, how many media sets to use, and how long the oldest backup should be.

**TP Monitor.**  Transaction Process Monitor, a form of middleware in which the client communicates with a special (usually dedicated) computer known as a *transaction server*, which then passes information on to an application server. Upon finishing its task, the application server communicates back to the transaction server, which finally responds to the originating client. TP monitors collect statistics, make those statistics available, and can act on the information contained in the statistics. See also **middleware.**

**Track.**  On hard disks, concentric circles denoting data storage areas. CD-ROMs use spiral tracks; most tape drives use parallel tracks.

**Transport Layer.**  Fourth of the OSI layers, where extra security, flow control, and error-handling abilities get added; NetBIOS, TCP, and SPX operate here.

**Travan.**  A popular 3M-developed tape standard using 0.315" tapes with longer lengths and higher densities, boosting the capacity of QIC-80, QIC-3010, and QIC-3020 drives.

**TSR.**  Terminate-and-Stay-Resident program, usually DOS pop-up utilities and network programs; usually loaded in AUTOEXEC.BAT. The TSR is, to some degree, a round-peg-square-hole situation in that it attempts to make single-tasking DOS a multitasking operating system.

**Twisted-Pair Cable.**  Popular network cable using twisted pairs of phone wire; may be shielded or unshielded. See also **Category 1, 2, 3, 4, and 5.**

**UDP.**  User Datagram Protocol, a connectionless (i.e., non-guaranteed-delivery) transport-level Internet communication protocol, as opposed to TCP, which is a connection-oriented transport protocol.

**UI.**  See **user interface.**

**UNC Path.**  The Universal Naming Convention format for a network file or print resource, in the format \\*server*\*queue* or \\*server*\*volume*\*directory*. Windows 3.x supported UNC paths over Microsoft networks, and Windows 95 supports them for Novell LANs as well.

**Uninterruptible Power Supply.**  See **UPS.**

**UPS.**  Uninterruptible Power Supply, a backup device that provides power to a server, workstation, or other device continuously from its battery, which is constantly being recharged from AC power.

**User Interface.**  The UI is concerned with getting information from the human user into the computer or from the computer out to the human user. The user interface includes data entry, automated data capture, character display, and graphical display. The UI involves all forms of input and output between humans and computers.

**User-Level Security.**  A network security model whereby administrators create user names, passwords, and resource access privileges, and security is established on a per-user basis. See also **share-level security.**

**UTP.**  Unshielded Twisted-Pair, the least expensive type of cabling for Ethernet LANs, using what is essentially phone cable and available in 2-pair, 4-pair, or 6-pair configurations. Used in 10BaseT networks.

**V.22bis.**  International data communications standard for 2400-baud operation, developed by the CCITT standards-setting organization. (The "bis" is a fancy Latin way of indicating that this extends the earlier V.22 standard.)

**V.32.**  A full-duplex data communications standard for 9600-baud operation.

**V.32bis.**  A full-duplex data communications standard for 14.4-Kbps operation, with fallback capability to V.32 for noisy lines.

**V.32terbo.**  Not a formal CCITT standard, this spec improved on V.32bis to provide speeds of 19.2 Kbps.

**V.34,**  Ratified in Fall 1994, it specifies 28.8 Kbps but boasts a few improvements over V.fast and is the current high-speed standard—possibly the last this side of ISDN.

**V.42.**  An error-correction standard that supports automatic resends of bad data with compatible modems. See also **LAPM.**

**V.42bis.**  Not, as you might think, a more advanced error-correction standard than V.42, but rather a *data compression* standard with the ability to only compress data that is likely to be compressible. Only works with modems that support it and V.42 error correction.

**V.fast.**  Also called V.FC for "V.Fast Class." An early (and somewhat premature) manufacturer-driven standard specifying 28.8-Kbps operation. Some V.fast modems are ROM upgradable to V.34.

**VBA.**  Visual Basic for Applications. See **Macro.**

**VCACHE.**  (1) The disk cache component of 32-Bit File Access in Windows for Workgroups 3.11; faster than SmartDrive. (2) The dynamic file system disk cache in Windows 95, available to all file system drivers.

**VESA.**  Video Electronics Standards Association; typically used to refer to the VESA local bus (formerly VL-bus), which provides higher performance than the standard ISA bus for video, disk, and network interface cards. The VESA bus can handle 32-bit cards and is well suited for 486 PCs, though it has been largely eclipsed by the PCI bus. See also **PCI.**

**Virtual Device Driver.**  See **VxD.**

**Virtual Disk.**  See **RAM disk.**

**Virtual Drive.**  A drive letter to which a remote drive or directory is logically connected.

**Virtual Machine (VM).**  An environment provided by Intel 386 and higher processors and associated software that allows a region of memory to be isolated and set aside for emulating an 8088 PC.

**Virtual Memory.**  A technique for allowing programs to access memory addresses that correspond to disk space instead of RAM. Windows' swap files are virtual memory constructs.

**Virtual Port.**  In Windows, a parallel port to which a remote printer is logically connected. It's not necessary to actually have a local port corresponding to the virtual port.

**VRAM.** Video RAM, often used in high-performance graphics boards; roughly twice as fast as DRAM, and twice as expensive.

**VSDN.** Voice Synchronous Data Networking, in which voice signals travel along the same wires used for data communications. VSDN is one way of providing redundancy for voice communications fault tolerance.

**VxD.** Virtual Device Driver; in Windows, a resource driver that can run in protected mode above 1 MB and that may be accessed by multiple Windows sessions and DOS sessions under Windows. The WfW and Windows 95 network drivers are VxDs.

**Watchdog Packets.** Packets sent by a network to inactive workstations to see if they're still connected. If the workstation doesn't respond to the watchdog packets, the network terminates the connection.

**Wide Area Network (WAN).** LANs linked over large distances, usually *via* communications protocols running on satellite, microwave or public data network links.

**Wiring Closet.** A utility closet where network hubs may reside, possibly cohabitating with telephone equipment.

**Workgroup.** A team of individuals who commonly work together and need to share programs and files and printers.

**Workgroup Application.** An application that requires, and provides for, communication between multiple users.

**WORM.** Write-Once, Read-Many, said of optical ROM technologies such as writable laser disks used for archiving large quantities of data. WORM has been supplanted by CD-R in many organizations.

**WYSIWYG.** What You See Is What You Get, the goal of matching printed documents precisely with their screen appearance.

**X.500.** A 1988 ITU-TSS standard with mail and directory name service features. X.500 is the foundation for NetWare 4.x's NDS architecture.

**XNS.** Xerox Network Services, the basis in part for Novell's network operating systems.

**ZIF.** Zero Insertion Force, said of processor sockets that permit the easy removal and replacement of microprocessors through the use of a clamping lever.

# Index

# About the Authors

RICHARD J. MARTIN is Principal of Atavista Associates, consultants and educators in the management of information technology. Before forming Atavista Associates, he was Director of Commercial Systems for INTELSAT, where he oversaw the creation of a corporate client/server computing architecture as well as several million dollars annually of system development projects.

GLENN E. WEADOCK is a computer consultant and popular seminar leader. He is President of Independent Software, Inc. and a longtime instructor and writer for Data-Tech Institute. He has written three other books in McGraw-Hill's popular Bulletproofing series, including *Bulletproofing Windows 95* and *Bulletproofing NetWare*.

# About the Illustrator

EMILY SHERRILL WEADOCK is the Director of Independent Software's Digital Art Studio. An award-winning computer artist whose work has been featured in international magazines, Emily's talent ranges from technical illustration to broadcast-quality 3D animation and multimedia development. She is the coauthor of *Creating Cool PowerPoint 97 Presentations* and has illustrated all the books in the Bulletproofing series. Before trading brushes for mice, Emily enjoyed success as a mixed-media construction artist and studied art at SMU and Baylor University.